SOCIAL WORK AND IRISH PEOPLE IN BRITAIN

Historical and contemporary responses to Irish children and families

Paul Michael Garrett

First published in Great Britain in June 2004 by

The Policy Press
University of Bristol
Fourth Floor
Beacon House
Queen's Road
Bristol BS8 1QU
UK

Tel +44 (0)117 331 4054
Fax +44 (0)117 331 4093
e-mail tpp-info@bristol.ac.uk
www.policypress.org.uk

British Library Cataloguing in Publication Data
A catalogue record for this book is available from the British Library.

Library of Congress Cataloging-in-Publication Data
A catalog record for this book has been requested.

ISBN 1 86134 411 2 paperback

A hardcover version of this book is also available

Paul Michael Garrett is a Senior Lecturer in the School of Sociology and Social
Policy, University of Nottingham, UK.

Cover design by Qube Design Associates, Bristol.
Front cover: photographs supplied by kind permission of Joanne O'Brien.
Printed and bound in Great Britain by Hobbs the Printers Ltd, Southampton.

List of tables and figures

Tables

Figure

Acknowledgements

Many people have provided me with diverse kinds of support and assistance in writing this book. These include: Clare, Ciaran and Geileis, Alan and Meryl Aldridge, Jennifer Bisnouth, Paula Brady, Becky Calcraft, Anita Cuddihy, Rita Duffy, Annie Dolan, Mark Drakeford and Ian Butler, Trevor Jones, Christian Karner, Noelette Keane, Ken Levine and Claire Bench, Elizabeth Malcolm, Brian McCarthy, Sarah Morgan, Sinead O'Donohue, David Parker, Sue Parker, Patrick Reynolds, Michael Ridge, Mary Tilki, Bronwen Walter and Patrick Webb. Outside an often insular academic world, my friends in the Nottingham Robert Hamill Campaign were also a source of solidarity and companionship. Many colleagues in AUT also reminded me that there is an alternative to neoliberalism in the higher education sector in Britain.

Some of the material featured in Chapters One and Two was presented to a seminar at the Renville Institute at the University of Helsinki in May 2002. I am very grateful to Pirkko Hautamäki for her invitation and for making me welcome in Helsinki. Specifically, in relation to Chapter Five, I am grateful for the help of John McDonnell and the All-Party Irish in Britain Parliamentary Group of MPs. Furthermore, the Association of Directors of Social Services provided assistance and cooperation and helped to facilitate the research featured in the chapter. Barry Luckock and his colleagues provided helpful suggestions on some of the material featured in Chapter Six, when I was invited to present a seminar paper in the School for Social Work and Social Care at University of Sussex in late 2003. The Action Group for Irish Youth, the Irish Youth Forum and the Irish Equalities Working Group at the Commission for Racial Equality provided invaluable opportunities to discuss some of the themes in the book. Dawn Louise Rushen and others at The Policy Press were efficient, patient and always willing to answer my queries. The two anonymous reviewers of my initial manuscript also furnished detailed and constructive comment and advice.

I have written this book as an individual product of the Irish diaspora. I was born in England, but am an Irish citizen. My formation, perspective and opinions in this book are, therefore, inseparable from my own diasporic experience. Indeed, the book can, in some senses, be read as autobiography, but without a subject. Needless to say, I am entirely responsible for any errors, or shortcomings, that readers may detect.

List of abbreviations

ADSS	Association of Directors of Social Services
BAAF	British Agencies for Adoption and Fostering
CIN survey	Children in Need survey
CPRSI	Child Protection and Rescue Society of Ireland
CRE	Commission for Racial Equality
DoH	Department of Health
ECRS	English Catholic Rescue Society
GSCC	General Social Care Council
IBRG	Irish in Britain Representation Group
IWG	Irish Workers' Group
LCC	London County Council
QP	Quality Protects
RRAA	2000 Race Relations (Amendment) Act
SSDs	social services departments
SSI	Social Services Inspectorate

This is in memory of my Mum and Dad
(but also for Maura and Jim)

Introduction

In the late 1990s and early 21st century, politicians and commentators in Britain have looked on, in puzzled wonderment, at the arrival of the so-called 'Celtic Tiger' economy in the Republic of Ireland[1]. It has even been asserted that the Irish, with their allegedly ostentatious new-found wealth, are the "playboys of Europe" (*The Observer*, 22 July 2001). Recent representations of Irish people have also tended to centre on popular culture: the Riverdance phenomenon, U2 and The Corrs (Stevens et al, 2000; see also West, 2002). Indeed, the popularity of a particular construction of Irishness led one British newspaper to contend, in the mid-1990s: "If you're hip, you must be Irish" (O'Sullivan, 1996). In the same article, a writer and cultural commentator mused: "Irish culture is seductive. It has become a signifier for hedonism with soul" (see also 'Dubliners come home to find boom prices in Cool Hibernia', *The Independent*, 30 May 1998, p 14). More generally, within the field of cultural studies, it has been claimed that 'Irishness' has 'cachet' and that it has attained the 'status of cultural capital' (Thompson, 2001, p 1; see also, however, Maddox, 1996).

All of these notions are, of course, highly debatable. Cultural commodification is, of course, a key characteristic of Late Capitalism and this can be related to what has also been dubbed 'Cool Hibernia' and the 'commodification of Irishness' (McGovern, 2002; see also Fish, 1997). Thus, throughout the late 1990s, this was evidenced in the marketing of alcoholic drinks (Armstrong, 1996; see also 'Special brew of trendy ales and blarney rakes in cash', *The Guardian*, 1 May 1997). More recently, it has been possible to detect a certain wane in corporate interest in utilising 'Irishness' to promote consumption (see, for example, 'Breweries call time on "Oirish" theme pubs', *The Irish Post*, 5 May 1999; 'Irish acts in doldrums as festival is axed', *The Observer*, 1 June 2003). Nonetheless, these developments do highlight the new centrality of Ireland and 'Irishness' in the field of cultural studies (see also Kirby et al, 2002b). In contrast, with social work – and social policy – in Britain, there has been an embedded failure to recognise the specificity of Irish people[2].

Social work and Irish 'invisibility'

Since the inception of social work in the late 19th century, despite historically having been the recipients, even *targets*, of social services, Irish people have been bypassed the profession's less regulatory, more enlightened discourses and practices[3]. In a contemporary context, the lack of an Irish dimension is institutionalised and has normally resulted in, for example, Irish people being encouraged to 'tick' either the 'White' or the (revealing) 'White Other' box on forms designed to monitor the 'race' and ethnicity of users of services[4]. Local authorities have also routinely failed to consult Irish people and Irish community groups when service plans are drawn up because the mainstream theoretical orientation, frequently grounded in a recourse to "lazy essentialisms" (Gilroy, 2000, p 53), continues to promote the notion that 'black' and 'ethnic minority' can simply be conflated and are discursively interchangeable. Importantly, this mainstream and dominant perspective fails to take account of the historical and contemporary racialisation of Irish people and other ethnicities not located in a 'black' category (see, however, Downey, 1997; Valios, 2002).

At present, otherwise informative studies purporting to provide comprehensive analyses of 'race' and ethnicity in terms social services provision for children and families do not interrogate the experience of either first- or second-generation Irish families in Britain (for example, Barn et al, 1997; Kirton, 2000; Thoburn et al, 2000). This omission reflects, moreover, the intellectual and sociological disposition of social work in Britain – its professional 'common sense' (see also Hickman, 1998). Irish people in Britain are rendered *invisible* by, for example, social work educators' anti-discriminatory discourse and by government guidance and reports, such as the Department of Health's *Adoption now: Messages from the research* (1999), where a black/white binary delimits debates on 'race' and ethnicity. This reductive approach is not unique to social work and reflects, more general, historical and culturally rooted factors. In brief, the dominant paradigm conceptualises discrimination in terms of skin colour and 'race' (see Dyer, 1997). This preoccupation with visible difference, while clearly immensely relevant, has, however, led to other immigrations, ethnicities and racism(s) being insufficiently analysed: the experiences of Irish people, Jewish people and many groups of asylum seekers and refugees (Parker, J., 2000; Roskill, 2000; Smith, 2000; Bloch and Schuster, 2002; Duvell and Jordan, 2002; see also, in this context, Anthias, 2002).

Despite this 'invisibility', Irish users of social services are likely to have specific needs that arise from their experience(s). This book, therefore, explores the Irish dimension as it relates to social work theory and practice. Clearly, social work and Irish people in Britain is a potentially vast subject, but the aims of the book are relatively modest in that the specific focus will be on social work with Irish children and families. Even more precisely, responses to Irish mothers and children in need of substitute care will be the chief interest. Sociologically, issues of 'race' and ethnicity are frequently enmeshed in discourses that are preoccupied with reproduction and motherhood (see Yuval-Davis, 1997), and this understanding will also provide part of the foundation for the book. Furthermore, 'unmarried motherhood' and unplanned pregnancy continue, in an Irish context, to be related to migration from Ireland (Mahon et al, 1998; Rossiter and Sexton, 2001; Oaks, 2002; see also 'Sharp rise in teens going to Britain for abortions', *The Irish Times*, 23 August 2002).

The book examines a range of archival sources and explores how, historically, Irish mothers and their children have been responded to by social work and related agencies in Britain. Is there any evidence to suggest that they were treated in a specific way that was disadvantageous for them? Alternatively, have Irish mothers and their children been regarded in the same way as their English counterparts? In a contemporary context, how have Irish children been viewed in terms of dominant anti-discriminatory paradigms? What, moreover, are social services separtments (SSDs) doing to address issues connected to Irish 'identity' and children 'looked after' under the 1989 Children Act? How do Irish social workers view the actions of their departments and issues related to service provision and Irish people in Britain? What are the key factors relating to social work with children and families from the Irish Traveller community? These are just some of the questions that this book seeks to examine.

In this Introduction, I begin with the concept of diaspora, which, it is argued, provides a helpful framework in which to locate the migration of Irish people. Next, the focus is on Irish people in Britain, and here it is acknowledged that the phrase 'Irish community' should be used with a sense of reflexive caution because it can be perceived as seeking to erase, or mask, internal differences *within* 'the community'. In short, while pressing for recognition of Irish specificity in social work and other social welfare discourses in Britain, there is also a need to recognise diversity within the Irish community. I then briefly highlight Irish vulnerability in Britain. The final part of the Introduction maps out how the book is organised.

The Irish diaspora

The term diaspora is now "loose in the world" (Clifford, cited in Gray, 2000, p 168). For Spivak (2002, p 47), large "movements of people – renamed 'diaspora' – are what defines our time". Certainly, the whole idea of an Irish diaspora can inform our understanding of some of the circulating concerns of this book. Gilroy (2000, p 123) observes:

> The idea of diaspora offers a ready alternative to the stern discipline of primordial kinship and rooted belonging. It rejects the popular image of natural nations spontaneously endowed with self-consciousness.... I[t] problematizes the cultural and historical mechanics of belonging. It disrupts the fundamental power of territory to determine identity by breaking the simple sequence of explanatory links between place, location, and consciousness.

Gilzean and McAuley (2002), among others, have also identified the different understandings of 'diaspora'. At its most basic, however, the whole notion of diaspora simply refers to the dispersion or migration of communities (see also Vertovec, 2000, ch 7).

Hickman (2002), however, has noted the absence of Irish people in 'diaspora studies' where African and Jewish history or cultures have tended to be the dominant focus (see, in this context, Braziel and Mannur, 2003). Nonetheless, certainly since the mid-1990s, a number of academics and commentators have located the Irish experience within this conceptual framework (see, for example, Akenson, 1996). Here, the work of the philosopher Richard Kearney (1997, pp 99-101)[5] has been particularly influential. He argues:

> When one speaks of the 'Irish community' today, one refers not merely to
> the inhabitants of the state, but to an international group of expatriates and
> a subnational network of regional communities. This triple-layered identity
> means that Irishness is no longer co-terminous with the geographical outlines
> of an island. The diaspora both within and beyond the frontiers of Ireland
> (over seventy million claim Irish descent) challenges the inherited definitions
> of state nationalism.... For as long as Irish people think of themselves as
> Celtic Crusoes on a sequestered island, they ignore not only their own
> diaspora but the basic cultural truth that cultural creation comes from
> hybridization not purity, contamination not immunity, polyphony not
> monologue.

Moreover, the contributions of the journalist and cultural commentator Fintan
O'Toole (1994, 1997) have been significant (see also O'Seaghdha, 2002). In
the 1990s, Patrick O'Sullivan's six-volume edited collection, *The Irish world
wide: History, heritage, identity* also appeared, as did the *Irish Empire* series, lavishly
produced by RTE (Ireland), BBC (Britain) and SBS (Australia) (see also
O'Sullivan, 2003). These programmes, screened by BBC in the autumn of
2000, looked at the themes of dispersal, emigrants' working lives, women's
stories, religion in the diaspora, as well as dreams of home.

Of greatest significance, perhaps, was a key intervention by Mary Robinson,
then President of Ireland, in 1995. In a speech, entitled 'Cherishing the Irish
diaspora', she stated:

> The men and women of our diaspora represent not simply a series of
> departures and loss. They remain even while absent, a precious reflection of
> our growth and change, a precious reminder of the many strands of identity
> which compose our story. (Cited in Gray, 1996, p 182)

Robinson's successor, Mary McAleese, has echoed these sentiments by her
references to the 'global Irish family'. In legalistic terms, resonance can also be
found in Article 2 of the Constitution of Ireland, as amended by the Referendum
held in 1998 following the Good Friday Agreement, which acknowledges that
the "Irish nation cherishes its special affinity with people of Irish ancestry
living abroad who share its cultural identity and heritage".

Certainly, Robinson's inclusive definition of 'Irishness' sent a powerful message
to the Irish diaspora. Nash (2002, p 34), for example, has commented on
Robinson's efforts to "rethink Irish identity thorough a focus on the circuits of
people and cultural forms between Ireland and other places". Gray (2002, p
124) has also maintained that the former President's "gesture re-coded Irish
identity as multilocated and legitimised new possibilities of Irish identification
and belonging" (see also Gray, 1997). However, while accepting that the diaspora
framework is of some conceptual usefulness, there are certain problems that
can be associated this approach.

One of the chief critics is David Lloyd (1999, p 12), who criticises the

sentimental invocation and celebration of the Irish diaspora. He disputes the
term in relation to Irish America and prefers to see *emigration*, as opposed to
diaspora, as the key factor[6]:

> In the four decades preceding the eve of independence ... close on two and
> a quarter million Irish people emigrated.... For the most part, they did not
> leave for mere adventure and the promise of a new life; they left in order to
> survive the economic and cultural devastation that colonialism had inflicted;
> they left because there was no obvious alternative. Their leaving has left a
> wake that works continually in Irish culture. It can neither be softened into
> the contours of a cultural diaspora nor ignored for the sake of exaggerating
> Ireland's twentieth-century prosperity: both remain predicated on the as yet
> unceasing pattern that for some cushions the neo-colonial history of our
> present.

MacLaughlin (1997, p 6) also notes that emigration "has long been a 'hidden
injury' of class which has affected the sons and daughters of small farming and
working-class families more than other sectors of Irish society"[7]. Three other
criticisms of the application of the diaspora concept can also be briefly identified.
First, there is the suggestion that mainstream discourses on the Irish diaspora
ignore the gendered experience of migration (Walter, 2001; see also Gray, 1997).
Second, it has been argued that there is often a failure to explore how there is
something of an 'elective affinity' between diaspora and a neoliberal or global
capitalism with its demands for labour mobility and ethnic commodification
(Gray, 2002). Finally, it could be argued that, for all the comments about
'cherishing the diaspora', the government of the Republic of Ireland has been
more apt to embrace "emigrants and their descendants symbolically" while
excluding them "as concrete individuals and voters" (Gray, 2002, p 125; see
also 'UCC closure of centre condemned', *The Irish Examiner*, 23 June 2003).

Despite these criticisms, the diaspora framework remains of some conceptual
use. The important point is that the Irish diaspora needs to be related to the
political economy because, as Bronwen Walter (2001, p 8) has argued, all
diasporas "must be seen as a product and constituent of international capitalism"
(see also Brah et al, 1999).

Irish people in Britain

Historically, of course, Irish people have migrated from Ireland in large numbers
and there is "hardly a corner of the world that does not have an Irish population"
(Task Force on Policy regarding Emigrants, 2002, p 28). Indeed, "about twenty
per cent of Irish-born people live outside (the island of) Ireland, which is a
high proportion for a modern industrialised society" (Walter et al, 2002a, p
96). It has also been maintained that:

Ireland occupies a very unusual place in the wider pattern of European emigration in the very large numbers of emigrants relative to the total population of the country, such that there was a continuous decline from 8.2 million people in 1841 to only 4.2 million in 1961. The peak years of outflow were the immediate aftermath of the Great Famine of 1847-51 and the loss by 1920 is estimated to be around 6 million people. The major destination in the nineteenth century was the USA, but from the 1920s the direction of the flow turned to Britain which has been by far the largest destination until the 1990s. (Walter et al, 2002a, p 1)

In the early 21st century, it is estimated that, of the three million or so Irish citizens abroad, almost 1.2 million were born in Ireland, the equivalent of 30% of the present population. Even today, despite increasing levels of prosperity, some 20,000 people continue to emigrate every year (Task Force on Policy regarding Emigrants, 2002, p 6). However, there have been two large peaks of outward movement from the Irish Republic. These are often referred to as the 'second wave' (the 1950s) and 'third wave' (the late 1980s), after the huge 'first wave' of the mid- to late 19th century (Walter et al, 2002a, p 3; see also Wickham, 1998). During the 1950s, the average outflow was 40,000 per year and in the late 1980s, 27,000 per year (Walter et al, 2002a, p 3). Although "less recognised than flows from the Republic, emigration from Northern Ireland has a very long history and has at different times both mirrored the pattern of movement from the Republic in the post-1945 period and diverged from it" (Walter et al, 2002a, p 2). Furthermore, whatever their religious background, people from Northern Ireland are usually simply regarded as 'Irish' in other countries (Walter et al, 2002a, p 2).

The experience(s) of Irish people varies, however, from one country to another. The largest Irish-born community in the world outside of Ireland is in Britain (Task Force on Policy regarding Emigrants, 2002, p 39). Indeed, more than:

[t]hree-quarters of the Irish-born living outside Ireland now live in Britain. In the post-1945 period Britain has replaced the USA as the largest area of settlement. Although numbers declined from a peak of 957,000 Irish-born in 1971 the total remained at 850,000 in 1991. It is estimated that a further 1.7 millions have been born to Irish parent(s). Many third generation children are also raised with a strong sense of Irish heritage, especially in large centres of Irish settlement. A three-generation Irish community could number 6 millions. (Walter et al, 2002a, p 30)

The lack of immigration restrictions set Britain apart from other destinations with which Ireland has a long association, including the US, Canada, Australia and New Zealand. Indeed, this apparent lack of immigration controls is frequently interpreted as proof that Irish people in Britain are, in truth, somehow *really* British, certainly not an 'ethnic minority' group. However, Britain is also the only country in which Irish people continue to experience more marked forms of discrimination. Although "vestiges of anti-Irish attitudes can be traced in British settler colonies, they appear to be far less marked" (Walter et al, 2002a, p 96). This partly reflects "the long history of hostility between the former imperial centre and its closest colony" (Walter et al, 2002a, p 96), but also the more recent 'Troubles' in Northern Ireland:

> The post-1945 Irish population has therefore being caught between two images. On the one hand their migrant experience and cultural difference has been denied because they are a 'white', 'British Isles' population group. On the other hand anti-Irish stereotypes persist in British society and have been fuelled by anti-IRA fears over the last thirty years. (Walter et al, 2002a, p 38)

Indeed, during the conflict in Northern Ireland, many Irish people simply "kept their heads down" in Britain (Walter et al, 2002a, p 40; see also Walter, 2000).

The Irish-born population is now an ageing and numerically declining population. According to the 1991 Census, 26.4% are aged 65+ and there is also a higher proportion of women (Walter et al, 2002a, p 32; see also Task Force on Policy regarding Emigrants, 2002, p 36). In terms of areas of settlement, the same Census indicated that Irish people in Britain are strongly clustered by region of settlement. Thus, a tendency to settle in the South East, especially in the Greater London area, strengthened in the post-1945 period. Within London, further clustering by boroughs and wards occurs; in Brent, for example, the Irish-born proportion was 9% in 1991 (over 20% including second generation), with Islington having 7.1% Irish-born (18% including second generation) and Hammersmith and Fulham 6.9% (17% including second generation) (in Walter et al, 2002a, p 32).

John McGahern's most recent (2002) and acclaimed novel, *That they may face the rising sun*, features a memorable character called Johnny, one of the many Irish men who found employment in the car industry in the British Midlands in the 1950s and 1960s (see also Valios, 2002). Indeed, during this period, large numbers were attracted to the employment opportunities in the industrial West Midlands (such as in Birmingham and Coventry). Although the Irish-born comprised only 1.8% of the total population of England in 1991, they formed, for example, nearly 6% in two Birmingham parliamentary constituencies, Erdington and Sparkbrook. Again, by adding the second generation, this brings each of those totals nearer to 20% of the total population (Walter et al, 2002a, p 32). In north-west England, which included 12.8% of the Irish-born in England, very large numbers of people are also of Irish descent, with Manchester, particularly, retaining a strong Irish presence (4.6% of Irish-born in 1991; estimated 9% including the second generation) (Walter et al, 2002a, p 32). Towns outside these two regions, such as Luton (5.4% Irish-born, estimated 12% including second generation), also had large Irish populations and, according to the 1991 Census, there were substantial clusters found in places such as Sheffield (Walter et al, 2002a, p 32; see also Gilzean and McAuley, 2002).

Initial statistical data relating to the 2001 Census were released in February 2003. In this, 1.2% of the population of England and Wales was identified as 'White Irish'. The highest proportion of 'White Irish' were found in the London boroughs of Brent, Islington and Hammersmith and Fulham. The 2001 Census also indicted that the percentage of the population born in Ireland had declined: 0.9% (472,000) from the Republic of Ireland and 0.4% (223,000) from Northern Ireland. London, particularly Brent, was the region with the highest percentage of those born in the Republic; the North West, particularly Corby, had the highest percentage of those born in Northern Ireland. The decline in the Irish-born population was also revealed in those London boroughs with the highest percentage of Irish-born in both the 1991 and 2001 Census exercises: Brent down to 6.95% from 9%; Islington 5.72% down from 7.1%; Hammersmith and Fulham 4.83% down from 6.9%. In terms of the age profile of the Irish community in England, the 2001 Census also revealed that only 5.9% of those featured in the 'White Irish' category were in the 15-and-under age group (compared with an average of 20.2%) and nearly one in four were 65 or over (compared with an average of 16.0%) (National Statistics, 2003).

Second-generation Irish and subsequent generations of Irish people in Britain

There is substantial regional variation in the size and composition of the second-generation Irish population in Britain. The ratio of second to first generation, for example, is "much higher in locations outside of London and the Southeast" (Task Force on Policy regarding Emigrants, 2002, p 45). Moreover, there is a much larger population with Irish links in some regions than is generally recognised (see Hickman et al, 2001). Indeed, those who were not born in Ireland yet who have an Irish identity are clearly important and given this book's focus and concerns it would be wrong to perceive only the Irish-born as possessing a *real* or authentic Irish identity. As Walter et al (2002a, p 29) observe, birthplace is "not the only way in which Irish populations can be defined. Children brought up in households where one or two parents are Irish-born may also feel themselves to be wholly or partly Irish and may pass significant elements of this identity on to their own children". This understanding, moreover, is important for children and families in contact with SSDs in Britain.

Clearly, second and subsequent generations would not feature in a definition of 'Irish' that is solely determined by place of birth. In the latter half of this book, which examines the contemporary picture, an inclusive definition of Irish people will, therefore, be used. That is to say, 'Irish' will be understood to refer to 'persons who come from, or whose forbears originate in, Ireland and who consider themselves Irish'. This inclusive definition of Irish was also recommended to the Ethnic Monitoring Committee of the Greater London

Council in the mid-1980s (Hickman and Walter, 1997, p 65). Here, the emphasis is placed on a person's own perception since, as Pearson et al (1991) observe, "there are dangers in inferring that a country of birth gives valid reflection of how people choose to describe themselves". This view was echoed in a recent report on *Ireland and the Irish abroad* (Task Force on Policy regarding Emigrants, 2002), which argued that for "many second and subsequent generation Irish, there is a wish to have their Irish identity properly acknowledged, both in Ireland and in the country in which they have grown up" (2002, p 28). The Task Force (2002, p 33) went on to maintain that:

> [E]xpressing and maintaining their Irish identity is not just an issue for Irish-born emigrants. Often, it matters as much to those born of Irish descent. The extent to which these people consider that they are Irish varies. For some, their Irish background is of no significance in their ethnic identity whereas many others wish to have their Irish background acknowledged and have opportunities to express the Irish dimension of their identity. Most of those for whom an Irish identity is important see no conflict between maintaining this identity alongside that of their country of birth while a minority take the view that only an Irish dimension is relevant for them.

It was because of an awareness of this issue that, after a long campaign by the Irish voluntary sector, a self-identifying Irish category was included in the 2001 Census. In the period leading up to the Census week in April 2001, this campaign continued with a 'Be Irish, be counted' publicity drive. However, even before the publication of the initial Census data, there were fears that the Irish community would be under-reported because the stark 'White Irish' category did not capture the complexity of Irish identities in Britain ('Census may not register all Irish', *The Irish Post*, 14 April 2001; see also Myles, 2003). Indeed, in terms of some of the themes at the heart of this book, it is recognised that identity is a complex issue for the children of Irish emigrants. Research has revealed, for example, that the "majority live with hyphenated identities that encompass their region and their Irish identity e.g. London-Irish or Leeds-Irish" (Task Force on Policy regarding Emigrants, 2002, p 45; see also 'Struggle for Irish Identity', *The Irish Post*, 23 November 2002).

Changes introduced in the 2001 Census were, as Mary Hickman et al (2001, p 1) observe, a "significant development which acknowledges that Irish identities are not simply confined to a migrant generation". However, unlike in North America and Australia, the 'Irish' category was singular rather than mixed or multiple choice. In England and Wales, the named 'White' ethnic categories were 'British' and 'Irish', without provision for a 'Mixed' category (Walter et al, 2002a, p 31). This still fails, therefore, to "account for the large proportion of people" who may see themselves as having "mixed or hybrid identitifications" (Walter et al, 2002a, p 40)[8]. Perhaps, in a more fundamental sense, this complexity highlights the need to acknowledge diversity *within* the Irish community in Britain.

Diversity and the Irish community in Britain

The idea of an Irish diaspora, referred to earlier, has been criticised for promoting "notions of simple ethnic identity that the concept of diaspora itself was actually meant to dispel" (Nash, 2002, p 34; see also Gray, 2000). However, as the sociologist and cultural theorist, Stuart Hall (1990, p 35) has argued:

> Diaspora does not refer us to those scattered tribes whose identity can only be secured in relation to some sacred homeland ... the diaspora experience as I intend it here is defined, not by the essence of purity, but by the recognition of a necessary heterogeneity and diversity; by a conception of 'identity' which lives by and through, not despite difference; by hybridity. Diaspora identities are those which are constantly producing and reproducing themselves anew, through transformation and difference.

Sharing Hall's approach, this book is underpinned by an understanding that Irish people in Britain do not form a homogeneous and socially static bloc (see Hall, 1996; Hobsbawm, 1996; Fraser, 2000; Commission on the Future of Multi-Ethnic Britain, 2000; Lentin, 2001). The aim here, therefore, will not be to promote 'simple' ideas of ethnic identity or – even worse – to champion a crude essentialism or dangerous 'ethno-dogma' (Gilroy, 1994; see also Brah, 1992; Dominelli et al, 2001).

Certainly, I refer to the 'Irish community', yet this is also done with a sense of wariness because 'community' – perhaps like 'empowerment' (Margolin, 1997; Forrest, 2000) – is one of those sentimental and seductive words that is frequently used to mask internal cleavages *inside of* communities (see Anthias and Yuval-Davis, 1993). As argued elsewhere, "like other communities, the Irish community is complex and diverse – potentially energised, in fact, as much by difference and hybridity as by a sense of commonality" (Garrett, 1998, p 38; see also Anthias and Yuval-Davies, 1993, ch 6). As Hall (2000, p 232) argues, the "temptation to essentialize 'community' has to be resisted". Moreover, people "belong to many different, overlapping, 'communities' which sometimes exert contrary pulls" (Hall, 2000, p 230). Related to this, McLennan (2001, p 391) observes that if "national and religious belonging are major types of cultural affiliation, there are plenty of other relatively coherent cultural formations too: those coagulating, for example, around work role, class experience, sexual identities, residential location, leisure habits, political and social movements" and so on. Alexander and Alleyne (2002) have also discussed the "reification of 'community'" (see also Alleyne, 2002). Meanwhile, Hobsbawm (1994, p 428) has argued that never "was the word 'community' used more indiscriminately and emptily than in the decades when communities in the sociological sense became hard to find in real life". Nonetheless, the comments of Hickman (2002, pp 20-1), while still somewhat problematic, are equally salient.

> The fact that the Irish diaspora is heterogeneous and composed of different imaginings of Irishness ... does not necessarily undermine the existence of a "diasporic community", as such communities are always hybrid phenomena.... The point is that "community" is highly symbolised with the consequence that members of the community can invest in it with their often very different selves. Its character is sufficiently malleable that it can accommodate all its members' selves at various different junctures. So although people will have different imaginings of the "community" in their heads some symbols or practices will unite larger groups of them, at one time or another, effectively forming alliances on an ethnic basis. On some issues and in some areas this will be more obvious than others.

Certainly, processes of racialisation and 'othering' cannot be detached from social divisions rooted in social class, gender and sexuality (Edge, 1995; Hickman and Walter, 1995; Walter, 1995; Kanya-Forstner, 1999; Gray, 2000; Walter, 2001; see also Marston, 2002). In addition, there are specific factors attached to the age and generation of Irish people in Britain (Norman, 1985; Ullah, 1985; Tilki, 1998a; Campbell, 1999). Historically, religion has, of course, been a significant factor (Gilley, 1999; Pooley, 1999). It is also increasingly being realised that Irish Travellers have been subjected to specific forms of 'othering' both in Ireland and Britain. More fundamentally, as McClintock (1994, p 5) has argued, social cleavages such as 'race', ethnicity, gender and class are "not distinct realms of experience, existing in splendid isolation from each other; nor can they be simply yoked together respectively like armatures of Lego. Rather they come into existence *in and through* relation to each other – if in contradictory and conflictual ways" (emphasis added).

The problem, however, is that social work in Britain has largely failed to recognise that there may be *any* Irish dimension to theory and practice[9]. As a result of this lacuna, therefore, while recognising the diversity *within* the Irish community in Britain, there is still – for those pressing for change in social work theory and practice – a case for "strategic essentialism" (Spivak, cited in Arrowmith, 1999, p 177). Perhaps this is particularly important given the vulnerability of certain groups of Irish people in Britain that might need to seek out the assistance of local authority SSDs.

Vulnerability and Irish people in Britain

It would, of course, be inaccurate and misleading to portray Irish people in Britain as being entirely beset by discrimination and multiple hardships. As a report produced for the Irish government has asserted, there is "an emerging Irish business and professional class who are fully integrated into British life while retaining their Irish identity" (Task Force on Policy regarding Emigrants,

2002, p 39). Furthermore, there is "a growing confidence among the Irish in Britain in expressing their identity, as evidenced by the unprecedented numbers" now taking part in the annual St Patrick's Day parades in London, Birmingham, Manchester, Nottingham and other cities in Britain (Walter et al, 2002a, p 41; see also 'Ambitious Irish scale job heights in Britain', *The Guardian*, 27 February 1998).

Nonetheless, it remains important to continue to recognise those in the Irish community who are vulnerable and socially excluded[10]. Walter et al (2002a), for example, have identified a number of interconnected groups that can be viewed as likely to be the 'most vulnerable' in Irish communities abroad. These include:

- new migrants;
- elders (including those who laboured in the unregulated sectors of the economy in Britain);[11]
- Irish Travellers;
- second-generation Irish people;
- drug users, including those 'ordered out' of Ireland by paramilitaries;
- people with mental health problems;
- homeless people (and those in poor housing);
- child migrants;
- disabled migrants;
- gay and lesbian migrants;
- children who are adopted and fostered;
- prisoners.

More broadly, while Irish people are "eligible for equal treatment in virtually all respects with British citizens, including employment, social security and health matters, research evidence shows that Irish emigrants in Britain suffer disproportionately from economic and social disadvantage" (Task Force on Policy regarding Emigrants, 2002, p 39). There is also "evidence that Irish Travellers experience particular difficulties both as Travellers and as emigrants, notably in relation to health, education and social services" (2002, p 44; see also Carr, 1999; Gaffney, 2001)[12].

Nonetheless, the mainstream discourses on 'race' and ethnicity, not only within social work, but also within the social sciences more generally, have tended to fail to take account of an Irish dimension:

> There has been a widespread assumption both by academics and by the public at large that the Irish unproblematically assimilate into the 'white' population within a fairly short space of time and that their children are simply 'English'. This reflects the 'myth of homogeneity' of British society, which represents Britain as a stable, unchanging 'white' nation only recently disrupted by the arrival of (black) immigrants. However, this picture has

existed alongside longstanding rejection of Irish people as alien 'others'. (Walter et al, 2002a, p 38)

In terms of the structural location of Irish people in Britain, the 1991 Census, which, pending the emergence of similar data from the 2001 Census on this question, remains the most up-to-date source for this type of information, revealed that Irish-born men's occupations were similar to those of the whole population. Irish women, in contrast, were strongly clustered in particular occupational groups (such as nursing) and personal services (such as domestic and catering work). This has led Buckley (in O'Connor and Goodwin, 2002, p 33) to observe:

> Overviewing Irish workers in Britain, we can see them rigorously channelled in to hyper-trophied gender-stereotypes, with millions of Irish women intensely engaged in the feeding, cleaning, healing, caring and teaching of millions of Britons and millions of Irish men focussed into clearing, constructing and fabricating the economic landscape of contemporary Britain.

O'Connor and Goodwin's (2002, p 47) own recent research has shown that, in the British labour market, the Irish-born tend to work longer hours than the UK-born.

However, Irish men and women under the age of 30 in 1991 were more likely to have a degree than men and women in the population as a whole (Walter et al, 2002a, p 33). In relation to social class, "Northern Irish-born men in England were more likely to be in the highest social class, Class 1, than the English-born" (Walter et al, 2002a, p 33). However, they were also more likely to be in the lowest Class 5 (2002a, p 33). The Republic-born men were "much more likely to in Social Class 5 than any other group of men, including Pakistanis and Black British" (Walter et al, 2002a, p 33). Indeed, overall the Republic-born were disproportionately located in the lower-ranked classes. The arrival, however, of "young, highly qualified people entering professional and managerial careers is likely to have produced significant changes in the overall profile during the 1990s" (Walter et al, 2002a, p 33).

Nevertheless, across a range of indices, the life opportunities of many Irish people in Britain continue to be impaired, yet this is rarely recognised in most mainstream discourses on 'race' and ethnicity. In terms of health status, Irish-born people in Britain suffer more ill health than the British population as a whole. That is to say, levels of ill health are higher than would be expected from demographic and socioeconomic status. Once the elderly profile (related to the high migration in the 1950s) and the class position of Irish people in Britain "has been accounted for, they are more ill than just these indicators would lead you to expect" (Walter et al, 2002a, p 42). Furthermore, Irish men are the *only* migrant group whose mortality rate is higher in Britain than in their country of origin (Hickman and Walter, 1997).

Research also indicates that Irish people are more likely to be hospitalised for mental distress, alcoholism, depression and schizophrenia and are more likely to be detained under mental health legislation and to be administered ECT (electro-convulsive therapy) (see, in this context, Moane, 2002). Irish women are particularly over-represented in admissions to mental health services facilities. Second-generation Irish people also have high levels of poor health and excess rates of mortality (Hickman and Walter, 1997; see also Pearson et al, 1991; Greenslade, 1992; Harrison and Carr-Hill, 1992; McCollum, 1994; Farrell, 1996; Mullen et al, 1996; Murphy, 1996; Tilki, 1996, 1998b; Walls, 1996; O'Brien and Power, 1998; Abbots et al, 1999; Foster, 2003).

In terms of housing, "a higher percentage of households with Irish-born heads ... lives in public sector rented property than either all White-headed or other ethnic minority headed groups" (Walter et al, 2002a, p 33; see also O'Flynn, 1992; Diaz, 2000; Cope, 2001; Warnes and Crane, 2001). On account of the war in the North of Ireland and operation of the Prevention of Terrorism Acts (Hillyard, 1993), Irish people were, of course, also subjected to differential policing with the Irish community being regarded as a "suspect community" (Hillyard, 1993). Even since the Belfast Agreement was signed in April 1998, indications remain that Irish people in Britain are subject to specific types of police surveillance (see 'Police watch ferry passengers', *The Irish Post*, 28 October, 2000; see also the editorial 'More revelations discredit the PTA', *The Irish Post*, 28 October, 2000; 'Treat all Irish as suspects, police ordered', *The Observer*, 10 December 2000; 'Police detain ferry couple', *The Irish Post*, 5 April 2003). Furthermore, other parts of the criminal justice system appear to relate to Irish people in a discriminatory way (Action for Irish Youth et al, 1997; Murphy, 1994; Mooney and Young, 1999; Carey, 2002; see also 'Irish ex-prisoners urged to help discover the truth of prison deaths', *The Irish Post*, 31 August 2002). Even more fundamentally, the prevalence and resilience of anti-Irish racism in Britain is rarely acknowledged (Miles, 1982, ch 6; Hickman and Walter, 1997; Commission on the Future of Multi-Ethnic Britain, 2000; Walter, 2000). The 'liberal' and 'quality' press, for example, frequently publishes contributions from 'star' columnists who make offensive remarks about Ireland and Irish people in Britain. Prominent in this respect have been contributions from Julie Birchall, Richard Ingrams and Lyn Barber. Derogatory and offensive representations of Irish people in British 'soaps', such as *Brookside* and *Eastenders*, have also been a recurring cultural trait even during a period when, as we have observed, being Irish is supposed to have had a certain 'cachet' (see, for example, 'BBC apologises to "backward and violent" Ireland', *The Guardian*, 24 September 1997; 'Brookside sparks a row', *The Irish Post*, 30 January 1999; see also the editorial 'The soaps that stain', *The Irish Post*, 16 January 1999)[13].

The specificity of the Irish experience in Britain may now, however, be beginning to be recognised by government. In 1995, the Commission for Racial Equality (CRE) recommended the inclusion of an Irish category in all UK ethnic-monitoring systems. This was followed two years later by the publication of a major CRE report, *Discrimination and the Irish community in Britain* (Hickman and Walter, 1997). Perhaps most significantly, as noted earlier, a self-identifying 'White Irish' category was also included in the 2001 Census. Furthermore, *all* issues associated with 'race' and ethnicity have a new resonance following the publication of the Macpherson Inquiry into the killing of Stephen Lawrence with the confirmation that the Metropolitan Police are 'institutionally racist' (Macpherson, 1999; Lea, 2000). In the light of this finding, *all* state and voluntary agencies need to interrogate their operational modalities, ethos and 'ways of seeing' questions concerning 'race' and ethnicity. Following the Race Relations (Amendment) Act 2000, the CRE has also published additional guidance for local authorities.

This book can also be understood as a response to the *Parekh report – The future of multi-ethnic Britain* (Commission on the Future of Multi-Ethnic Britain, 2000)[14]. This report highlighted the specificity of the Irish community and acknowledged that three million Irish people in Britain are "by far the largest migrant community" (2000, p 31). However, "all too often they are neglected in considerations of race and cultural diversity. It is essential that all such considerations should take their perceptions into account" (2000, p 31).

The Parekh report also draws attention to the significance of language in the discourse on 'race' and ethnicity. Important here is the report's reluctance to use the terms 'ethnic' and 'ethnic minority'. This book, although mindful of these comments featured in the Parekh report does, however, use the phrase 'ethnic minority'. In this context, the comments of Aspinall (2002, p 804) are also noteworthy. He observes that the Parekh report:

> explicitly avoids use of the term 'ethnic' on the grounds that its popular meaning may obscure its specialised usage. It also argues for a moratorium on the on the term 'minority' – consequently such terms as 'ethnic minority' and 'minority ethnic' – on the basis that 'the term "minority" has connotations of "less important" or marginal [and] in many settings is not only insulting, but is also misleading or inaccurate'. Such narrow policing of language is jejune in the context of debates about terminology for describing ethnicity and ethnic relations in Britain. While "minority", like any appellation, is open to misuse, this is not an argument to proscribe a term that is salient and has well established meaning: that of a 'statistical' minority rather than a connotation of lacking political and economic power.

The organisation of the book

It has been argued that "British child welfare practice has suffered from a lack of historical reflection" (Stevenson, 1998, p 154). Acknowledging the accuracy of this assertion, the first part of the book is concerned with the historical dimension to social work with Irish children and their families in Britain. In examining this issue, the book, therefore, critically analyses documentation, including both government and voluntary organisation sources, in Ireland and England. Chapter One begins in Ireland with an examination of the migration of Irish 'unmarried mothers'[15]. Up until the early 1970s, many Irish women temporarily fled from Ireland to England because of their fear of a type of incarceration in Ireland's Mother and Baby Homes (see also MPRH, 1941). Importantly, in contrast to Ireland where an 'unmarried mother' might spend two years or more in a Mother and Baby Home, the length of stay in such homes in England was only four months. Related to this was the lack of legal adoption in the Republic of Ireland until 1952 (Newman, 1951). This chapter draws on the archives of a child protection and rescue society, based in Dublin, in order to chart Irish concerns about what was termed the 'abnormal flight' of 'unmarried mothers' from Ireland to England. It also shows how thousands of migrant 'unmarried mothers' were 'repatriated' back to Ireland.

Chapter Two explores the process of repatriation in greater detail. Since the 1960s, of course, the whole idea of repatriation has more frequently been associated with discourses centred on racist projects to create a 'white' Britain. However, during the 1950s and 1960s, a particular construct of 'repatriation' was applied in a different sense in relation to pregnant, 'unmarried' Irish women. This is not to suggest that all Irish 'unmarried mothers' were repatriated, because some women were successful in their plans to leave home, in Ireland, give birth in England and then to return to Ireland with their child left behind and placed for adoption. Moreover, the repatriations were not underpinned by force of law. The repatriations were, however, an exclusionary process that was bound up with a range of discourses and practices that centred on the 'otherness' of these Irish women.

Importantly, British social work and associated welfare services were central in this process. Indeed, in the 1950s and 1960s, the initials PFI, or 'pregnant from Ireland', was part of the everyday vocabulary of the social workers dealing with 'unmarried mothers' arriving from Ireland. A number of case papers, from the late 1950s, examined in one Catholic Rescue Society in England are the focal part of this chapter. Chapter Three then examines the actions of the London County Council (LCC) and its 'daring experiment' to discharge children from 'care' to Ireland in the 1950s and 1960s. Here, it is maintained that dominant constructions of 'Ireland' played a role in the scheme. In addition, the LCC policy is examined and viewed in the context of other exclusionary practices centred on Irish people in Britain in the mid-20th century.

The second half of the book concentrates on the contemporary picture. Chapter Four, therefore, critically analyses Department of Health and other policy documents which, in effect, have tended to erase or render invisible Irish children and families in Britain. Here, it is argued that a critical factor is the failure to interrogate pivotal ideas about 'whiteness'. As Hazel Carby observes, there is a need to "think about the invention of the category of whiteness as well as that of blackness and, consequently, to make visible what is rendered invisible when viewed as the normative state of existence; the (white) point in space from which we tend to identify difference" (cited in Giroux, 1997, p 326). If the 'category of whiteness' is explored, in a British context, Irish experiences become apparent. Less theoretically, this chapter also comments on ways in which social workers might evolve more sensitive practices relating to Irish children requiring placements with substitute carers.

The foundation of Chapter Five is a discussion on the answers by directors of SSDs to a questionnaire that invited them to comments on their organisations' responses to Irish children and families. The key aim of this initiative was to map out how local authorities are operationally relating to Irish children and families and to identify ways in which services might be improved. Chapter Six then goes on to explore, in detail, the perceptions of a small number of Irish social workers currently working in London. These respondents cannot be seen as representative of *all* Irish social workers in Britain, yet they do provide insights into six significant themes: the approach to 'race' and ethnicity in social work; Irish identities in Britain; racism and stereotyping; placements and the non-recognition of Irish children; social work with children and families who are Irish Travellers; an agenda for the future. Mindful of the changing organisational shape of social work and social care services in Britain (Chief Secretary to the Treasury, 2003), the book's concluding chapter seeks to bring together key themes that have emerged in the book and considers these in the context of what has been referred to as the 'politics of recognition'.

Notes

[1] The US investment bankers Morgan Stanley coined the term 'Celtic Tiger' in 1994 (see the critical discussions in Allen, 1999; Kirkby et al, 2002a; Coulter and Coleman, 2003). Mayer (2003, p 27) has recently observed that we are "now in the post-Celtic Tiger phase as each day brings fresh news of an increase in inflation or unemployment". Moreover, Walter et al (2002a, p 97) have argued that that "Northern Ireland has not shared in the Celtic Tiger prosperity of sections of the Republic's workforce and more young people are still leaving than returning".

[2] On account of specific cultural and political factors, social work and Irish people in Scotland will not be included in the following discussion (see Devine, 2000; Walter et al, 2002a, pp 46-50; Walls and Williams, 2003). Wales, moreover, has had a "very small Irish-born population during the post-War period" (Walter et al, 2002a, p 31). This book, therefore, is mainly focused on England, although Chapter Five includes data from Wales. In his book *Cultural competence in the caring professions*, O'Hagan (2001, ch 11) includes a fascinating discussion on efforts to promote Irish culture and the Irish language in Northern Ireland and the responses of social work and social care professionals.

[3] 'Social work' will be broadly conceived in what follows. Most of the latter half of the book will focus on local authority social work: that provided by SSDs. However, elsewhere – especially in the more historical chapters – the discussion will also encompass charitable provision, particularly 'rescue' services provided by the Roman Catholic Church. Still related to social work, this book will not seek to explore and precisely define distinctions between, for example, 'anti-discriminatory social work

practice' and 'anti-oppressive practice'. Others have spent worthwhile time and energy in providing theoretical clarification: Preston-Shoot (1995) and Dominelli (1996) have provided their own definitions of 'anti-oppressive practice'. Mallinson's (1995) preferred formulation is the somewhat bland 'non-oppressive practice'. Both anti-discriminatory social work practice and anti-oppressive practice have been usefully explored and discussed in Harlow and Hearn (1996, pp 5-8), Thompson (1993) and O'Hagan (2001). Throughout this book, 'anti-discriminatory social work practice' is the preferred phrase.

[4] How race and ethnicity are, more generally, conceptualised in Britain is discussed, in detail, in Anthias and Yuval-Davis (1993), Mason (1995) and O'Hagan (2001). Hall (2000) also contains a useful discussion. More recently, Gilroy (2000, p 17) has made the case for the "deliberate and self-conscious renunciation of 'race' as a means to categorize and divide humankind". He goes on to promote a "pragmatic, planetary humanism". See particularly chapter one of Gilroy's book. His compelling and controversial perspective is criticised in, for example, St Louis (2002).

[5] For a similar 'cosmopolitan point of view', see Waldron (2000).

[6] A number of writers have observed that Lloyd's critique is firmly located in an American context and is not, in truth, entirely transferable to Britain (see Kenny, 2003). Ryan (1994) has also provided a critique of the idea of an Irish diaspora.

[7] Miles (1982, p 123) has observed that "Irish labour was a crucial component of capitalist development. Indeed, in the case of the west of Scotland, it is difficult to see how capitalist industrialisation could have occurred at the scale and speed it did without Irish labour". Jim MacLaughlin (1997, p 28) is also correct to point out, in relation to those who left for America, that the Irish "gravitated to the urban centres of the east coast of North America but also played a significant role in clearing native Americans from the interior" and "were among the chief benefactors of white colonial and capitalist expansion in North America".

[8] Related to this are Hickman's (2002, p 16) comments on the 'plastic Paddy', a "term deployed in order to deny and denigrate the second-generation Irish in Britain". This epithet, quite common in the 1980s was, she observes, "frequently articulated by new middle-class Irish immigrants in Britain, for whom it was a means of distancing themselves from established Irish communities".

[9] This is not, of course, to disparage the work of those organisations that are currently providing specialist social work and social care services specifically for Irish people (Kowarzik, 1994; Korwarzik, 1997). *Díon* means roof, or shelter and the *Díon* Committee, established by the government of the Republic of Ireland supports 97 voluntary sector jobs in Britain (Task Force on Policy regarding Emigrants, 2002, p 48).

———

[10] It is recognised that ideas that pivot on 'social exclusion' are somewhat problematic (see, for example, Byrne, 1999; Garrett, 2003).

[11] See also 'Bodies lay unnoticed for weeks', *The Irish Post*, 9 August 1997. Here it was reported that that one of these bodies, that of a 75-year-old cancer sufferer, had lain for three weeks in his flat, four floors above the local SSD office. O'Connor (1972, pp 127-8) has written about how the deregulated sector of the building industry worked in the early 1970s. Here, 'the lump' referred to sub-contracted labour, which was paid for by the hour or day and was neither insured, registered, nor officially recorded. Many Irishmen in Britain worked in this way (see also the stories of MacAmhlaigh, 1966, 2001). Ruth Dudley Edwards (1998) provides a rather dismissive and scornful interpretation of the vulnerability of some older Irish people in Britain. It is increasingly recognised that some older people in Britain may also have been subjected to 'institutional abuse' in Ireland (see Hunter, 2002). The Irish Survivors Outreach Service (ISOS) can be contacted at the London Irish Centre; Haringey Irish Centre; Coventry Irish Centre; Sheffield Irish Centre; Manchester Irish Community Care.

[12] Irish Travellers are considered as an ethnic group under the terms of the 1976 Race Relations Act. However, the National Lottery has been pilloried for funding a research project on Irish Travellers (see 'How your lottery money goes to Rwandan potters, Yorkshire male prostitutes and Irish Travellers – but is denied to British war heroes', *The Daily Mail*, 11 October 2002). Nevertheless, *Room to roam: Britain's Irish Travellers* is an important social research project on Irish Traveller communities in Britain. Focusing on London and Manchester, the project is based at St Mary's College, Strawberry Hill, Twickenham, TW1 4SX (http://www.smuc.ac.uk/irishstudies/roomtoroam.htm). The 1994 Criminal Justice and Public Order Act relieved local authorities of their duty to provide authorised sites for Travellers and it also made it much easier to evict Travellers when they are parked illegally and removed central government grants for new council-run sites. In a number of areas, this legislation has contributed to the severe overcrowding and worsening conditions on existing sites. Vanderbeck (2003, p 365) has argued that the act "has increased the already strong pressure on Traveller families to move onto official sites (which are often little more than state-sponsored ghettos)". The Traveller Law Reform Bill, designed to counter discrimination against Gypsies and Travellers, was introduced in parliament in 2002. In the interviews with Irish social workers, featured in Chapter Six of this book, it is clear that the situation of Irish Travellers and their engagement with social work and social welfare agencies should be a major concern for those seeking to promote anti-discriminatory social work practice.

[13] See also the reports: 'Family say they're being terrorised', *The Irish World*, 19 March 1999; 'Irish race slur', *The Irish Post*, 17 July 1999; 'Tories brand Irish "aliens"', *The Irish Post*, 5 February, 2000; 'Irish Centre suffers third strike by racist vandals', *The Irish Post*, 18 May 2002; 'College to pay damages to racially-abused teacher', *The Irish Post*, 21 June, 2003. Curtis (1997) discusses historical representations of Irish people in Victorian caricature. In this context, McClintock (1994, p 52) has correctly observed that the

"English stereotype of the Irish as a simianized and degenerate race also complicates postcolonial theories that skin colour (what Gayati Spivak usefully calls 'chromatism') is the crucial sign of otherness". Eagleton (1998) makes a number of telling, pithy remarks on this body of theory and Duncan (2002, p 323) argues that the Irish do not "fit the racial and geographic borders assumed by most postcolonial scholars".

[14] Pilkington (2003, ch 8) contains a summary of the media's response to the publication of the Parekh report. He argues that this report "served as a 'proxy target' for the resentment felt [by some] towards the earlier Macpherson report" (Pilkington, 2003, p 273; see also 'British tag is "coded racism"', *The Guardian*, 11 October 2000).

[15] In the more historically focused chapters of the book, the term 'unmarried mother' will be used because this is how some women were referred to, identified and labelled during the period being discussed (see Fink, 2000). However, as Fink and Holden (1999, p 234) have argued, "married and unmarried womanhood" are not coherent oppositional or stable categories either in their "assumptions about women's sexual and reproductive behaviour or in their definition of marital status". It is conceded that Irish men, as fathers, do not feature in the account provided in this book. Indeed, this is certainly an area that merits further research.

ONE

Fleeing Ireland: social exclusion and the flight of Irish 'unmarried mothers' to England in the 1950s and 1960s

Luckier girls, on board a ship, watch new hope spraying from the bollard.
(Austin Clarke, 'Unmarried mothers', cited in McCormack, 1992)

Carol Smart (2000) has maintained that archival research is vitally important and provides us with an additional way to comprehend the evolution of social policy and the discursive practices of the welfare state. Perhaps this is particularly significant in terms of how questions related to 'race' and ethnicity have been constructed. This and the following two chapters will examine, therefore, how Irish mothers and their children were responded to in the 1950s and 1960s. We will begin in Ireland where official concerns about the migration of 'unmarried mothers' in the period after the setting up the Irish Free State in 1922 provide part of the historical foundation for some of the issues examined in the rest of the book. An exploration of the situation *within* Ireland at this time enables us to examine how one particular group of Irish citizens felt compelled to make a brief, but expeditious, 'flight'. Using more contemporary vocabulary, it could be maintained that the women who are the focal concern of this chapter left the national territory because they were socially excluded. Many, however, were then subjected to exclusionary practices in England and pressurised to return to Ireland.

As Walter et al (2002a, pp 15-19) argue, social exclusion has rarely been perceived as a cause of Irish emigration in academic literature (see also Powell, 1992). Here, the dominant explanatory models have tended to interpret post-1945 emigration as being prompted by economic factors with the employment situation 'at home' being viewed as the key determinant. More recently, Irish emigration has also been perceived in a more positive light in the context of more encompassing global mobility generated by the spread of the free market economy and technological changes (Brah et al, 1999). Nonetheless, in an historical and contemporary context, processes of social exclusion can be seen to have influenced decisions to leave Ireland. This relates to pregnant 'unmarried mothers' in the past and, perhaps, to the women currently travelling from the island of Ireland to Britain for abortions (Oaks, 2002). This form of migration "constitutes an important migration flow which is undercounted and usually omitted from discussions on emigration" (Walter et al, 2002a, p 18). Indeed, it has been argued that "the experience of abortion represents Ireland's hidden Diaspora" (Ruane, cited in Walter et al, 2002a, p 18). Current estimates of numbers of women travelling from the Republic of Ireland to Britain for terminations are at 7,000 per annum (Walter et al, 2002a, p 18). However, the real figure is likely to be much higher. Each year, thousands of women are also travelling from Northern Ireland in order to have abortions in Britain (Rossiter and Sexton, 2001).

Clearly, other groups in Irish society can be regarded as having migrated to Britain because of social exclusion in Ireland. This could encompass gay and lesbian emigration; the emigration of some of those who had been in care in Ireland (Kelleher et al, 2000); 'political' migration from Northern Ireland, particularly in the 1970s and 1980s. Moreover, many of these groups and individuals are likely, of course, to have contact with social work and social care services in Britain. However, here the aim will be specifically to examine the situation of 'unmarried mothers'. In this context, the annual reports of the Child Protection and Rescue Society of Ireland (CPRSI) and official reports produced by the Irish government provide valuable documentary sources[1].

We begin by briefly examining the response to Irish 'unmarried mothers' after the inception of the Irish Free State in the early 1920s. This will be followed by an exploration on the opposition to legal child adoption and the dominant discourse on child adoption and 'unmarried mothers' in Ireland from the early 1950s until the late 1960s. Being still focused on the situation within the relatively new state, the aim will then be to chart and to interpret 'official' concerns about the migration of 'unmarried mothers' to Britain. This will provide part of the foundation for the next chapter, which will reveal how some of these women were apt to be responded to after they had made the journey across the Irish Sea.

'Unmarried mothers', social authoritarianism and the Irish Free State (1922-37)[2]

Initially, it is important briefly to refer to the wider societal context in which policies toward 'unmarried mothers' evolved in the state that emerged after (part of) Ireland had attained a limited form of independence in 1922 (Garvin, 1996). In brief, this was a period when the role of women was increasingly constrained and some of the hopes of socialists, feminists and others involved in the struggle for independence were shattered (Lloyd, 1999, pp 39-40)[3]. Heather Ingman (2002, p 254) has recently and succinctly identified some of the key legislative changes for women in this period:

> [F]ixed constructs of gender played a key role in the building of the new
> Irish State and became institutionalised in its juridical structure. Despite
> the declaration of equal rights in the 1916 Proclamation, repeated in the
> 1922 Free State Constitution, as well as the prominence of Irish women in

the suffrage movement, women's position after 1922 saw a gradual erosion of their political rights. Political and public life were regarded as masculine spheres; women were subjected to efforts by the political and ecclesiastical authorities to confine their activities to the home and to a single identity, the domestic. Among the measures taken were the imposition of marriage bars, restrictions on women's employment in the civil service (1925), restrictions of industrial employment (1935), the Juries Bill of 1927 which exempted women from jury service, the Criminal Law Amendment Bill of 1934 banning the sale or importation of contraceptives. These efforts on the part of the authorities to restrict women to the home culminated in de Valera's 1937 Constitution founded on the family unit.

These developments helped to shape the social location and fix the cultural milieu for Irish women in this period. Equally important, however, were the consequences for those women who acted in a way that ran counter to the dominant order. Here, sexual transgression was important and how this was responded to and the types of sanctions put in place was of significance in terms of how 'unmarried mothers' were viewed and treated.

The official statistics for 'illegitimate' births remained low throughout the period of the Irish Free State. In 1921-22, these births amounted to just 2.6% of all births in the 26 counties (that is, the Free State, now the Republic of Ireland). In 1933-34, the percentage peaked at 3.5% (Whyte, 1971, p 31). What began to appear during the late 1920s, however, was a bifurcated policy towards 'unmarried mothers'. This policy, for example, was apparent in the report of the Commission on the Relief of the Sick and Destitute Poor, including the Insane Poor (1927). Here 'two classes' of 'unmarried mothers' were delineated: "those who may be amenable to reform" and "the less hopeful cases" (1927, p 68). The language and tone of the Commission's report indicates, moreover, a shift toward the criminalisation of such women in that it was reported, on 27 March 1926, that "there were in the County Homes and Dublin Workhouse, 629 'unmarried mothers' classed as first *offenders* and 391 women who had fallen more than once" (1927, p 8; emphasis added). The Commission next advocated treatment techniques, which were intended to set apart 'first offenders' from the 'less hopeful' cases. Thus, it went on, the treatment of the former "must necessarily be in the nature of moral upbringing" and be characterised by the traits of firmness and discipline, but also charity and sympathy. This would take place in special establishments and a prototype, founded by the Sisters of the Sacred Hearts of Jesus and Mary, was opened in 1922 – the Sacred Heart Home, Bessborough, County Cork. Here, only those 'unmarried mothers' likely to be "influenced toward a useful and respectable life" were placed (Department of Local Government and Public Health Annual Report 1928-29, p 113). By the late 1920s, some 65 mothers were situated at Bessborough and trained in domestic work, poultry keeping and gardening. They also received instruction in religion and, at length, were "provided with a suitable situation" and their children were boarded out with foster mothers

(Department of Local Government and Public Health Annual Report, 1928-29, p 113). Other special establishments for 'first offenders' were established and – unlike Bessborough – operated by the local authority, although still staffed by nuns. These were located at Pelletstown (Dublin), Tuam (Galway) and Kilrush (Clare). However, 70% of 'unmarried mothers' remained in the county homes or former workhouses. The policy aim, however, was to try to ensure that 'unmarried mothers' were placed in establishments similar to the one at Bessborough.

In respect of the other category, the so-called 'less hopeful case', or "residue composed probably of those who are the least open to good influences", the Commission, reporting in 1927, proposed that a period of detention was fitting. In circumstances where an 'unmarried mother', pregnant for a third time, applied for relief to a poor law institution, the Board of Health, it was proposed, should have the "power to detain" the mother for "such a period as they think fit, having considered the recommendation of the Superior or Matron of the Home" (Commission on the Relief of the Sick and Destitute Poor, including the Insane Poor, 1927, p 69). The authors of the report observed:

> The term of detention we recommend is not an irreducible period and is not intended to be in any sense penal. It is primarily for the benefit of the woman and her child, and its duration will depend entirely on the individual necessities of the case. We are not in favour of the rigid application of fixed periods of detention ... the widest possible discretionary powers should be exercised. The object of the recommendations is to regulate control according to individual requirements, or in the most degraded cases to segregate those who have become sources of evil, danger, and expense to the community. (1927, p 69)

Prior to discharge from a poor law institution, it was mooted that these 'unmarried mothers' should also fulfil the requirements of the Board of Health in terms of being demonstrably able to "provide for her child or children, either by way of paying wholly or partially for maintenance in the Home or boarding it out with respectable people approved by the Board of Health" (1927, p 69).

These proposals seem to have had a swift impact. The Department of Local Government and Board of Health report, published in the early 1930s, stated that "intractable" 'unmarried mothers' were finding themselves admitted to Magdalen asylums in Dublin and elsewhere throughout the country. Many of these women, it was alleged, were "feeble minded" and in need of "supervision and guardianship". Thus, the Magdalen asylums offered "special provision" for this "class" (Department of Local Government and Public Health Annual Report, 1931-32, p 129). Despite this, many of these 'intractable' mothers, or 'hopeless cases', continued to find their way into the county homes or workhouses. One of the Free State's two inspectors for boarded-out children, Miss Litster, condemned them for their "weak intellect" and lack of "moral fibre", and her report concluded with a further call for "the power of detention in special cases" (Department of Local Government and Public Health Annual Report, 1931-32, p 294). Her inspector colleague, Miss Fitzgerald-Kenney, who called for the detention of 'unmarried mothers' of "an unstable character" also shared this view (Department of Local Government and Public Health Annual Report, 1931-32, p 289).

Opposition to legal child adoption

The response to 'unmarried mothers' in Ireland was also connected to the issue of child adoption. Legal adoption had been introduced in England and Wales in 1926, in Northern Ireland in 1929 and in Scotland in 1930. However, no legal adoption existed in the Republic of Ireland until 1952. Whyte (1971, p 184), moreover, has stated that no question was asked in the Dáil, the Irish parliament, on the introduction of legal adoption until 1939.

A campaign had begun for its introduction in 1948 with the formation of a skilled pressure group, the Adoption Society (Ireland), but even in the early 1950s and despite the wide coalition of support for adoption there was opposition to such plans (Newman, 1951). General MacEoin, Minister of Justice in the inter-party government (1948-51) opposed any attempt to introduce reform, and it was suggested by Charles Casey, the Attorney General, that a statute on adoption might breach the constitution. Fears were also expressed that legal adoption might run counter to the teaching of the Roman Catholic Church (Maguire, 2002; Keating, 2003). In this latter respect, perennial concerns were voiced about 'illegitimate' children being adopted by "kindly people not of her faith" (Casey, cited in Whyte, 1971, p 190). Indeed, Whyte's view is that this fear that reform "would facilitate proselytism ... was probably the strongest objection to legal adoption" (Whyte, 1971, p 191). Having won the approval of the Church, a private member's bill was introduced, however, and this became law in 1952 (Whyte, 1971, pp 275-77). This act made it plain that adopting parents were to be of the same religion as the 'illegitimate' child.

One further component of the opposition to legal adoption should be identified and this was summed up by a rural deputy's contention that legal adoption, in interfering with the line of succession, was "like interfering with a stud-book" (Whyte, 1971, p 187). This crudely put sentiment was attached to rural concerns about patterns of land and property inheritance being disrupted. Perhaps more significantly, however, this critique highlights the fact that frequently in Ireland, and particularly in the context of the post-Famine restructured agrarian economy, every issue *returns*, in some respects, to more fundamental questions that are rooted in discourses centred on patriarchy and land ownership (Gibbon, 1973; Kinealy, 1994; Gibbon and Curtin, 1978). Specifically in this context, and as Catherine Nash (1993, p 44) observes, the "moral code supported the economic and social system of family farming, which demanded the regulation of sexuality for the control of inheritance".

Despite there not having been legal child adoption in the 26-county state until the early 1950s, there had, however, been de facto adoptions (Barrett, 1952, p 11) and what one anonymous writer referred to as "the export of Irish children in the name of lonely souls everywhere" (MPRH, 1941; see also Maguire 2002). In the 1950s, particularly, many 'illegitimate' children born in Ireland were 'handed over' to childless couples in the US. Indeed, despite the Church being somewhat hesitant about the introduction of legal adoption, it remained complicit, throughout the 1950s and 1960s, in covert and legally dubious endeavours to provide childless American couples who were Roman Catholics with children. Furthermore, these 'adoptions' frequently occurred without there having been full and rigorous assessments of the potential adoptive parents. These arrangements were also characterised by a racist subtext in that, for many white citizens of the US, Ireland was the place where a child could be acquired who had little chance of possessing any "negro blood" (Milotte, 1997, p 56). However, in the mid-1960s, the CPRSI began to comment on specific factors associated with finding adoptive parents for black, or 'coloured', children who were 'illegitimate' and born to Irish mothers:

> The pressing challenge which faces our Adoption Department at the moment is the finding of suitable adoptive parents for children of mixed race. This is a particularly difficult problem and one which causes us much concern. Every deprived child is in need of the love and affection which the adoptive home provides. The need is even greater in the case of the coloured child, for the security provided by loving adoptive parents is essential if he is to be able to face life with what some at least regard as *the added disability of colour* (CPRSI Annual Report, 1966, pp 2-3; emphasis added).

Child adoption and 'unmarried motherhood' following the introduction of the 1952 Adoption Act

Following the introduction of legal child adoption, a more embracing professional and international discourse on child adoption and 'unmarried motherhood' had an impact on the way in which 'experts' in Ireland addressed and framed the issue (see Bowlby, 1990; Spensky, 1990). So, for example, a member of *An Bord Uchtala* (the Irish Adoption Board), writing in the religious periodical *Christus Rex* in the mid-1950s, stressed the importance of John Bowlby's assertions concerning the "permanency of the mother substitute" for those children who were unable to live with their birth mother. The dominance of this approach was such that it was "not too far removed from common ordinary sense" (Macauley, 1955). Within Ireland, however, there were also a small number of individuals who played a key role in mapping out an authoritative conceptual framework for the theory and practice of child adoption. Perhaps the central figure here was Cecil J. Barrett, "the acknowledged clerical expert on child fostering and adoption" in Ireland (Milotte, 1997, p 30; see also Barrett, 1955)[4].

Barrett's *Adoption*, was published in 1952 and at the time it was regarded as the "definitive guide to adoption practice" (Barrett, 1952, p 176). The book reflected the contemporary understanding in that adoption was regarded as a 'closed' system. That is to say, once the mother and her child were separated they were never to see each other again. Perhaps not surprisingly, however, although being informed by dominant secular discourses on child adoption, Barrett was also preoccupied with the spiritual – or, more specifically, Catholic – component and this was most apparent in his approach to 'unmarried mothers'. Here, for example, Barrett adumbrated how the Roman Catholic social worker was different from her secular counterpart:

> The efforts of non-Catholic social workers in other countries on behalf of the unmarried mother are tending more and more to become purely humanitarian. The emphasis is laid on her social and economic difficulties to the disregard of her moral problems. While her fall may be deplored because she has a child to provide for, only too often it is readily condoned and excused. Her condition is referred to as the unfortunate consequence of a slip or a mistake on her part. She has been the victim of bad luck resulting in an unhappy embarrassment and she is advised to be more careful next time! No cognisance is taken of the gravity of sin or the beauty of the virtue of purity. The very idea of sin would sometimes appear to be outside the ambit of their ministrations. (Barrett, 1952, p 23)

For the Catholic social worker, therefore, "material assistance" was of "no avail, unless the rents in the mother's spiritual fabric" were "repaired" (Barrett, 1952, p 24). Here, the provision of accommodation fulfilled a central role. Mother and Baby Homes run by the Sisters of the Sacred Hearts of Jesus and Mary were, as observed earlier, available to 'assist' in such circumstances. The first of these establishments was opened, as we saw earlier, at Bessborough, in 1922. By the early 1950s, similar institutions had also been opened in Roscrea (1930-69) and Castlepollard (1935-71). These so-called 'extern institutions', still reflecting the recommendations of the Commission that reported in 1927, only accepted the "girl expecting her first baby", and "every effort" was "made to safeguard her secret". Consequently, each woman entering such a home was given a "new name" and each resident was left unaware of the true identity of other residents (Barrett, 1952, p 42; see also Luddy, 1995, ch 4).

A number of disadvantages existed, however, for the unmarried mother. First, the centrality of the secrecy inherent in such arrangements was likely to reinforce the sense of shame and sin. Indeed, this was an essential aim of such homes which remained intent on imprinting on the minds of such mothers what Barrett referred to as the "gravity of sin" (see also Viney, 1966; Wallace, 1995; Torode and O'Sullivan, 1999). Second, and still associated with the notion of secrecy, this arrangement reinforced patriarchal power; this is reflected in the various ways that this secrecy aided anonymous birth fathers and "protected men and male reputations" (Milotte, 1997, p 195). Despite the day-to-day control of such establishments remaining with nuns, it was men, and particularly priests and doctors (Barrett, 1952, p 43; see also Goulding, 1999), who performed the important functions of gate keeping and referring women who were to be admitted to such homes. Finally, but crucially for the 'unmarried mothers' directly concerned, they might be, in effect, incarcerated for a number of years to enable their spiritual and moral regeneration to take root. On account of this situation, Barrett conceded that most "girls do not like going to a Mother and Baby Home because they consider that they will have to remain there too long" (Barrett, 1952, p 44; see also Creegan, 1967). Indeed, as an anonymous author reported in the literary periodical *The Bell*, many women refused to go to such homes because it meant "in effect, two years imprisonment". Moreover, there was "about the two year period of restraint a suggestion of 'punishment' and 'moral regeneration'" (MPRH, 1941, p 82). The same author also castigated the standard of the state provision available in Dublin (St Patrick's, Pelletstown) and Galway (Children's Home, Tuam) for 'unmarried mothers' pregnant for a second, or more, occasion.

The threat of a type of incarceration in semi-penal institutions, therefore, was likely to be one of the main reasons why so many pregnant 'unmarried mothers' were intent on fleeing to Britain to give birth and have children adopted. However, many were, as we shall see later, thwarted and compelled to return to Ireland.

Official concerns about the migration of expectant 'unmarried mothers' from Ireland to Britain

Since the inception of the Southern Irish state and running parallel to the evolution of policy relating to 'illegitimacy' and child adoption, there had been official concerns about the migration of 'unmarried mothers'. In the late 1920s, for example, it was noted that evidence had been received from the Catholic Aid Society in Liverpool that a number of expectant mothers were migrating from Ireland to England (Commission on the Relief of the Sick and Destitute Poor, including the Insane Poor, 1927, p 73). At this time, however, the commission was "not prepared to put forward any scheme for repatriation". It was similarly noted that these women "become public charges in Great Britain" and, indeed, this aspect was to become a recurring theme connected to the way in which English agencies responded. In 1927, the Commission was of the view that "better organisation ... of the machinery for dealing with expectant 'unmarried mothers'" would reduce "the number impelled to cross to Great Britain".

In 1931, the Committee on the Criminal Law Amendment Acts (1880-85) and Juvenile Prostitution returned to the subject. Once again, evidence had been provided from Liverpool, and the committee concluded that migration of expectant mothers was increasing. The Liverpool Society for the Prevention of the International Traffic in Women and Children, which met female travellers on the docks and at Lime Street Station, reported that between 1926 and 1930, it met 1,947 Irish expectant mothers. Other voluntary organisations in

Liverpool, Leeds and London also identified a similar trend (Committee on the Criminal Law Amendment Acts, 1880-85 and Juvenile Prostitution, 1931, pp 10-11). The Department of Local Government and Public Health also observed that "several complaints" had been received from English rescue societies about "the number of girls who having got into trouble leave the Free State and go to England" (Department of Local Government and Public Health Annual Report 1931-32, pp 129-30). Such was the concern that a special conference took place involving representatives of the English agencies and inspectors from the department where it was "agreed that every effort should be made to discourage girls going to England and in such circumstances to bring them back when possible". Since the conference, a number of women had already "been sent back" and arrangements made in Dublin for "their reception". No connection was made, however, between the migration of these expectant mothers and the punitive and semi-penal regimes they faced had they remained inside the Free State.

In the Department's annual report for 1934-35 (p 180), a specific paragraph was devoted to 'Repatriation of Irish 'unmarried mothers". One of the key agencies facilitating this arrangement in Ireland was the CPRSI. By the late 1930s, and at the "special request of the Cardinal and Archbishops of Ireland", the CPRSI had taken 'charge' in terms of assisting in the return of expectant 'unmarried mothers' to Ireland (CPRSI Annual Report, 1940, p 4). Indeed, the CPRSI's annual report for 1948, reflecting the increased amount of time and energy being devoted to such work, began to carry a special section on 'Repatriation Cases' (see Table 1.1)[5].

During 1948, for example, "40 of these girls, either before or shortly after confinement" had been "brought home" and parents of "girls" were warned to be "on their guard if a daughter unexpectedly and without apparent reason hastens off to England" (CPRSI Annual Report, 1948, p 2). However, the following year the CPRSI injected a new note of urgency with the claim that "Irish unmarried expectant mothers are constantly going to England for their confinement", and 50 had been repatriated during the year. Similar to the writer in *The Bell*, eight years earlier (MPRH, 1941), the report, perhaps because of the organisation's direct contact with the women concerned, referred to perhaps the prime reason for these women's migration:

> Reports from English Catholic rescue workers show that many girls refuse to return home because of the long period which they must spend in the Special Mother and Baby Homes in the country. We have little doubt that many of the girls would never willingly go to England or would willingly return if the term to be spent in the Special Homes here was shortened. (CPRSI Annual Report, 1949, pp 2-3)

In the annual report for 1952, the year of the Adoption Act, the CPRSI reported that the number of repatriated mothers was on the increase: 85 had been repatriated and there "were many times that number who refused to return to

Table 1.1: Annual totals of Irish women repatriated via the Catholic Protection and Rescue Society of Ireland (1948-71)

Year	Number of women	Year	Number of women
1948	40	1960	113
1949	50	1961	181
1950	55	1962	185
1951	51	1963	135
1952	85	1964	173
1953	112	1965	195
1954	115	1966	213
1955	121	1967	183
1956	123	1968	120
1957	100	1969	145
1958	85	1970	91
1959	89	1971	33

Ireland" (CPRSI Annual Report, 1952, p 2). Here, the CPRSI again linked the length of these women's confinement in institutional provision in Ireland with their wish to give birth in England:

> Apart from the services of a few voluntary societies in Dublin, such as ours, all of which are constantly in financial difficulties, the only facilities available for the unmarried mother are County Homes and three special Mother and Baby Homes. The local authorities maintain the girls in these institutions, and a girl has little chance of going free until she has remained almost two years with the child in the institution. How can any girl remain such a long time out of touch with her home and her friends and still preserve her secret? The result is the abnormal flight to England with the consequent danger to both mother and infant. (CPRSI Annual Report, 1952, p 2)

In the 26-county state, there were reported to be 806 'unmarried mothers' in County Homes and the three Special Homes for 'unmarried mothers' on 31 March 1953 (Commission on Emigration and Other Population Problems, 1955, p 265), but that year alone the CPRSI had assisted in the repatriation of 112 'unmarried mothers' (CPRSI Annual Report, 1953, p 2) and the following year the number had reached 115 (CPRSI, 1954, p 2). In 1955, the CPRSI claimed that the "situation appears to be particularly bad in the London area and the Crusade of Rescue, while doing magnificent work in helping our Irish girls, reports that it cannot cope with the large numbers – estimated to be many hundreds annually" (CPRSI, 1954, p 1). The fear that had dominated the early reports of the CPRSI was also apparent in the worries expressed that the children of Catholic mothers might be "lost" to non-Catholics adopters and a new note was introduced in that it was suggested that "some girls place their children with English non-Catholic adoptive parents" because of "their preference" for "adoption rather than institutional care for their children". This meant, however, that they were "prepared to sacrifice a child's Faith for its apparent material welfare". The point about Irish women's opposition to institutional care for their children will be returned to later, but the comments about the availability of "apparent material welfare" in England hints, perhaps, at a more fundamental cultural malaise and disappointment about the lack of affluence in the 26-county state (Commission on Emigration and Other Population Problems, 1955). The contrast with Britain might, moreover, have appeared to be particularly pronounced in the 1950s when Harold Macmillan was telling the public that they had "never had it so good" (see Hall et al, 1978). The CPRSI soon returned, however, to its chief preoccupation in the 1950s:

> We believe that a partial remedy lies in the hands of those who control the Mother and Baby Homes in this country. In no other country in the world has the unmarried mother to remain for two years in a Home with her child. A few months is regarded as sufficient to allow the mother time to decide on the future of her child and is also believed to be adequate in helping her towards moral rehabilitation. Any longer period is regarded as punitive and it is becoming increasingly obvious that our girls will not submit themselves voluntarily to punitive treatment. (CPRSI, 1954, p 2)

In 1955, the Commission on Emigration and Other Population Problems (1955, p 264) also made it clear that there was no legal basis for 'unmarried mothers' being detained in this way, but the matrons of these establishments, who were religious sisters in the three Mother and Baby Homes for 'first offenders', had wide discretionary powers as the local managers of such institutions. The Commission also reported that the illegitimacy rate had fallen in the early 1950s; the annual rate for illegitimate births per 100 total live births was 3.5 for 1914-50, but for 1951 and 1952 this had dropped to 2.5. It was conceded, however, that these figures were likely to "'understate the problem". One reason for this was because of the "births of illegitimate children whose conception took place in the Twenty Six Counties but whose birth occurred elsewhere" (Commission on Emigration and Other Population Problems, 1955, p 101). In 1955, the year the commission published its report, the CPRSI assisted in the repatriation of "121 Irish girls with their babies from England" (CPRSI Annual Report, 1955, p 1).

In following year, the CPRSI responded to criticisms that had apparently appeared in the press suggesting that Irish "unmarried mother's" going to England "did not receive the help they needed in their own country". It set out, therefore, "emphatically to nail this inaccuracy" by stressing its various activities, which included authorising welfare officers of the Catholic Social Welfare Bureau, who worked on the boats leaving Dublin for Liverpool and Holyhead, to offer the help of the CPRSI to migrant 'unmarried mothers'.

The annual report for the following year stated that 100 mothers had been repatriated and also listed those Diocesan Rescue Societies – in Westminster, Birmingham, Southwark, Liverpool, Salford, Nottingham, Clifton, Portsmouth, Shrewsbury and Glasgow – that had been responsible for requesting repatriation and the assistance of the CPRSI. The majority of these requests came, and continued to come, from the Crusade of Rescue in Westminster.

The CPRSI defined 'repatriation' as follows:

> It means simply this: that we bring back to Ireland those pregnant girls who go over to England seeking help from already burdened English Rescue Societies. When a girl, pregnant from this country, seeks the assistance of our counterparts in England or Wales, we authorise those to who she turns to offer our help in providing her with ante-natal and post natal accommodation and with the provision for care of her child. If she is willing to accept our offer and return to Ireland, we arrange her accommodation and promise her help in planning for her child. The English worker provides her with a ticket to Dublin and puts her on a train; our worker meets her at the boat and we interview her at our office, provide her with meals and a ticket to her destination here. Her 'destination' is always far removed from her own native place and she herself has the right to choose it. When her baby has been born she writes to us and then we help her in the manner chosen by her. All this work goes on quietly and confidentially and absolute secrecy is guaranteed to each girl. (CPRSI Annual Report, 1960, pp 2-3)

In 1961, 181 'unmarried mothers' were repatriated, the highest number the CPRSI had been involved in until that year. Indeed, by 1964, such was the amount of work that repatriation was engendering, that 'Repatriation' (together with 'Child Care and Adoption' and the 'Unmarried Mother') began to feature on a new masthead for the CPRSI's annual reports. Concerns existed, however, not only about the children of these mothers finding themselves adopted by non-Catholics; there were also worries, in the new era seemingly heralded by the reforms of the administration of Sean Lemass, that 'unmarried mothers' travelling to England were betraying the nation, since "with each such girl who arrives in England, the false impression abroad of Ireland as a cruel, intolerant land gains momentum" (CPRSI Annual Report, 1964, p 4; see also Bew and Patterson, 1982).

Despite such criticisms, the number being repatriated increased to 213 in 1966. The majority of these repatriations continued to be from the London area. In 1967, the CPRSI warned of "an added and very grave danger" – the legalisation of abortion – which "placed a temptation of a very serious nature before the distraught unmarried mother". However, possibly related to the availability of legal abortion in England, the numbers repatriated with the cooperation of the CPRSI began to decrease. A fall in the number of women being repatriated might also have been related to more 'unmarried mothers' being prepared to retain their children during a period of relative social liberalisation. Importantly, also, there are indications that, by this time, 'unmarried mothers' were unlikely to remain in the Mother and Baby Homes in Ireland for the same lengthy period as they had in the past.

> Some girls express the fear that if they go into a Mother and Baby Home in this country they will have to remain there for a very long time. Such fears are groundless nowadays. Any girl whom we have promised to help is assured that she will not have to spend too long a time in the Home after her baby is born. A mother is expected to remain with her baby until provision has been made for his care otherwise. Such care is usually provided either by adoption or, should the mother be undecided as to her plan for the future of her child, by temporary nursery or foster care. In either case, this usually takes about six to eight weeks. Many factors affect the timing in each individual case, but our efforts are always directed towards avoidance of leaving any girl unduly long in the Home. (CPRSI Annual Report, 1969, p 2)

The CPRSI continued to stress, however, that it "is our view that the various needs of the unmarried mother are best met in Mother and Baby Homes".

By the time of the publication of the CPRSI report for 1972, repatriation did not even feature as an item to be reported. The final reference to repatriation occurred in 1971 when only 33 'unmarried mothers' were repatriated with the help of the CPRSI. (Only four years before it had helped to repatriate 235 women.) However, between 1948 and 1971, the CPRSI had assisted English authorities in the repatriation of over 2,500 'unmarried mothers' back to Ireland.

Conclusion

Prior to examining the response of social work and related agencies in England (see Chapter Two of this book), it is perhaps necessary to comment briefly on the 'official' Irish context for these concerns about the migration of 'unmarried mothers'. Certainly, in the period discussed, there were more embracing preoccupations about female emigration. Travers (1997), for example, has argued that Irish female emigration from Ireland, more generally, has been largely "ignored by historians", despite the annual average emigration rate for females being higher than that of males during the period 1871-1971. A number of female historians and sociologists have now begun, however, to explore aspects of female emigration and, specifically, the Irish female experience of the diaspora (see, for example, Lennon et al, 1988; Hickman and Walter, 1995; Walter, 1995; Gray, 1996, 2003; Ryan, 2001a, 2001b, 2002a, 2002b, 2003).

After the Second World War, particularly, fears began to be expressed about the consequences of Irish female emigration because of the impact on the "blood stock" (Travers, 1997, p 154). Concern was also expressed and advice provided on account of worries about the impact of life in England on the spiritual life of vulnerable young Irish women. The ostensible fear that these women's Catholic faith might be undermined was complex, however, because it can also be associated with ideas rooted in notions of racial or ethnic purity. In the early 1950s, writing in the Catholic periodical *The Furrow*, a priest from Belfast commented, for example, that one girl returned from England regarding as "a great joke" the fact that she and others had been "dumped into a hostel with negro men" (see Culchane, 1950). Similarly, a guidebook for 'Irish girls' emigrating to England warned against "foreign jews" (Travers, 1997, p 163; see also Ryan, 2001a). Concerns such as these possibly also contributed to John Charles McQuaid, the Archbishop of Dublin, setting up the Emigrant Section of the Catholic Social Welfare Bureau in 1942. Indeed, according to McQuaid, the "chief activity" of the organisation was the care of emigrants, but "especially women and girls" (McQuaid, cited in Kelly and Nic Giolla Choille, 1997). Furthermore, in the 1950s, the Roman Catholic Church in England also began to respond to what it saw as the culturally specific needs of the Irish in Britain and to put in place an inchoate social work or social welfare service (Godfrey, 1956; Woods, 1956). Not infrequently, however, Irish Catholic clergy felt compelled to remark on the "patronising attitude" held by "their fellow Catholics" in England (see Culchane, 1950, p 411).

Turning specifically to repatriation in the late 1960s, this began to taper off and the availability of legal abortion in England was one possible factor accounting for the redundancy of this practice. In this context, Ackers (1996) has identified how the extent of women's right to reproductive self-determination and their migration can be viewed as related issues (Ramirez and McEneaney, 1997). Perhaps some similarities also exist in terms of the 'secret' journeys made to England to have children adopted in the past and the 'secret' journeys made to abortion clinics today (Conroy Jackson, 1992). Indeed, the 'silences' associated with 'secret' births and adoptions and 'secret' abortions are, perhaps, not entirely dissimilar in the context of this discussion (Fletcher, 1995). Furthermore, Powell's (1992) suggestion that Irish 'unmarried mothers' travelling to England to have children born, then adopted, was not wholly displeasing to the Irish authorities since it served to distort the nation's illegitimacy rate and artificially push it downwards can, perhaps, also be connected to the current situation in respect of Irish women travelling to abortion clinics in Britain in that, once again, unresolved tensions and problems centred on the denial of women's reproductive rights are being exported (see also Smyth, 1992; Oaks, 2002).

Perhaps the chief reason 'unmarried mothers' fled to England to give birth in the 1950s and 1960s was bound up with their fear of a type of incarceration in Ireland's Mother and Baby Homes. The anonymous writer in *The Bell*, in the early 1940s, identified the significance of this issue (MPRH, 1941). In addition, the reports of the CPRSI indicate, as observed earlier, that the staff of the CPRSI were consistently unhappy with the length of time 'unmarried mothers' were expected to remain in the Mother and Baby Homes in Ireland. The seemingly low-key campaign of the CPRSI to promote changes in this policy, reflected in the annual reports, also reveals that the discourse on 'unmarried motherhood' and child adoption in Ireland was more pluralistic than some present-day accounts have acknowledged[6].

A second possible reason for the brief migration might be related to fears about the mortality rate for 'illegitimate' children in Ireland. A difficulty existed in terms of identifying potential adopters after legal adoption was introduced in 1952. Consequently, most 'illegitimate' children, if not looked after by grandparents or other extended family members, were placed in institutions. The Department of Local Government and Public Health had observed that "one out of every four illegitimate infants died within the first year of life" (Department of Local Government and Public Health Annual Report 1931-32, p 58). Similarly, in 1955 the Commission on Emigration and Other Population Problems reported that the death rate for illegitimate children in Ireland was higher than the rate in Britain and other countries (Commission on Emigration and Other Population Problems, 1955, p 112). Moreover, the disparity between death rates for 'legitimate' and 'illegitimate' children was wider than in "neighbouring countries"[7].

Identifying this as a factor motivating the journey of these women is entirely speculative, and to explore the issue more fully one would need to interview surviving birth mothers and allow them to define *their* own motivations. The point here is that the high death rate for 'illegitimate' children in institutional care in Ireland *might* have prompted an expectant 'unmarried mother' and expectant mother to seek to give birth and have the child cared for in England. No evidence appears to be available to support the assertion that many Irish women "were sent specifically from Ireland, through the auspices of the CPRSI, to deliver their baby and were returned soon afterwards" (Marks, 1992). Although the CPRSI disagreed with the long periods women were confined in Mother and Baby Homes in Ireland, it did not facilitate women travelling to England to give birth. Although, as we shall see later, the CPRSI did cooperate with agencies intent on repatriating Irish women, the impetus appears to have come from English agencies.

The focus of this chapter, therefore, has been on factors that influenced many pregnant women to leave Ireland and travel to Britain. The next two chapters, while remaining focused on historical responses, will examine how social work services in Britain perceived these women. Is it the case, for example, that voluntary and statutory services treated them in the same way as other English women who were faced with, what are now often termed, 'crisis pregnancies'?

Notes

[1] An earlier version of this chapter was published as 'The abnormal flight: the migration and repatriation of Irish 'unmarried mothers'', *Social History*, 2000, vol 25, no 3, pp 330-44, (www.tandf.co.uk/journals/routledge/03071022.html). I am grateful to Taylor & Francis for granting permission to me to use substantially reworked parts of that article. The Child Protection and Rescue Society of Ireland (CPRSI) was founded in

1913 largely because of concerns about the children of Catholics being taken care of by "Protestant proselytising bodies" (CPRSI Annual Report, 1916, p 11). In 1992, its name was changed to '*Cunamh*: Child care agency', but it has been located at 30 South Anne Street, Dublin since 1921. Elizabeth O'Flynn, secretary of *Cunamh*, allowed me to have access to the archives of the agency. Throughout this chapter, it will be referred to as the CPRSI, or simply 'the society'. See also Earner-Byrne (2003) for a recent interpretation of some of the issues referred to in what follows in this chapter.

[2] 1922-37 covers the period from the inception of the new Irish Free State to the introduction of a new Irish constitution, *Bunreacht na h-Éireann*, in 1937 (see also Scannell, 1988; Lee, 1991; Collins and Hanafin, 2001). Early exchanges on the unmarried mother 'problem' include Glynn (1921), MacInerny (1922) and 'Sagart' (1922).

[3] Lloyd (1999, p 103) comments on "the political and economic power of the large and middling farmers who have been described as the 'nation building class'":

[T]he nation-state they built, for numerous reasons, largely conformed to their interests and ideology: conservative, principally agricultural and dominated by the most conservative type of Catholicism imaginable. The classes among the opposition to such a polity thrived, and who throughout the War of Independence stood for quite radical transformation of the society, created soviets and maintained if not an anti-clerical at least an anti-episcopal stance, were decimated by emigration.

[4] Barrett was also a leading figure in the CPRSI, and his role is also discussed in Maguire (2002). Pilkington (2002) has observed that it would wrong to perceive Protestantism in Ireland as being, unlike Roman Catholicism, enlightened and more progressive on social issues.

[5] These figures are extracted from the CPRSI annual reports.

[6] Interesting film archive material and oral testimony was provided in a Channel 4 documentary screened in Britain in 1998 (*Witness: Sex in a cold climate*, 16 March 1998). The programme was undermined, however, because it failed to take account on the plurality of opinions in relation to how best to respond to and manage 'unmarried mothers' in Ireland in the 1950s and 1960s. The plight of 'unmarried mothers' and other 'fallen women' was also highlighted in 2002 when *The Magdalene Sisters*, written and directed by Peter Mullen, won the Golden Lion award at the prestigious Venice Film Festival. See Dunne (2002-03) and Raftery's (2003) related pieces. In 2002, the BBC also screened Lizzie Mickery's not-dissimilar drama *Sinners*. Barton (2000) has written about the operation of a range of 'semi-penal' institutions for 'wayward women and wicked girls' in England.

[7] Perhaps the deaths of 35 girls in a fire at St Joseph's Orphanage, Cavan, in February 1943 was more meaningful and traumatic for the general public than this type of statistical information (see Arnold and Laskey, 1985).

TWO

Responses in Britain to the PFIs: the repatriation of 'unmarried mothers' to Ireland in the 1950s and 1960s

A ticket for three pounds and six
To Euston, London via Holyhead.

Well, mount the steps; lug the bag:
Take your place. And out of all of the crowd,
Watch the girl in the wrinkled coat,
Her face half-grey. (Brendan Kennelly, *Westland Row*, 1966)

The aim of this chapter is to focus specifically on those pregnant 'unmarried mothers' who travelled from Ireland to Britain to give birth 'secretly'. How did social work and social welfare agencies respond to them once they had arrived? All migrant Irish 'unmarried mothers' were not, of course, repatriated back to Ireland and some women were successful in their plans to travel to England, give birth, have the baby placed for adoption and return home to Ireland. Here, however, the aim is simply to focus on a few of those Irish 'unmarried mothers' who were subjected to repatriation[1]. The period covered by this chapter will largely be the late 1950s, when the initials PFI ('pregnant from Ireland') were part of the everyday vocabulary of the social workers that dealt with 'unmarried mothers' arriving from Ireland (O'Hare et al, 1983). Indeed, most of the case records discussed relate to women and children repatriated in 1958, partly because, on account of economic changes triggered that year, "sociologically 1958 dates the beginning of the contemporary period in Ireland" (Breen et al, 1990, p 5).

At least a dozen Catholic child adoption and rescue societies in England were involved in repatriation schemes (CPRSI, Annual Report 1959, p 2). Here, we will explore the case records of just one agency, the English Catholic Rescue Society (ECRS)[2]. This agency had a working relationship with the Child Protection and Rescue Society of Ireland (CPRSI) and the two organisations regularly liaised with each other about women and children being repatriated. This chapter begins by examining some of the case papers on the so-called PFIs and then comments on how more encompassing professional discourses on 'unmarried mothers' and child adoption were likely to impact on these women when they arrived in Britain. The final part of the chapter places the treatment of the PFIs in the context of other discriminatory discourses and practices concerned with Irish migrants to Britain.

PFI (pregnant from Ireland)

Most of the women who were repatriated, whose ages ranged from 19 to 36 years of age, appear to have contacted the ECRS soon after their arrival from Ireland. In terms of the papers examined, this ranged from three days to two months after arrival. Moreover, case papers held by the ECRS make it clear that 'the possibility of returning to Ireland' was addressed during a woman's initial interview with one of the caseworkers at the ECRS office.

In her study on Irish 'unmarried mothers' who were repatriated to one particular Mother and Baby Home in Ireland, Creegan (1967, para 6.21) refers to the situation of one woman who left Ireland when she was eight years old on account of the death of her parents. Astonishingly, having been 'brought up' by her sister in Britain, she did not even know anyone in Ireland when she became pregnant and was repatriated years later.

In the ECRS case papers, the idea of returning to Ireland was touched on with Ciara, who had only arrived from Dublin three days previously and had passed her baby's expected date of 'delivery'[3]. She was staying in a B&B that she had managed to locate through an advertisement section in the Catholic newspaper *The Universe*. Aged 36, "well dressed ... well spoken" and educated at a convent school in an affluent Dublin suburb, she worked as a wages clerk. Her husband, she told her caseworker, died the previous year. The caseworker was not convinced, further investigated Ciara's marriage and contacted the CPRSI. The caseworker's opinion was that Ciara had "woven a story to give a semblance of respectability to her position" and her investigations appeared to substantiate this suspicion when no evidence was available of any marriage ever having taken place. The child was born in hospital and a place for Ciara and the baby was located in a Mother and Baby Home in the same city with the cost of their stay being met by the local council in accordance with Part 3 of the 1948 National Assistance Act. After the birth of her baby, Ciara conceded to her caseworker that she had lied about her marriage. She wanted her child to be adopted and was prepared to have an Adoption Society in Cork coordinate this for her.

Ciara's decision to accept the plan for the repatriation both of her and her child, however, was likely to be influenced by her unhappiness in the Mother and Baby Home. Less than a month after the baby's birth, the caseworker noted:

> Ciara is inclined to take a rather high-handed attitude and gave the impression she would stop at nothing (or very little!) to "get out of this place".

A priest had also been contacted (presumably by Ciara or her former landlady with whom she still kept "in touch") and he had spoken to the chaplain of the

Mother and Baby Home about Ciara's "length of stay" in the home, "all she had to do in the laundry" and the fact she "never got out etc etc". The chaplain's prompt response, according to the caseworker, was "that as far as he could see the girls were never in – always hanging about the roads etc!".

A few weeks after Ciara's discharge from hospital, the Reverend Mother of the Mother and Baby Home had shown her a letter from a women in Arklow who was "looking for foster children". She already had two children placed with her after their mothers had spent time at the home. Ciara agreed to take her child there and the Cork Adoption Society was then to organise the legal adoption. Following her return to Ireland, Ciara exchanged letters with her caseworker, Sister Teresa, for the rest of the year. Six months after the child's birth, in England, he was taken to the prospective adopters in Arklow and Ciara wrote:

> Poor little Stephen was taken from me before I realised what had happened, and he had been so good on the long journey.... It is dreadful to have to part with our own flesh and blood and I hope and pray it is all for the best, and please God he will get a good home.

Ciara, despite her apparent unhappiness in the Mother and Baby Home, thanked her caseworker for the "great kindness" the ECRS had shown her in England.

Case papers reveal, however, that some of the women felt pressurised on account of moves to have them repatriated. Maura, aged 19 and working as a cashier in a butcher's shop, had arrived from Dublin[4]. She had travelled to England a month prior to her visit to the offices of the ECRS. The putative father had taken "advantage of her after he had been drinking" and her baby was due in five months. Maura was described as a "very nice type of Irish girl" and both her father and her mother knew of the pregnancy and were "standing by her". Her "mother wanted her to remain at home", but Maura decided she "wanted to save her the embarrassment of the neighbours and came over ... with the help of her father" who was working locally.

During Maura's initial visit, it was proposed that she should return to Ireland and go to a Mother and Baby Home in the Dublin area. Maura, however, "nearly collapsed" because the home was "just around the corner from her home and the women helpers would know her and her family". The following month she rang and stated that her mother had been in contact with the CPRSI in Dublin and that she was, instead, prepared to go to the Mother and Baby Home in Castlepollard, Westmeath. She was to travel the month before her baby was due and her mother was to "meet her off the boat and take her to Castlepollard". The caseworker noted: "girl is very lonely and homesick over here and longing to get home". Unfortunately, the local authority in Dublin was not prepared to pay "for a girl from their area in any other Home". The CPRSI was prepared to make arrangements for Maura to go to Castlepollard, but only as a "private patient", paying three guineas per week, and if she was prepared to have her child adopted.

Carmel, one of 11 children, was aged 21 and came from Tipperary[5]. She was working as a shop assistant in a Woolworth's store and arrived at the offices of the ECRS four months before she was expected to give birth. A "thin, white faced, poorly looking girl the first thing she did was burst into tears". The putative father had travelled to England with her, but had since "disappeared". None of her family was aware of the pregnancy. As was the practice, the ECRS caseworker recorded whether the pregnancy had occurred in Ireland and, on learning that it had, she "explained position re PFIs". At this time, Carmel was "willing to go back to Eire".

By the time of the second interview Carmel's attitude had changed:

> Carmel arrived for interview in a very determined state of mind – she reiterated throughout the interview that she would not go back to Ireland. Stated she knew a lady – a non-Catholic who had offered to adopt her baby.

The case notes subsequently record that Carmel agreed to travel to the Mother and Baby Home in Castlepollard the month before her baby was due to be born. However, when Carmel began to miss appointments, perhaps after further fears about returning home, the caseworker stated that if she failed to cooperate "I shall insist on you going back to Ireland straightaway". The following month letters sent to Carmel started to take on a more coercive tone:

> I am very surprised that you have not yet got in touch with me nor with the clinic.... If you don't keep this appointment I will ring the personal manageress the next morning and tell her you are pregnant and refuse to have proper anti-natal care and would she please help us in this matter. I don't want to do that Carmel as it may cost you your job – so please come here on Thursday.

Later that month, three months prior to her child's birth, Carmel had still to visit the antenatal clinic. Her caseworker wrote again stating that she would inform Carmel's landlord there was a "pregnant woman in the house, who refuses to have proper medical care". Even though Carmel was aged 21, it was also added:

> You are under age and we are responsible for your welfare at the moment. It you are not going to cooperate, I will write to your mother and tell her that we cannot accept the responsibility.

The month before her baby was born a letter to the CPRSI in Dublin revealed that Carmel was returning to Ireland:

> Carmel arrived up here this morning and announced that she had told her mother about the baby and her mother had written and told her to go

home and not go to Castlepollard. Carmel has a sister over here and the pair are travelling back to Ireland on Saturday and are returning to their home in Co Kerry.

Carmel's relationship with the ECRS highlights the fact that certainly some of these Irish 'unmarried mothers' were very concerned about the prospects of being repatriated. Her experience, only hinted at on her case file, also indicates that, in travelling from Ireland to give birth, 'unmarried mothers' did not find England more emotionally conducive. However, the files also indicate that many of these women struggled hard to define their own experiences and tried to find solutions that were at odds with plans put in place by the network of disciplinary social welfare agencies in England.

Bridget, from Dundalk and working in a cinema locally, was a "very ordinary type, of mediocre intelligence"[6]. At her first interview at the offices of the ECRS, her caseworker quickly formed the view that she was the type "who might take the easy way out of her difficulties". She was "very reluctant" to even consider returning to Ireland. Her mother had died and her father would "kill her" if he "knew of her position". According to Bridget, going to a Mother and Baby Home in Ireland, especially Castlepollard, was just like going to "a prison". The caseworker recorded:

> Thought she could go into a Mother and Baby Home here, or have the baby adopted straight from hospital, or get the baby from hospital into a nursery where she could pay for it pending adoption (a nurse had told her the latter, an idea of which I disabused her!).

> I told her that if she remained here she would have no alternative but 'part 3 accommodation' on discharge from hospital, and that the only help we could give regarding baby would be to ask Father G. if he would accept for a 'Cork Adoption'… I urged her to accept Irish arrangements…. I told her very clearly that all the vague talk about provision of foster mother, nursery accommodation etc practically invariably came to nothing in the end, and that she was very likely to find herself in serious difficulties if she did not take our advice. She knows that we reserve the right to inform her father if a non-Catholic adoption is contemplated.

Case files reveal that staff at the ECRS were not only intent on delineating the choices (or lack of choices) they viewed as available to these 'unmarried' Irish mothers, they were apt, in some instances, to pressurise them if alternative, more independent, plans or course of actions were embarked on. Indeed, once the ECRS, often in consultation with its counterparts in Ireland, had decided that repatriation was the desired outcome, there was sparse room for these women to manoeuvre and progress their own plans. This was in the context of their being in a foreign country, often alone and concealing a pregnancy from employer and landlord in England and family back in Ireland. As we have seen with the case of Carmel, some of the letters sent to these women not only threatened to divulge their 'secret', but were also couched in quasi-legal language. Sinéad, for example, but were written to by the Administrator of the ECRS who advised[7]:

> My committee has considered your application and believes that you should, as a matter of strict justice, return to Ireland with your son.

The files of the ECRS indicate that caseworkers were attentive to the class origins of the unmarried Irish women who presented in their office. Teresa, for example, was "a pleasant girl" who reflected in "her manner and bearing the result of living in close quarters with refined people"[8]. Similarly, Nora's parents were "of some local standing and highly respected, on intimate terms with the Administrator and other clergy of their Cathedral parish"[9]. A variety of Irish women from different class backgrounds arrived at the office of the ECRS and the class component to the interaction between the social workers and the women seeking their help is likely to have had some influence on the character of that engagement. However, evidence from case papers suggests that, irrespective of the pregnant woman's class and social standing, if her child was conceived in Ireland, then she could have found herself repatriated. Moreover, once the decision to repatriate had been taken and 'agreed', the practical steps to organise the return of the women – and usually their children if they had already given birth – proceeded quickly and in a business-like fashion, with the ECRS issuing brusque instructions via letter. Mona, for example, received a letter informing her of the following[10]:

> We have heard that your baby can be accepted in Cork this weekend. Will you be at the office with him by 3.00 p.m. at the latest on Friday 23 January. You should bring with you his vitamin and milk tokens books, also his medical card, one dozen nappies and any clothing which he may possess. If you have feed already prepared, this can be heated up on the train and the next feed prepared freshly on the boat. There will be two other mothers travelling with you....

We can only speculate, of course, how these women felt, originally having planned to give birth and have the child adopted in England, but now compelled to travel, with the new baby, back home to Ireland. Once repatriated, this was likely to then entail a lengthy stay in one of Ireland's hated Mother and Baby Homes, the prospect of which, discussed in Chapter One, was likely to have prompted the migration in the first place.

Ordinarily, when the boat docked in Dublin, a worker from the CPRSI met the returning mothers. Noreen, for example, was told[11]:

Mrs Riordan will be easy for you to identify when she speaks to you, as she will be wearing a white armband.... Please do not leave the boat until you have seen Mrs Riordan.

Returning mothers then went to the office of the CPRSI and, subsequently, on to the Mother and Baby Home identified for them.

An almoner, or hospital social worker, in the area where the ECRS was located refused to have his department pay the accommodation costs of Geileis, an Irish 'unmarried mother', because he was "not prepared to foot the bill for another of our wayward Irish girls!"[12]. The remark suggests, if not an anti-Irish sentiment, perhaps the patronising hautiness of the colonial administrator. Implicit also might be the notion that these migrant Irish women were a burden on the welfare state and post-war reconstruction. The case papers held by the ECRS contain no evidence of an overt anti-Irish racism, but the entire repatriation endeavour was perhaps founded on the entrenched idea that these Irish women, although likely to be Catholic like the staff of the English agency, did not belong, that they were 'other', alien and had no right or entitlement to remain in Britain; hence, the energetic efforts to ensure that they were returned to Ireland.

'Unmarried motherhood' and child adoption in the 1950s and 1960s

It might be argued, of course, that busy child welfare staff were acting in an entirely pragmatic fashion and ensuring that the welfare of the children was safeguarded during a period when there was frequently a lack of Catholic adopters available to some English agencies. Moreover, it could be contended that the seemingly callous way in which some Irish women appeared to have been treated simply reflected the dominant professional discourse on child adoption and 'unmarried motherhood' during this period. In order to examine these assertions, it is, therefore, important to briefly examine the contemporary discourse on 'illegitimacy' and 'unmarried mothers' because this provides part of the contextual framework in which migrant Irish 'unmarried mothers' were responded to, assessed and set apart from their English counterparts.

It has been suggested, for example, that until the Second World War 'unmarried motherhood' "had been considered as being the result of the seduction of an overcredulous girl, who was particularly weak in character, ignorant or mentally defective" (Spensky, 1992, p 106; see also Humphries, 1988, ch 3). This dominant response began to change in the 1950s, however, when 'unmarried mothers' began to be pathologised. In Britain, this new tendency was never as pronounced as in the US, but it was still reflected in the highly influential work of John Bowlby (1990). In 1953, for example, he observed that it was "the opinion of many social workers with psychiatric knowledge and experience" that "with many girls, becoming an unmarried mother is neurotic and not just accidental".

Meanwhile, in "other cases the girls are chronically maladjusted or defective" (Bowlby, cited in Spensky, 1992, p 108).

The reasons for the way 'unmarried mothers' were constructed and perceived are complex and, indeed, a full exploration of this specific topic lies outside the scope of this book. In brief, however, three contributory factors can be identified. First, there were official concerns about the increase in the numbers of 'illegitimate babies' born during and after the war (Ferguson and Fitzgerald, 1954). Second, there was the conformist ambience of the 1950s, which saw the promotion of a specific construct of family life and gender relations within deadening political and cultural order being principally shaped by the Cold War. In the area of popular culture, for example, this was reflected in the British films of the 1950s and early 1960s featuring 'unmarried mothers' and in the "significant determination to re-assert the pleasures and benefits which companionate marriage, family life and the home purportedly offered women" (Fink and Holden, 1999, p 250). Third, these years also saw the growth of 'expertise' and of those professions and disciplines (social work, psychology and criminology) that made particular claims about human behaviour. These 'psy professions', despite their gender, class and 'race' bias, made confident assertions and 'objectively' delineated the 'normal' from the 'deviant' (see Rose, 1989). Moreover, these dynamics and the social context in which they evolved were to have particular consequences in relation to social casework with 'unmarried mothers'.

In 1953, only one in five 'unmarried mothers' entered a Mother and Baby Home in England and Wales (Spensky, 1992, p 110). However, such homes had a wider impact in that they were used as a "disincentive for other young women to engage in pre-marital sex and risk a pregnancy" (Spensky, 1992, p 41). By 1956, there were 27 local authority Mother and Baby Homes with 397 beds in England and Wales. This was NHS provision and no charge was made on the mother. In addition, there were 170 voluntary homes being used by local authorities and these had 1,666 beds (Wimperis, 1960, p 180). The regimes in such homes varied, but all of them remained intent on regulating the behaviour of the 'unmarried mother' and on ensuring that she did not err again. In Britain,

> From the mid-1950s until the 1967 abortion legislation had time to have an effect in the 1970s, the home for 'unmarried mothers' became a producer of legitimacy. The unmarried expectant mother would enter it for a few weeks before confinement, then she would give birth, either in the Home itself or in hospital and finally she would return to the home for a few weeks after which the baby would be adopted. The baby would be legitimised through adoption, the childless couple would acquire more legitimacy by having a child, and the mother would come out – apparently – as if nothing had happened, cured of her pathological unconscious urges. She would then be able to get married and, in her turn, bear legitimate children, this time, driven by more healthy, unconscious urges. (Spensky, 1992, p 112)

This assessment accurately describes the crudity of the approach to 'unmarried mothers' and adoption in the 1950s. Moreover, even as recently as 1969, one writer could observe that the granting of an Adoption Order marked "the end of the unmarried girl's status as a mother" and her "restoration as a *normal* member of the community" (Pochin, 1969, p 128; emphasis added).

Significant also was the perception that 'unmarried mothers' were frequently childlike and viewed as not having the ability to make informed choices. In the late 1950s and early 1960s, for example, Felix Biestek (1957, p 25), an American Jesuit and one of the primary definers of what constituted the philosophical foundation for social work, could observe:

> Caseworkers have differed in their evaluation of the capacity of 'unmarried mothers' as a group, to make sound decisions. Some feel that 'unmarried mothers' are so damaged emotionally that they are incapable of arriving at a good decision themselves.

In short, there was little acknowledgement of what we might refer to today as the human rights or therapeutic needs of all birth mothers, not solely those of the migrant Irish mothers who are the focal interest of this chapter (Howe et al, 1992; Logan, 1996; see also Garrett, 2002). Simply put, 'unmarried mothers' did not have the 'motherhood mandate' in this era (see Wheeler, 1998, p 120)[13].

These points, although at risk of implicitly undermining the hurt likely to have been experienced by the repatriated women, do contain elements of truth. However, the entire issue, and specifically the response of the English agencies, can also be viewed as a good deal more complex. Initially, in seeking to briefly explore some of these issues and to interrogate the 'situatedness' of the women migrants who are the focal interest of this chapter (see Brah, 1996, pp 182-3), it needs to be emphasised that legally they had the right to be in Britain despite the efforts of, for example, the ECRS to segregate them from British 'unmarried mothers' and to, in effect, expel them. Nevertheless, as we have seen, some of the exchanges between the ECRS and the women (as narrated by casework staff) strongly implied that the whole repatriation endeavour was legally underpinned, yet this was not the case. Similarly, in Ireland, despite the practices examined in Chapter One, there was no law that provided for the detention of 'unmarried mothers' in Mother and Baby Homes for specific periods of time (see Osborough, 1975, p 117). In short, what these women were confronted with, both in England and Ireland, were 'welfare'-oriented social control strategies that were not grounded in any specific laws or legal process. This is not, however, to deny the power and persuasive authority of such strategies.

The women at the centre of the repatriation endeavour, however, should not be perceived as merely passive victims (see also Luddy and Murphy, 1990). Indeed, it is possible to detect their "initiative and resourcefulness in manipulating the system" in the face of adversity (Cullen, 1991, p 43). Furthermore, this chapter has frequently referred to the women's obduracy and tenacity when confronted with a panoply of regulatory and disciplinary forces in Britain. Put more theoretically, there are traces of resistance, and what Foucault refers to as "reverse discourse" (Mahood, 1990, p 12), in their efforts to evade and disrupt the plans of the ECRS. Equally important, however, the strategies of the ECRS and associated agencies should be viewed in the light of more entrenched British perceptions and practices in relation to Irish immigration.

Examining the repatriations as a British exclusionary practice

In the 19th century, for example, Irish migrants seeking relief in England were liable, under the 1847 Poor Law Removal Act, to be deported back to Ireland. In 1847 alone, 15,000 Irish people were 'removed' from Liverpool because they had been recipients of relief, and during the period 1846-53 some 72,781 Irish people were 'removed' from the city and returned to Ireland (Neal, 1988, p 97; see also Gray, 1999). Indeed, it was not until 1948 that the law of settlement and removal finally disappeared from the statute book (Rose, 1976). Clearly, debates centred on whether or not an individual was entitled to claim relief within particular spatial boundaries and localities related to *all* paupers in England and not just Irish paupers. The suggestion here, however, is that discourses pivoting on the 'removal' of Irish people, which continued into the 20th century, may also have helped define and shape the cultural and institutional responses of English welfare agencies to pregnant Irish women travelling to England to give birth and have children placed for adoption. In short, the discursive practices of these English agencies – which prompted some to involve themselves in repatriation schemes – may have been informed by an ideology and operational orientation that was historically rooted and not simply pragmatic and expedient.

Enda Delaney, for example, has examined the responses of the British state to Irish immigration during the period stretching from Ireland's partial independence in 1922 until the end of the Second World War (Delaney, 1999; see also Delaney, 2000). He has revealed that, in the late 1920s, various concerns were expressed, frequently by Scottish Presbyterian churches, over the extent and impact of Irish immigration (see also Douglas, 2002). The government responded by holding a number of interdepartmental meetings and by instigating "investigations by various arms of the state into Irish immigration" (Delaney, 1999, p 243). A work permit scheme for Irish workers was also mooted, but rejected. However, in the late 1930s, concerns were apt to resurface and, as in the previous decade, the Irish government was approached about cooperating with the repatriation of Irish migrant workers having recourse to poor law assistance. Ramsey MacDonald, prime minister in the national government, appeared to be particularly fixated about the "perfect scandal" of Irish citizens becoming a charge on the poor law (Delaney, 1999, p 248). Indeed, the issue of deportation – more specifically British ruminations on the viability of enforcing deportation – featured as a recurring subtext in Anglo-Irish relations during the late 1920s and 1930s. In the Commons, an inquiry was even made, in March 1937, to ascertain if it would be "possible to put an import duty on Southern Irish human beings as it is placed on Southern Irish animals?" (Hansard, 321, col 147, March 1937). This suggestion was not reflective, perhaps, of mainstream elite opinion in Britain (see, for example, the more reasoned and temperate approach of the Secretary of State for Dominion Affairs in Hansard, 329, cols 2411-14, 3 December 1937). However, it does reveal the depth of opposition to Irish immigration and racist tenor of aspects of the discourse during this era. Lunn (1992) has also highlighted a 'concerted campaign' in the 1930s, led by some Conservative MPs and certain sections of the civil service, to focus on racist stereotypes of the Irish as abusers of the social services, as receiving privileged access to jobs and operating as a local political mafia in cities like Liverpool (see also Ryan, 2001a).

In July 1939, the Prevention of Violence Act compelled all Irish citizens to register with the police. With the outbreak of war in September 1939, all persons aged 16 and over travelling to Britain were required to possess identity cards that were issued in Ireland. The following year, a wholesale ban on travel to Britain was introduced, except for those on "business of national importance" (Delaney, 1999, p 252). The British need for labour, however, led to a good deal of flexibility and recruitment of Irish workers took place. However, "in particular areas of the wartime economy, the response to Irish migrants was less than enthusiastic" (Delaney, 1999, p 257). Moreover, despite a pragmatic approach by elites in Britain, in the "inter-war years Irish migrants were rarely regarded as a desirable addition to the population by politicians and civil servants" (Delaney, 1999, p 259).

As observed earlier, the Irish women at the centre of this discussion had a legal right to migrate to England because Irish people had been granted a privileged position, in relation to those from other countries, under the 1948 British Nationality Act. Irish citizens were also exempted from the provisions of the 1962 Commonwealth Immigrants Act (see Miles, 1993, p 133). This exemption largely related to continuing labour shortages in Britain after the Second World War, which resulted in 1951, for example, in Irish women comprising 11% of nurses and midwives in Britain (Wheeler, 1998, p 36). However, Irish exclusion from the tightening up of the immigration process should not necessarily be interpreted as representing tolerance and acceptance of the Irish compared with people from black communities in Britain. In this context, it has been argued that the control "of Irish people takes a very different form ... and the fact that it does not mirror strategies adopted by the state towards black people in no way lessens the fact that the Irish are a problematised and targeted population and this is achieved through the prism of racialisation" (Hickman, 1995, p 210). Indeed, the Commonwealth Immigrants Bill *had* made the Irish subject to immigration control and some British MPs were of the view that Irish immigrants might undermine and contaminate Britain. In the House of Commons, for example, one MP stated that the Irish, on account of tuberculosis, were "far more likely to cause danger of infection to other people" than were Commonwealth immigrants. He also proposed that Irish people should only be able to remain in Britain for "a certain period only" (Hansard, cols 753-7, 6 November 1961; see also the comments of Denis Healey MP in Hickman, 1998, p 302).

In late 1961, it was reported "forty Conservatives may withdraw support [from the government] if Butler fails to solve the problem of Irish workers coming to this country" (see 'Tory threat to Immigration Bill', *Liverpool Daily Post*, 1 December 1961). The eventual legislation did not subject the Irish to immigration control, but Section 7 of the Act provided for the deportation of citizens of Commonwealth countries and the Republic of Ireland if they were aged 17 and over, had not been continuously resident for the past five years and had been convicted of a criminal offence punishable by imprisonment. By May 1963, courts in Britain had recommended that the Home Secretary issue deportation orders against 624 Irish citizens (Russell, 1964, pp 136-49).

More specifically related to the case of repatriated Irish 'unmarried mothers', it is clear that some of the concerns about Irish immigration in the post-war period were also grounded in specific concerns about 'Irish girls' because "the hierarchy of belonging", developed in Britain during the period of post-war reconstruction, "was not only raced, but also gendered" (Wheeler, 1998, p 27). Thus, the criminality of 'Irish girls' in Britain, as reflected in the proportion they comprised of the prison population, was highlighted (Russell, 1964, p 144). Minutes of the Liverpool Vigilance Association reveal that, in the mid-1950s, "several letters had been received from probation officers in the London area asking for ... assistance with deporting Irish girls"[14]. In addition, fears were also expressed concerning the involvement of 'Irish girls' in prostitution, with the BBC, for example, screening a documentary about "good time girls", including Irish immigrants, who "drifted" to London[15]. In the early 1960s, a member of the House of Lords set up a 'social offences group', and one of the group's concerns was 'Irish girls' operating as prostitutes:

> [O]ne of the problems they wished to investigate was the dilemma of the pretty Irish teenage girl who steps off the boat at Liverpool, penniless and without friends and with little prospect of employment. Alone and bewildered, she often falls unwittingly into the grip of a call-girl network, said Lord Stonham and once she has accepted the fatal offer of help what the innocent young girl considers to be an offer of a room for the night, she has probably passed the point of no return. She is condemned to a life of slavery as a prostitute. ('MPs probe call girl racket in Liverpool', *Liverpool Daily Post*, 7 December 1961)

Interestingly, the Liverpool Vigilance Association, whose national umbrella organisation operated an Irish Girls Sub-Committee on account of its concerns, was of the view that there was little substance to Lord Stonham's assertions since their 'boat and station' activity indicated that there were fewer "Irish girls arriving without work or money"[16]. However, this moral panic about 'Irish girls' who were allegedly turning to prostitution continued throughout the early 1960s and, on occasions, the issues of illegitimacy and prostitution were fused (Russell, 1964, p 144).

Conclusion

This chapter has concentrated largely on the actions of a Roman Catholic agency and its response to Irish 'unmarried mothers' in England in the late 1950s. Here, it was revealed that many of these women were treated in a harsh way and, often with their newborn babies, sent back to Ireland. The practice of 'repatriation', however, should also be placed alongside other historical measures that have been focused on Irish people migrating to Britain.

Chapter Three will next examine how mainstream social work services – specifically the London County Council's Children's Department – responded to Irish children and families in the 1950s and 1960s.

Notes

[1] It is acknowledged that the chief disadvantage with this approach is that there is no scrutiny of the case papers of those pregnant Irish women who were *not* repatriated. Thus, there will be no specific discussion in what follows concerning, for example, how decisions were made about which Irish women were viewed as candidates for repatriation and which were not. However, in the case papers examined, it appears that all expectant 'unmarried mothers' from Ireland were viewed as potential candidates for repatriation. Future research might also examine case files on women who self-identified as 'English' to compare and contrast their treatment to that of Irish women in the 1950s and 1960s. For example, were English 'unmarried mothers' apt to be treated in the same harsh way as many of the Irish women featured in the case records below? It would also be interesting to find out if there were differences in the treatment of women travelling from the six counties of Northern Ireland. Additionally, if access is permitted, research might focus on the case papers of a number of English adoption and rescue agencies and not simply the one agency as we do here. No interviews were conducted with any mothers who became embroiled in the repatriation process and this may also be an area for additional research. Marks (1992), focusing on archival sources, has explored how pregnant Irish (and Jewish) 'unmarried mothers' were dealt with in London during the period 1870-1939.

[2] The director of an English adoption society granted me permission to have access to case files and other documents including annual reports (1948-73) held by his agency. It is not possible, however, to refer to him by name, nor to specify the name of his agency, referred to throughout as the English Catholic Rescue Society (ECRS), because this might undermine the right to confidentiality of a number of the Irish women referred to in this chapter who had recourse to the agency in the late 1950s. The real names of the 'unmarried mothers' and their children have been altered; so have the names of the agency staff and, where appropriate, some of the place names used. An

earlier version of this chapter appeared as 'The hidden history of the PFIs: the repatriation of 'unmarried mothers' and their children from England to Ireland in the 1950s and 1960s', *Immigrants and Minorities*, vol 19, no 3, pp 25-44. I am grateful to the publisher, Frank Cass, for permitting me to make use of some of this material.

[3] Case papers on 'Ciara' begin on 8 September 1958.

[4] Case papers on 'Maura' begin on 12 May 1958.

[5] Case papers on 'Carmel' begin on 14 May 1958.

[6] The extracts from the case file on 'Bridget' are from case notes dated 30 October 1958. A number of repatriations were undertaken in co-operation with an adoption society in Cork, not simply with the CPRSI. See also 'Kit's story' in MacAmhlaigh (2001), which tells of a pregnant young woman's journey from Ireland to a Mother and Baby Home in England in 1958.

[7] The extract from the letter to 'Sinead' is dated 14 November 1958.

[8] The extract from the case file for 'Teresa' is dated 10 February 1958.

[9] The extract from the case file on 'Nora' is dated 3 October 1958.

[10] The extract from the letter to 'Mona' is dated 20 January 1959.

[11] The extract from the case file on 'Noreen' is dated 14 October 1958.

[12] The comments about 'Geileis' feature in a letter dated 13 May 1958.

[13] A survey published after the Second World War revealed that in terms of maternity services, although 'unmarried mothers' "rarely had their babies delivered by doctors" and that in the past, "a few authorities entrusted the delivery of unmarried women to pupil midwives". Evidence also suggested that 'unmarried mothers' were less likely to be given "some kind of analgesic or anaesthetic" (Joint Committee of the Royal College of Obstetricians and Gynaecologists and the Population Investigation Committee, 1948, p 198). In the mid-1960s, there were also "instances of staff discriminating between married and unmarried patients; of nurses who deliberately tried to embarrass 'unmarried mothers' by talking pointedly of adoption, and enquiring loudly whether a girl was returning to the Mother and Baby Home; and of pressure put on mother by nursing staff to either keep or part with her baby" (Nicolson, 1968, p 111). These responses, therefore, were likely to have impinged on Irish migrant women and are likely to have provided an additional source of worry.

[14] Minutes of meeting taking place on 11 March 1957. The Merseyside Record Office, Liverpool, holds minutes of the Liverpool Vigilance Association committee meetings and other related papers (1908-76), (reference 326VIG).

[15] The programme was *Special enquiry* and the BBC screened it on 24 October 1956. See the minutes of the Liverpool Vigilance Association committee meeting, 8 October 1956.

[16] Minutes of the Liverpool Vigilance Association committee meeting, 11 December 1961.

THREE

The 'daring experiment': London County Council and the discharge from care of children to Ireland in the 1950s and 1960s

In February 1955, the chairman of London County Council's Children's Committee was asked if there was any evidence that "increased immigration from the West Indies in recent years" had led to an increase in "coloured children" coming into care? The chairman responded that the number of children taken into care was available on a monthly basis and it "would be undesirable to give any appearance of segregation … by giving details as to colour or nationality" (1 February 1955, London County Council Minutes of Proceedings). However, despite this reply, from the mid-1950s until the mid-1960s, the Council *was*, in fact, intent on sifting, logging and demarcating Irish children on the basis of their nationality. Related to this process of classification, hundreds of children were removed from Britain and taken to live outside the jurisdiction of the British government, in Ireland.

The aim of this chapter, therefore, is to chart the approach of the England's largest local authority to Irish children in public care in the middle of the 20th century. More specifically, the central focus will be on the activities of the London County Council Children's Committee and its efforts to discharge children from care to Ireland. The key period stretches from 1954 until 1965 since, as we shall see, it was during this time that that the council appeared to have been most preoccupied with Irish children in its care. This part of the book will refer to the publicly available minutes of the proceedings of the council. However, it will also make more extensive use of the 'closed' minutes of the Children's Committee (1948-65) and related presented papers. In addition, reference will be made to the similarly 'closed' minutes of the Special Sub-Committee of the Children's Committee on Nurseries (also known as the Special Sub-Committee on the Clearance of Welfare Nurseries) and associated presented papers (1954-55)[1].

Crisis in the nursery: the evolution of a policy of discharging children from care to Ireland

In 1954, the Children's Committee of the London County Council (LCC) set up a special sub-committee to deal with a crisis relating to two of the local authority's residential welfare nurseries at King's Mead and Hillside. The Home

Office had expressed concern in 1953 that these establishments were being used to accommodate children 'in care' who were younger than three years old. As a consequence of these official concerns, the Home Secretary granted his approval to continue to use the nurseries for only another six months, until the end of June 1954. Furthermore, even this brief renewal of approval was only granted on the basis that the LCC had definite plans for the provision of suitable alternative accommodation (13 May 1954, LCC/MIN/2723).

Officers of the LCC, therefore, were set the task of expeditiously clearing the two nurseries of their young residents. The job was made immensely difficult because there were almost 40 children involved. King's Mead alone, for example, was reported to be housing 28 children in early June 1954 and there was even discussion about removing some of the children to Devon because of the lack of alternative accommodation, or substitute carers, in the London area (1 June 1954, LCC/MIN/2723; 29 June 1954, LCC/MIN/273). On account of the crisis and the failure to remove the children quickly, the Home Office granted approval for a further six months.

When the special sub-committee first began to meet to try to resolve the crisis, there was no indication that there might be an 'Irish solution' available to these local government officers. Indeed, an initial audit of the religious affiliation of the children resident in the King's Mead residential nursery, for example, did not hint at a preponderance of Irish children. Early in June 1954, for example, the Children's Officer had reported that of the 28 children resident in the nursery, 13 were Roman Catholics, 13 Church of England and two of other religious affiliations (1 June 1954, LCC/MIN/2723). Later in the year, Hillside nursery was reported to be housing 21 children: eight Roman Catholics ("1 coloured"), 10 Church of England ("2 coloured"), one Protestant, one "Hebrew" and one Presbyterian (24 September 1954, LCC/MIN/2723). However, at a sub-committee held in July, the same Children's Officer reported that a "considerable number of children in King's Mead nursery with whom the sub-committee is concerned have Irish (Roman Catholic) mothers who come to London for the birth of their babies (often illegitimate)" (21 July 1954, LCC/MIN/2723). Consequently, it was resolved:

> that a child welfare officer in the children's dept be authorised to go to Ireland to visit the families of Irish mothers whose children are in the care of the Council at King's Mead nursery, with a view to the children being discharged to the care of relatives in Ireland. (21 July 1954, LCC/MIN/ 2720)

A Child Welfare Officer made this visit in August 1954 and, over the next 10 years, she was to prove pivotal to the scheme that the LCC was to put in place[2].

In September 1954, revealing how intent on its plans the LCC was becoming, it was also resolved:

that the Children's Officer report to the Committee as to the possibility of arrangements being made whereby the Council is advised of the admittance to hospital of Irish girls who are about to have a baby so that early efforts may be made to prevent the babies being received into care. (24 September 1954, LCC/MIN/2720)

It is not clear from the archival sources examined how this particular aspect of policy, subsequently endorsed by the main Children's Committee, was put into operation. However, it is apparent that, by the end of 1954, the LCC was in the process of evolving a very distinct policy toward Irish children and their families. Furthermore, a policy departure, ostensibly concerned with dealing with a local crisis involving children in two residential nurseries, was going to have far wider implications.

'Unfriendly eyes': initial doubts about the new policy

As 1954 drew to a close, however, it was becoming clear that that doubts were beginning to arise with regard to the new policy triggered by the crisis at the King's Mead and Hillside nurseries. Here, a key area of debate focused on whether or not the new means of discharging children from care to Ireland breached the 1948 Children Act. In November 1954, the Children's Officer, perhaps becoming a little wary about the unguarded enthusiasm of some politicians and officers for the discharge to Ireland plan, reported that:

> In some instances … it has seemed that through unfriendly eyes the discharges might well be made to appear as though they were effected more from the point of view of getting children out of the Council's care than from that of placing them in a manner consistent with their welfare: and it is desired to draw the Committee's attention to the dangers which might arise if the children are discharged with little or no knowledge of what will happen to them afterwards, and often to strangers about whom little or nothing is known. (11 November 1954, LCC/MIN/2704)

The 'instances' that troubled the Children's Officer included "discharge to relations in Ireland who *nominally* accepted full care", but in reality made "private arrangements" for the child (11 November 1954, LCC/MIN/2704; emphasis added). Alternatively, "*nominal* discharge to relations in Ireland where, with relatives concurrence, the child went direct to a children's home" or for "immediate placement with 'foster parents' or 'adopters' who have been 'matched' with him and whose suitability cannot be properly investigated by the Council" (11 November 1954, LCC/MIN/2704; emphasis added).

On receiving this report (which was sceptical at best) from its senior child care officer, the Children's Committee resolved nonetheless that "in regard to children in the care of the Council whose parents come from Ireland (Eire or Northern Ireland)", 'nominal' discharge to relatives remained, along with a number of other options, acceptable[3]. However, each proposed discharge of a child to Ireland had to first go before another layer of the child welfare bureaucracy, the Adoption and Parental Rights Sub-Committee. Moreover, the Children's Officer was asked to prepare an additional report on "all aspects relating to the discharge from care of children whose parents come from Ireland to relatives in that country after discussions with the Secretary of State for Home Affairs and the Roman Catholic authorities" (11 November 1954, LCC/MIN/2692). Perhaps freshly mindful of the concerns of its Children's Officer, the Children's Committee also stated that "attempts" needed to be made to "obtain reports as to the welfare of children discharged from the care of the council to Ireland".

In October 1955, therefore, having made a number of further inquiries, the Children's Officer was before the Children's Committee once again. As instructed, he had consulted the Home Office. Specifically in terms of whether of not the consent of the Secretary of State was required before a child could be removed, it was of the opinion that:

> Emigration under section 17 of the Children Act does not include travel from Great Britain to Ireland. In practice, the Irish packets in both directions are crowded with children travelling without documents and in the care of many kinds of people; it is not the policy to control the travel of British subjects across the Irish Sea. Emigration is not defined in the Act, and in common parlance one would not speak of emigration to Ireland, which is still partly, and, within living memory was wholly, within the United Kingdom. The Secretary of State's consent is, therefore, not required to the discharge of children to Ireland. (6 October 1955, LCC/MIN/2706)

The Home Office was also of the view that boarding-out payments should only be paid "in the exceptional case" when a child was placed in Ireland (6 October 1955, LCC/MIN/2706). In short, the Home Office fully supported the policy of the LCC. However, this might be viewed as an unduly sanguine and relaxed response, given that one interpretation might be that many of these 'Irish' children, born to Irish mothers in London, were (as the Home Office response actually suggests) 'British subjects' and were, in effect, being removed from the jurisdiction of the UK government. Paradoxically, the discharge to Ireland scheme can, perhaps, be interpreted as, in effect, discursively *producing* 'Irish' children in order to deal with a specific childcare crisis.

The question of discharge from care to Ireland was also discussed at one of the regular liaison meetings that the Children's Officer had with the "Roman Catholic authorities and it was considered that the matter should be dealt with solely by the Council and not through the Catholic Rescue Societies in London" (6 October 1955, LCC/MIN/2706). This response would not seem to be indicative, however, of any principled opposition to the practice of removing children in this way because these same rescue societies were, as discussed earlier, actively involved in 'repatriating' Irish 'unmarried mothers', often with their newborn babies, back to Ireland.

The Children's Officer was also able to report that LCC's female Inspector of Child Care, accompanied by the Child Welfare Officer now associated with the scheme, had visited Ireland in early 1955. Her report remains illuminating, moreover, and merits further exploration because of the way it represents Ireland and Irish people during this period.

Picturing Ireland: the construction of the Irish 'other'

The visit to Ireland had commenced on 27 February 1955, and the energetic local government officers from London visited "children's homes, foster homes, and parental homes to whom children had been returned". In addition, they visited other households and investigated the possibility of grandparents or other relatives accepting responsibility for the care of children now in England (6 October 1955, LCC/MIN/2706). It was also reported that meetings took place with government inspectors in Ireland and with the Secretary of the CPRSI.

The actual 'programme' undertaken by the pair of LCC officials was based on "new work submitted" by the Child Welfare Officer. That is to say, "investigations regarding children in England having relatives in Ireland": a "review of cases of children already placed in Ireland". In addition, "interviews took place with administrative and field officers of statutory and voluntary bodies, in an attempt to assess the general feelings among them regarding the transfer of children to Ireland" (6 October 1955, LCC/MIN/2706).

As we have seen, the initial plan to discharge children from care to Ireland was sparked by a crisis prompted by the refusal of the Home Office to continue to sanction the use of nurseries as accommodation for children 'in care' who were under the age of three years. This reason may then have been used – opportunistically and in a more widespread manner – to rid the LCC of part of the financial burden of maintaining other Irish children in public care. However, the suggestion here is that the scheme was more fundamentally rooted in an understanding that Ireland and Irish people were alien or 'other', despite their 'whiteness' (in this context, see also Kiberd, 1996; Graham and Maley, 1999). This is not to maintain, however, that the identification of 'Irish children' was a process entirely bled of ambiguities. The Children's Officer argued, for example, that:

> it would not seem desirable in many cases to send to Ireland children who have been in this country for some long time and had grown up as *English children with English contacts and outlooks*.... The areas could, however, give an approximate number of children in care who have relatives in Ireland, ie recent cases within memory of existing staff, say during the last two years, for whom no definite arrangements for adoption or boarding out in this country is envisaged. (6 October 1955, LCC/MIN/2706; emphasis added)

The notion of 'English children' with 'English outlooks' was clearly founded on a range of implicit and inescapably unstable ideas about 'England' and an essential 'Englishness' (see Giles and Middleton, 1995). England as an 'imagined community' was, however, juxtaposed to that of an Ireland portrayed as backward, traditional and pre-modern (see also Anderson, 1991). Moreover, in representing Ireland in this way, an idea was being reinforced that Irish children who were 'in care' in England were somehow 'out of place'.

This, moreover, was a view about Irish migrants reinforced in the British popular press throughout the 1950s. In April 1957, for example, an unmarried Irish woman called Annette Killackey found herself on the front page of one of Britain's popular newspapers. The headline, in bold capital letters, implored: "Who wants my baby?". Annette had moved to London 18 months previously. However, "London was too big for the girl from Ireland" and soon she found herself pregnant. Her child was now 10 weeks old and, still living in a Mother and Baby Home, Annette was becoming inpatient because the placement and adoption of her child was taking too long. On account of her situation, she contacted a newspaper to try to speed up the adoption process (*The Daily Sketch*, 4 April 1957). Annette, therefore, was a desperate young woman who was 'out of place' both spatially (first Irish, and second, in a city that was 'too big' for her) and in terms of the normative values of the late 1950s and the dominant construct of the 'ordinary devoted mother' (see Winnicott, cited in Lewis, 1986, p 41).

The LCC Inspector of Child Care visiting Ireland, perhaps possessing the "stigmatising gaze of a culturally dominant other" (Fraser, 2000, p 109), reported to the Children's Committee that "in rural areas at any rate, life still flows along pretty clearly defined traditional channels" (6 October 1955, LCC/MIN/2706). Her 'modern', metropolitan perspective was also brought to bear on family relationships and specifically on the role of Irish women. One "girl" of "nearly 18 ... hoped to train as a teacher, yet she has not even been to her first dance yet". In commenting on why young Irish women emigrated to England, she told the Children's Committee:

> In discussing how their daughters had come to grief in England several mothers described them as "wild and wayward".... These [those going to England] must have been the more spirited girls irked unbearably by the drudgery of their lives and the restrictions upon their freedoms. Their response to the tempting prospects of work in England can be well understood. The mothers can be tempted too, by the prospect of money to be sent home; they told how they resisted the idea at first, fearing for the girl's safety, but eventually let them go. (6 October 1955, LCC/MIN/2706)

In terms of the substance of her visit, the same officer was of the view that there remained "scope for further work" in Ireland and that such work "might be expected to produce satisfactory results both in terms of 'child care' and financially to the Council". The discharge from care to Ireland schemes were also thought to be likely to deter Irish female immigration into Britain because it seemed "likely that an awareness of the measures being taken to restore Irish children of Irish parentage to their own country will make parents wary of allowing their young daughters to go to England". In short, the discharge plan was viable, but she counselled that certain factors had to be "borne in mind" and importantly these factors were again embedded in an understanding that Irish people were *different* and had, for example, lower standards of childcare. This is apparent in her remarks relating the 'matching' of children discharged from LCC care to foster homes in Ireland:

> Clearly, this could not be carried out along accepted lines. Impressions suggest, however, that this would matter less in Ireland than England.... The prevailing attitude to young children seemed that of "have 'em, love 'em and leave 'em be"; the foster child would be included and find himself very quickly "one of the family"; I felt that the whole foster-relationship, including the supervisor's role, would involve less anxiety, less critical evaluation (e.g. what we would consider overcrowding just would not matter), and a more instinctive approach than obtains in England. There is much to be said for this way. (6 October 1955, LCC/MIN/2706)[4]

This assessment was rooted, perhaps, in key colonial and racist tropes about Irish fecundity, instinct and lack of cleanliness (Spinley, 1953; McClintock, 1994). It also implies that the substitute care to be provided for the discharged children warranted "less critical attention" than might ordinarily have been the case and so increased the chances of their being placed in risky or harmful placements. Indeed, in the late 1960s, evidence was to become available that illustrated the dangers, for children, of this happening (see 'Amazing traffic in babies exposed', *The People*, 31 March 1968).

Of prime importance in the entire discharge to Ireland initiative, avowed the inspector, was a "knowledge and understanding of the Irish". For her, this was "essential" and the Child Welfare Officer the LCC designated to fulfil the pivotal role possessed this understanding. Perhaps, like a benign official in an African colony, she was reported, for example, to have a "warm sympathy for them, but this does not blind her to their weaknesses" (6 October 1955, LCC/ MIN/2706; see also Pratt, 1993). Equipped with this appropriate "knowledge and understanding of the Irish", the Child Welfare Officer had a specific "method for individual cases", which involved "getting the grandmother to consider taking an interest in her daughter's illegitimate child"; "enlisting the cooperation of the parish priest and/or CPRSI in finding a suitable foster home"; "making use of the statutory machinery which operates very much as in England.... Though possibly supervision is not as close, nor visits by the authorised officer as frequent as in England, impressions suggest that this is not a course for undue anxiety"; "furthering in every way the eventual return of the child to his grandparents or other relatives"[5].

In terms of practical matters, the Child Welfare Officer felt that she might be able to make 'office' arrangements with friends in Ireland. In addition, because of the gathering pace of the discharges, she was becoming "well known to transport officials and stewardesses" on her night-time journeys conveying children "by rail and boat" to Ireland (6 October 1955, LCC/MIN/2706).

Policy into practice: the identification of Irish children and their removal to Ireland

By the spring of 1956, therefore, the removal of children to Ireland was underway, with 48 children having been taken to Ireland since the new policy was adopted (19 April 1956, LCC/MIN/2707). An appendix to a report presented to the Children's Committee established the ages of the children concerned (see Table 3.1) (19 April 1956, LCC/MIN/2707).

The information featured in Table 3.1 is significant in that it reveals that older children were also being discharged from care to Ireland. As mentioned earlier, the initial LCC concerns centred on children who were under three years old living in the residential nurseries at Kings Mead and Hillside. However, half of the children taken to Ireland were aged five years and over. The information presented to the Children's Committee also contains important gaps that, if filled, might further illuminate key aspects of the process of discharge. No information is furnished, for example, on the country of birth of the children, nor how long they had been resident in England, or their eventual placement location in Ireland. Significantly also, no information is provided on the question of parental consent, nor on how the views of children were obtained on plans to remove them to Ireland.

The Children's Committee was also provided with information about other children who might be potential candidates for discharge to Ireland. Thus, all of the LCC's Area Children's Officers had been contacted and they arrived at the conclusion that there were 142 children in care whose circumstances suggested that detailed "case enquiries about them might be made in Ireland with a view to the discharge of at least some of them to the care of relatives there" (19 April 1956, LCC/MIN/2707). Sixty-one of the children had "Irish relatives where addresses in Ireland" were known (eight in Northern Ireland),

Table 3.1: Number of children discharged by the LCC from care to Ireland, by April 1956

Age	Number of children
0-2	6
0-5	18
5-11	15
11-15	5
15+	4
Total	48

but the majority (81 children) had "Irish relatives where addresses would need to be discovered in Ireland".

According to the Children's Officer, there appeared to be "sufficient work" in Ireland to justify a Child Welfare Officer being based in Ireland for six months each year. Financial savings were likely to accrue to the LCC if the relevant officer continued to be put to work in this way:

> [I]t must be borne in mind that, on the nine visits already paid by the child welfare officer to Ireland, she has been successful in arranging for 48 children to be returned to their relatives. It seems likely that the knowledge that the babies of Irish mothers are liable to be returned to relatives in Ireland if they come into care may deter some Irish mothers from abandoning their children so that they come into care. Some receptions into care may thus be avoided, although no estimate of probable numbers is possible.... If this successful effort could continue for a full period of six months, it may be that up to 100 children would be returned to relatives and on the basis that the average cost to the Council per child is a minimum of £5 a week (and considerably more if the majority are in nursery care), this could result in a saving of the order of £500 a week. (19 April 1956, LCC/MIN/2707)

Thus, this active identification of Irish children was bound up with determining which families were to have access to child welfare services in Britain. Furthermore, this focus on Irish children became even more pronounced the following year when a chart was made available to the LCC Children's Committee, which mapped out the numbers of people living in the LCC's nine administrative areas who were, according to the 1951 Census, from the Irish Republic (21 February 1957, LCC/MIN/2708)[6]. It was also reported that the "various authorities" in Ireland were fully cooperating with the activities of the Child Welfare Officer from London. For the Children's Officer, this cooperation was not only reflected in the relationship with the CPRSI, but was also "epitomised by the allocation of 66 gallons of petrol" to her "at a time when the local staff had to use public transport" because of an economic crisis in Ireland.

In general, it appeared, asserted the LCC's Children's Officer, that the discharge to Ireland scheme was now a success and had "more than justified itself from a financial point of view and from the standpoint of the welfare of the children concerned" (21 February 1957, LCC/MIN/2708). Arguing for an extension of the scheme, he recommended that there were over 100 children in care who were "known to have Irish *antecedents*" and that the scheme should be "continued until the supply is exhausted" (21 February 1957, LCC/MIN/2708; emphasis added)[7]. Moreover, there appeared to be grounds for expanding the operation of the discharge to Ireland initiative. Thus, it was suggested that the Child Welfare Officer might begin to undertake "similar enquiries (on reimbursement of the Council's expenses) for other local authorities" in order to "get the maximum from the experience and technique" that she had "in this field" (21

February 1957, LCC/MIN/2708). Perhaps on account of the Children's Officer's confidence and plans for the future, the Children's Committee not only agreed to further extend the scheme, it also agreed, in principle, for a second Child Welfare Officer to be trained as an assistant to the one already involved. Soon, however, the entire scheme was to be subjected to greater scrutiny when its existence was brought to the attention of the wider public.

The 'export-only' babies and the opposition of Irish mothers to the removal of their children from the UK

In April 1957, a popular British Sunday newspaper reported on the "daring experiment" that was underway in London and the activities of the Child Welfare Officer who was regularly "touring" Ireland to "find homes" for babies. These babies, "born in Britain to unmarried Irish girls" were "being shipped to Eire every week for adoption by Irish Catholic couples". This experiment was being undertaken because "no Catholic adopters" could be "found for these babies over here". The newspaper report maintained that some "children's homes particularly in the vast LCC area already have far too many children in care where chances of adoption have been hampered because their mothers have labelled them Catholic at birth" ('The "export only" babies', *The Sunday Pictorial*, 14 April 1957). Perhaps underpinning the 'story', therefore, was the idea that English Protestant couples who wanted to adopt were being deprived of the chance to adopt these children.

Two days after this press *exposé*, the 'chairman' of the LCC Children's Committee was asked if she had seen the newspaper article and to comment on the policy of discharging Irish children from care to Ireland. She responded:

> Over the last two years about 100 Irish Roman Catholic children who were in the Council's care have been taken to Eire to live with relatives who are willing to receive them; in some instances the children's mothers have been found and later joined the children in Eire. Before going to Eire the children have been living in nurseries and children's homes in this country and, owing to a shortage of Roman Catholic foster homes, could not be boarded out. With the cooperation of the Eire authorities the children will be able to lead happy, normal lives with their own families. (16 April 1957, LCC *Minutes of proceedings*)

The policy of removing children in care from London to Ireland, to be "able to lead happy, normal lives", was, however, encountering opposition in another domain. In short, some Irish women were refusing to cooperate with the plans of the LCC to take their children across the Irish Sea. This reluctance to go along with the local authority's plans had, in fact, proved something of an obstacle since the inception of the scheme earlier in the decade. As early as September 1954, for example, the Children's Officer told the Special Sub-Committee on the Clearance of Welfare Nurseries:

A factor of considerable importance, but not yet clear in most cases, is what the attitude of the mother is going to be to the suggestion that she should return to Ireland with her child or that she should allow her child to go there alone. It is becoming apparent that good offers of care, including possible adoption, may founder on a mother's refusal to leave this country or to allow her child to do so. At this stage the reasons for this attitude can only be surmised, but there are suggestions that some mothers, having chosen to quit the simpler rural life of their childhood and adolescence, usually spent in conditions bereft of many of the amenities available to city dwellers, are now so accustomed to city life that they have no intention of returning, or of allowing their children to return to their former homes. (24 September 1954, LCC/MIN/2723)

Later also, some mothers' active opposition to the scheme was referred to in committee meetings. The same Children' Officer claimed, for example, that "more children might have been sent to Ireland, but their mothers refused to allow them to go" (21 February 1957, LCC/MIN/2707). Clearly, the somewhat arid – and not infrequently intentionally evasive – tone of minute books mute, or omit entirely, the 'voices' of the women who opposed the scheme. Similarly, the views of the children who were the focal concern of the scheme are rendered subordinate in the 'official' discourse of the LCC. However, the fact that opposition to the scheme often featured as a recurring item in the minutes hints at the scale of the reluctance to cooperate by some mothers. Moreover, this opposition from these Irish women – frustrating 'official' plans for themselves and their children – was also apparent, as we have seen, in Chapter Two.

On 30 May 1957, the Children's Officer reported that:

Three mothers have refused to agree to their children (10 in all) being discharged from the Council's care in this country to the care of relatives in Ireland under the arrangements approved by the Committee…. [It] is likely that further instances will arise where parents refuse to consent to the action. (30 May 1957, LCC/MIN/2708)

Perhaps in the context of the 'daring experiment' now being in the public domain, this led the Children's Officer to speculate if discharging from care to Ireland, despite parental objections, was actually "consistent with the welfare of the child". Here, he suggested, it was important to recall that most of the children concerned in these cases were in care, under Section 1 of the 1948 Children Act. That is to say, they were in public care on a voluntary basis with the LCC having "no parental rights over them as against their parents" (30 May 1957, LCC/MIN/2708). Therefore, this entailed a parent's right to "resume the care of the child from the Council". Thus, it was "normally assumed that care will be provided … *in this country*; if despite the parent objecting the child is discharged from care to relatives outside the country, the parent is in effect deprived of the right to reclaim the child from the Council" (emphasis in original). Furthermore, "to discharge to Ireland a child whose mother in this country objected, would, in addition to removing the child from all normal contact with her (either now or in the future), leave her with the financial burden of paying fares etc, for his return if she wanted to bring him back, the Council having no power to bring back from Ireland any child not in care and in respect of whom it has no form of parental rights" (30 May 1957, LCC/MIN/2708). The Children's Officer concluded that "to send children out of the country in which their parents are living and out of the jurisdiction of the statutes under which the children have been in care, against the expressed wishes of the parents, would appear to be unjustifiable". "On balance", therefore, he was of the professional opinion that "children should not be sent to Ireland to be discharged from care against the wishes of the parent" (30 May 1957, LCC/MIN/2708). Nonetheless, the Children's Committee resolution left a margin of space to enable its officers to remove children to Ireland *despite* parental objections. It resolved:

> that children in the care of the Council be not discharged to the care of relatives in Ireland against the parents wishes *unless the district committee after considering all the circumstances are satisfied that such discharge is in the child's best interests.* (30 May 1957, LCC/MIN/2694; emphasis added)

On 20 February 1958, the Children's Committee asked the Children's Officer to report on the reasons why it was thought "unnecessary or inadvisable in the children's interests to undertake enquiry work in Ireland in respect of some of the children in the Council's care with relatives or connections in Ireland" (20 February 1958, LCC/MIN/2694). This resolution is of interest in that it implies that politicians on the LCC Children's Committee were becoming inpatient with what may have been perceived as certain reluctance, on the part of some of its officers to pursue the discharge to Ireland policy with sufficient enthusiasm. Moreover, the resolution can also be interpreted as revealing that the 'daring experiment' was creating some discord within the LCC. On another level, the phrase "relatives or connections" suggests that an attempt was being made to increase the pool of potential child candidates for removal. More specifically, 'connections' has, of course, an ambiguity that would provide for this type of expansion.

By this time, a different Children's Officer was in place at the LCC and he reported that with 233 children it had been deemed "inadvisable or unnecessary in the children's interests" for them to be removed despite their having Irish relatives or connections (9 October 1958, LCC/MIN/2709). His explanation is conveyed in Table 3.2[8].

Clearly, there can be no suggestion that all children in care across the LCC area with 'Irish relatives or connections' were dispatched across the Irish Sea. Nonetheless, the identification of Irish children continued and the scheme remained in place in the 1960s. Periodically, the position of the Child Welfare Officer, who spent six months in Ireland each year, was reviewed and a further

Table 3.2: Irish children in care and not sent to Ireland by the LCC

Reasons for failure to remove	Number of children
Enquiry work would have been abortive as the children were short stay or soon to be discharged from care	132
Enquiry work was not required as the parents were in this country and were in close contact with the children	36
Children were boarded out or placed for adoption	10
Children were home on trial in this country	2
The parent or the child himself did not want enquiries made and it was considered that in the child's interests, they should not be made	16
The Irish relatives were known to be unwilling, or were considered on evidence already available in this country to be unsuitable, to care for the child	19
The Area Children's Officers were awaiting developments before deciding whether to initiate enquiries in Ireland	9
The decision not to cause inquiries to be made at the time had been reversed. Child Welfare Officer is now investigating these in Ireland	7
Enquiries were not required because the children were happily settled in establishments and it was thought that the situation ought not to be disturbed by the making of enquiries	2
Total number of children	233

extension to the arrangement was authorised. The LCC also used the scheme to discharge from care children based in other local authorities: Bedfordshire, Hertfordshire and Middlesex. Furthermore, another seven local authorities made it clear that they would "like to make use of the service should the occasion arise" (25 February 1960, LCC/MIN/2711). The core task of the scheme remained, however, discharging from care those children who were the responsibility of the LCC and the emphasis in the reports of the various Children's Officers was on the money being saved by the LCC (23 February 1961, LCC/MIN/2712).

By the mid-1960s, 298 children had been removed to Ireland (19 March 1964, LCC/MIN/2715). Given the changing composition of London's population during this period, there were also suggestions that the scheme could be extended to children from other ethnicities and national backgrounds. However, given that children's services were soon to cease being the responsibility of the LCC, it was thought that there was insufficient time available to look into this dimension. Thus, the Children's Officer "saw no possibility of investigating before 31 March 1965 a scheme for the repatriation of West Indian children in care on the lines of the Irish scheme" (19 March 1964, LCC/MIN/2696).

Irish children and families as a 'problem' population

As with the 'repatriation' of Irish 'unmarried mothers' discussed in earlier chapters of this book, it could be argued that the 'daring experiment' was simply an instance of a hard-pressed council child welfare agency acting expediently. Indeed, there was a manifest need to 'clear' two residential nurseries of children as soon as possible. Some of these were the children of Irish parents, many were Roman Catholics and there was, at this time, a lack of Roman Catholic foster carers in Britain. It could also be suggested that the government in Ireland and at least one voluntary child welfare agency – the CPRSI – supported the scheme that the LCC put in place. However, the suggestion here is that underpinning the scheme was a more rooted and entrenched cultural (and, perhaps, political) idea that Irish children and families in Britain were 'out of place', a potentially problem population. This is reflected, moreover, in the contemporary social construction of 'problem families' in Britain.

In the 1950s, many families of the urban poor were characterised as 'problem families' who were indolent, feckless, dirty and a drain on the resources of the post-war welfare state (see Philp and Timms, 1957; Hall, 1960, ch 10; Starkey, 2000). Welshman (1999) has explored how social work in Britain related to 'problem families' and his contribution is timely because this construct emerged, once again, in social work and social care discourses in the late 1990s and early 21st century. Prime Minister Tony Blair has also been apt to use the term (see *The Guardian*, 26 July 1993). Furthermore, this ideological category is being uncritically deployed once again in professional exchanges centred on children and families (Cleaver and Freeman, 1995, pp 51-3; Eisenstadt, 1998; Steele, 1998; see also the editorial 'The division bell', *Community Care*, 15-21 February, 2001, p 17). 'Problem families' are, of course, also central to the official discourse on 'antisocial behaviour'[9]. However, in the context of some of this book's concerns, this construct can be interpreted as part of a matrix of ideas partly preoccupied with Irish people in Britain.

In the early 1950s, for example, Spinley (1953) provided an account of "one of the worst slums in London". She went onto describe a district that was "notorious ... for vice and delinquency ... a major prostitution area" and the "blackest spot in the city for juvenile delinquency". In this area, she asserted "a large proportion of the inhabitants are Irish; social workers say: 'The Irish land here, and while the respectable soon move away, the ignorant and the shiftless stay'" (Spinley, 1953, p 40). The author then sought to provide her readers with a picture of a typical house in the locality:

> The most noticeable characteristic of the house is the smell, indeed on a first visit the middle-class stomach may find it impossible to stay longer than five minutes. These strong odours are partly due to the fact windows are not opened and so no current of air can carry away the smells of cooking, lavatory bucket, mattress wet in the night, and the baby's vomit hurriedly wiped up. (Spinley, 1953, p 40)

Portrayals such as this are recursive in that similar descriptions of the living conditions of Irish people were produced in the 19th century and were a key component of the "bourgeois Imaginary" (Stallybrass and White, 1986, p 126; see also Engels, 1926)[10]. Such accounts are also reflective of more embedded and pervasive processes in that the experience of Irish people in Britain has frequently been framed by the "construction of the Irish (Catholic) as a historically significant Other of the English/British (Protestant)" (Hickman, 1998, pp 290-1; see also Gilley, 1999). In this context, the identification of 'dirt' and 'dirtiness' has, moreover, fulfilled a significant function. Indeed, it is often the case that racist discourses have associated black people "in various ways with dirt ... notably in the repeated perceptions" that they or their food smells (see Dyer, 1997, pp 75-6). The idea of a black presence "swamping" Britain was, of course, used by in the 1980s by the then prime minister, Margaret Thatcher (Scraton, 1987), and it has recently been reactivated by Home Secretary David Blunkett in his more comments on asylum seekers and refugees. However, even in the 1970s, a key social work textbook had observed that "fears have sometimes been expressed" that Irish immigrants will "swamp the social services with their demands" (Cheetham 1972, p 18).

John Marriot (1999), moreover, has convincingly argued that that the centrality of 'dirt' in social reform discourses of the second half of the 19th century cannot be separated from concerns about the arrival of Irish people in parts of London, geographical zones at the heart of the British Empire. Furthermore, as Spinley's account clearly highlights, similar concerns about Irish people, found in the unclean spaces of urban enclaves, were still being aired in the 1950s in debates within social work and social policy on 'problem families'[11].

Conclusion

As we shall see in Chapter Four, in terms of social work today, government guidance, reports and commentaries for practitioners and students largely omit any reference to Irish children and their families. Fundamentally, this is because the dominant approach to 'race' and ethnicity is founded on the idea that there exists a unitary and homogeneous 'white' identity in Britain against which a 'black' population can be tidily juxtaposed. Within this schematic approach, 'ethnic minority' and 'black' are conflated and the historical and contemporary cultural specificity of Irish children is not normally referred to in, for example, protocols concerned with addressing and promoting the 'identity' needs of children who are 'looked after', or 'in care', under the 1989 Children Act.

However, returning to the so-called 'daring experiment', the archival research featured in this chapter helps to reveal that official approaches to Irish children in the 1950s and 1960s were rooted in the understanding that these children were 'other' and could be identified and segregated from their British counterparts. In short, in its modalities of intervention in the 1950s, the LCC can be seen to have been actively structuring and organising – albeit in a largely negative way – the Irish *difference* that today's anti-discriminatory discourses have been frequently apt to deny. It has also been highlighted how the scheme, initially related to just two welfare nurseries, prompted an exercise that led to all Irish children and families in London being identified, classified and logged. It addition, it has been argued that, because of dominant ideas about Ireland and Irish forms of parenting, LCC officers accepted potentially lower standards for children. Issues bound up with the consent of Irish parent, usually mothers, were also discussed.

Thus far, therefore, the book has explored how social work and associated sectors responded to Irish 'unmarried mothers' and children in need of substitute care in the past, particularly the 1950s and 1960s. Next, however, we will turn to look at the contemporary picture by examining social work's more general approach to Irish children and their families in the early 21st century.

Notes

[1] Throughout this chapter, the London County Council will be referred to by the acronym LCC. The LCC established the Children's Committee in December 1948 to administer a number of its functions under the 1948 Children Act. This it did until April 1965 when, under the 1963 Local Government Act, children's services became the responsibility of the London Borough Councils. No names of any officers of the LCC will be used. All archival references to the minutes and presented papers of the LCC include the date on which the meeting took place, or at which a report was presented and the specific file held in the London Metropolitan Archives. I am particularly grateful to Rhys Griffiths, senior archivist, for allowing me to have access to materials that are ordinarily closed. An earlier version of this chapter appeared as 'The "daring experiment": the London County Council and the discharge from care of children to Ireland in the 1950s and 1960s', *Journal of Social Policy*, vol 32, no 1, pp 1-18.

[2] Up until her involvement in the LCC scheme, the Child Welfare Officer had been "fully occupied in supervising 100 Roman Catholic girls (most of them 15 years old) under after care arrangements". A Roman Catholic herself, she had "developed very good personal relationships with Roman Catholic societies and voluntary homes" (11 November 1954, LCC/MIN/2706).

[3] The discharge of children from care to Northern Ireland is a dimension that clearly merits fuller exploration elsewhere.

[4] The inspector did, however, rule out discharged children being placed in county homes, or former workhouses in Ireland. In this context, see Raftery and O'Sullivan (1999).

[5] This 'method' appeared, of course, to have little regard for the parent's right to confidentiality.

---

[6] Other information included: "Roman Catholic children in care a proportion of whom will be Irish; the number of children returned to Ireland during the past six months and the number returned from each area since the scheme first started". The phrase 'a portion of whom will be Irish' is written in pen and not, unlike the rest of the minutes, typed. It is not clear, however, whether this was added prior to the presentation of the report by the Children's Officer on 21 February 1957 or whether it was added during the course of the Children's Committee following debate. The reference to 'returned' disguises, of course, the fact that some of the children may *never* have lived in Ireland.

[7] The phrase 'until the supply is exhausted' is deleted by pen. Once again, it is not clear, however, whether this deletion took place prior to the presentation of the report by the Children's Officer on 21 February 1957 or whether it was done during the course of the Children's Committee following debate.

[8] Sixty-six of the 132 children where it was thought enquiry work would have been "abortive" were, it was reported "actually returned home during the investigation". In respect of the 10 children 'boarded out or placed for adoption', it was observed that such children did not fall within the "scope of the scheme". Interestingly, 16 children were placed in a category where either they or their parents did not want enquiries made. This is the *only* reference in the archives to children's own wishes being expressed on the discharge from care to Ireland scheme.

[9] The government White Paper, *Respect and responsibility – Taking a stand against anti-social behaviour* (2003), draws attention to the 'Problem Family Manual' produced by Kent Police (Home Office, 2003, p 55).

[10] The perspective of Engels is strikingly similar to that of Spinley. He observed, for example, that wherever "a district is distinguished for especial filth and especial ruinousness, the explorer may safely count upon meeting chiefly those Celtic faces which one recognises at the first glance as different from the Saxon physiognomy of the native" (in Miles, 1982, p 140). Interestingly, as Francis Wheen (2000, pp 261-2) has reminded us, Mary Burns, an Irish woman, was Engels' companion and lover for many years.

[11] Indeed, although not a central concern here, it is possible to argue that these ideas also help to illuminate some statements made about the Catholic population in Northern Ireland during the period of the 'Troubles'. In 2000, for example, it was reported that shortly after Bloody Sunday, a Foreign Office memo had proposed that the no-go areas of Derry should be "encouraged" to rot with the spread of disease (see 'Let Derry rot, FO man advised', *The Guardian*, 25 November 2000). It is surely also the case that if "your propaganda machine can convince soldiers that their opponents are not really human but are 'inferior forms of life', then their resistance to killing their own species will be reduced" (Grossman, cited in Gilroy, 2000, p 300). Perhaps related to the notion that Irish Catholics are an inferior or less valued form of life

have also been perennial fears, expressed by some in 'the North', about Catholics 'breeding' to outstrip the size of the allegedly beleaguered Unionist population.

FOUR

'Race', ethnicity and Irish 'invisibility'

Having put in place an historical foundation for the second half of this book, the focal argument in this chapter is that social work's theoretical approach to questions of 'race' and ethnicity, associated with a more embracing academic discourse, fails to address the specificity of Britain's largest ethnic minority, Irish people[1]. This is not to argue that Irish people are *entirely* omitted, even within Department of Health (DoH) publications that provide guidance for social workers (see, for example, DoH, 1991, p 106; DoH, 2001). Nonetheless, it is apparent that the hegemonic, or dominant, approach is apt to shrink the discourse on 'race' and ethnicity and does not allow for a more complex understanding. Similarly, there is a failure to examine some of the historical patterns of involvement with Irish children and families discussed in earlier chapters of this book.

Providing part of the context for an exploration of contemporary responses to Irish children and families, the chapter begins by briefly highlighting social work's more general interest in promoting what is loosely referred to as 'anti-discriminatory social work practice'. This has been subjected to a good deal of political criticism in recent years. Next, it looks at social work's dominant orientation in relation to 'race' and ethnicity, then goes on to examine contemporary and official guidelines for practice, revealing how these have tended to ignore Irish children and families. It is suggested that there may be some signs of change with the evolution of newer approaches, which take account of the diversity *within* black *and* white categories. However, it will be maintained that there is still a need properly to interrogate 'whiteness' and to recognise Irish specificity.

Anti-discriminatory social work practice, 'race' and child placement

Since the 1980s, social work's professional value base has been rhetorically underpinned by a commitment to anti-discriminatory social work practice. This has been defined as:

> practice which is rooted in a critical analysis of the history of economic, state and cultural processes which seek to either marginalise, stigmatise or exploit different collectivities. Anti-discriminatory social work practice seeks to understand social work's complicity in such processes and tries to evolve forms of practice which challenge these processes. (Garrett, 1998, pp 445-6)

In this context, social work students in the mid-1990s, for example, were required to demonstrate that they "respect and value uniqueness and diversity". Furthermore, they had to "identify, analyse and take action to counter discrimination" (CCETSW, 1995; see also Banks, 1995; Dominelli, 1996; Patel, 1999).

However, for 18 years, social work in Britain was also shaped by the political project of the right wing of the Conservative Party that had a deep antipathy for such ideas and values (see Gledhill, 1989). Social work's value base and awareness of factors connected to class, 'race', gender and oppression also led to the charge of 'political correctness' (Hopton, 1997; see also 'Cut the "ologies" and "isms", social workers told', *The Independent on Sunday*, 13 December 1992; 'Who's racially naive?', *Community Care*, (editorial), 9 September 1993). Significantly, child adoption, or more broadly child placement, was one of the key sites of the welfare state where the battle against so-called 'political correctness' was waged. Frequently, this focused on the issue of 'race' and placements[2].

Throughout the last quarter of the 20th century, 'race' featured as a key component in debates on adoption and child placement. In the early 1980s, for example, the Association of Black Social Workers and Allied Professionals challenged the hegemony of child placement policies and practices founded on a liberal and assimilationist perspective. Here, the critique focused on the damaging consequences for black children of being placed with white adoptive and foster carers, but it also, more broadly, drew attention to the impact of racism in British society (Small, 1982; Small with Prevatt Goldstein, 2000). Associated with this critique were specific social work practice innovations, such as the influential New Black Families scheme, launched in the London Borough of Lambeth in 1980, which set out to recruit substitute black families for black children in the care of the local authority. Partly on account of such ideas and projects, a new attentiveness to questions of 'race' and ethnicity was gradually incorporated into practice guidelines for children in contact with social services and into the 1989 Children Act. This Act, specifically Section 22.5, mandated that, with 'looked after' children or those in public care, local authorities had to give "due consideration" to their "religious persuasion, racial origin and cultural and linguistic background".

During the 1990s, this more progressive approach came under attack. The then prime minister, John Major, asserted that he was not "interested in trendy social theories, only in good homes for needy kids" (see 'Adoption "trendies" attacked by PM', *The Guardian*, 14 July 1993). In the summer of 1993, for example, media and political attention focused particularly on the case of James and Roma Lawrence whose application to adopt had been rejected by Norfolk County Council because, it was claimed, of their lack of understanding of 'race' issues (see also Clark, 1993). Significantly, in terms of the construction of the case, James was white and Roma was Asian.

Following the General Election in 1997, Paul Boateng, then junior minister at the DoH, attacked social services in a way similar to his Conservative predecessors. He was particularly concerned about an alleged social work fixation with 'same-'race" placements (see Valios, 1998), despite empirical evidence published by British Agencies for Adoption and Fostering (BAAF) highlighting the fact that this alleged preoccupation was not apparent in terms of social work practice in the area of adoption (see Valios, 1997, p 5). Nonetheless, in the late 1990s, it appeared that Boeteng was on something of a personal crusade to promote transracial adoption. Moreover, a good deal of his rhetoric appeared entirely at odds with the principles featured in the 1989 Children Act and social work policy and practice that had evolved in the 1980s and 1990s.

Specifically in terms of Boeteng's interventions, developments in the US may have played a part in terms of the inchoate backlash against a professional sensitivity to the 'race' and ethnicity of children in need of placements (Garrett, 2000)[3]. In the US, following the passage of the 1994 Multiethnic Placement Act and the 1996 provisions on Removal of Barriers to Interethnic Adoption, it is no longer possible to use 'race' "categorically or presumptively to delay or deny adoptive or foster care placements" (Brooks et al, 1999, p 167). Less emphatically, but somewhat similarly, *Adoption – Achieving the right balance* (DoH, 1998), a circular issued in August 1998, stated that the "Government has made it clear that it is unacceptable for a child to be denied loving adoptive parents solely on the grounds that the child and adopters do not share the same racial or cultural background" (1998, para 14).

In Britain in the late 1990s, there appeared, therefore, to be attempts to dilute the significance of a child's 'race' or ethnicity when substitute care was being considered. This development was, moreover, likely to have detrimental consequences for Irish children and families because of the traditionally rooted failure even to begin adequately to address these issues with and for them. Significantly, however, *Adoption now: Messages from research* (DoH, 1999), an overview of adoption research published in October 1999, appeared to run counter to New Labour's evolving position. The study concluded:

> The requirement of the Children Act 1989 to seek to place children with parents who are of a similar cultural and ethnic background and who meet their needs provides a sound basis for policy. Placement with a family of a different ethnic and cultural background should be unusual and should be based on specific reasons for individual cases. (DoH, 1999, p 159)

Following the publication of the inquiry into the death of Stephen Lawrence and, perhaps, a fresh alertness to 'institutional racism', this was clearly a more restrained intervention on the question of 'race' and child placement than was apparent in some of the remarks of Boeteng (Macpherson, 1999). More measured, informed by research evidence and what was actually taking place in practice, *Adoption now* cautioned, therefore, against any radical departure from the principles of the 1989 Children Act and the dominant approach that had evolved and been implemented in the 1980s and 1990s.

Although the DoH approach to such questions remained conceptually problematic (because of the omission of an Irish dimension), subsequent reports and guidance for social services have reinforced the importance for children and their families of 'race' and ethnicity (see Dutt and Phillips, 2000; O'Neale, 2000; SSI, 2000, ch 6). The *Prime Minister's review: Adoption* (PIU, 2000) also failed to signal any radical departures in terms of 'race' and the placement of children. There was, moreover, nothing significantly new on 'race', ethnicity and child placement in the 2002 Adoption and Children Act, which was introduced in order to relocate the adoption of 'looked after' children at the heart of social work with children and families.

Bypassing the Irish dimension: social work's hegemonic discourse on 'race' and 'ethnic minorities'

Although not always explicit in any of the legislation or guidance, the high-profile interventions on 'race', ethnicity and placements in the late 1990s and early 20th century have been centrally concerned, however, with the circumstances of black children in public care (see Kirton, 1996). Irish children and their families were entirely absent, therefore, in the political and professional discourse that resulted in the 2002 Adoption and Children Act. Here again, a black/white binary dominated discussions on 'race', ethnicity and children in need of substitute care (DoH, 1999, pp 41-5, 115-17). Indeed, it was only when the debate's primary definers had regard to the placement of Romanian children that the issue of 'white' ethnicity or 'heritage' was usually acknowledged (DoH, 1999, pp 128-30). Importantly, this is because national, or cultural, difference tends only to be recognised in relation to 'white' children originating outside the so-called 'British Isles' (see also Walter, 2001, p 107; in this context, see also Taylor, A., 1997; Drakeford and Morris, 1998).

Nonetheless, as discussed earlier in this chapter, the 1989 Children Act places a more encompassing duty on local authorities to have regard to a 'looked after' child's "religious persuasion, racial origin and cultural and linguistic background". Furthermore, the significance of these factors was emphasised in guidance issued by the DoH both before and subsequent to the legislation becoming operational in the early 1990s. In 1991, for example, a number of principles in relation to the care of children were identified, including the statement:

> Since discrimination of all kinds is an everyday reality in many children's lives every effort must be made to ensure that agency services and practices do not reflect and reinforce it. (DoH, 1990, p 11)

Thus, "ethnic minority children should be helped to be proud of their racial and cultural heritage" (DoH, 1990, p 11). However, despite this general guidance, the specific needs of Irish children and young people have frequently been ignored in policy documents and this is likely to have adversely influenced practice. A central factor here has been the dominant conceptual paradigm that suggests that childcare issues associated with 'ethnic minorities' are solely meaningful in relation to children who are black. In what follows in this chapter, therefore, the intention is not to diminish the importance of identity issues for black children (some of whom might also be Irish), but to illuminate the omission.

The influential *Patterns and outcomes in child placement*, while not exploring the issue in any depth, suggests that "Irish children may experience a distinct culture at home" (DoH, 1991, p 106). However, the more recent plethora of publications associated with the heavily promoted Looking after Children system (Parker et al, 1991; Ward, 1995; see also Knight and Caveney, 1998; Garrett, 1999) failed even to refer to Irish children who are 'looked after', and this has reinforced Irish 'invisibility'. Action and Assessment Records (AARs), the system's prime innovation, has, for example, a developmental section devoted to the 'identity' dimension of a child's development. Here, the somewhat overly simplistic question is posed: "Do you know what 'race' or ethnic group you belong to?". The AAR continues, "How would you describe yourself (e.g. black, white, Italian, mixed parentage, Asian, Chinese, African)?". In ways such as this, Irish children in Britain are simply eased out of the dominant child welfare discourse.

Indeed, a brief survey of contemporary DoH policy documents, produced in relation to social work with children and families, reveals that Irish children and families continue to be omitted (see also Barn et al, 1997; Thoburn et al, 2000). In 2000, the Social Services Inspectorate (SSI) published a report that purported to be an authoritative examination of services provided for "ethnic minority children and families" (O'Neale, 2000). Typifying the dominant approach, it was asserted: "Ethnic minority families face many issues that white members do not...." (DoH, 2000, p 1). A brief section of the report then set out how the term 'ethnic minority' was to be used: "It specifically covers families from Africa, the Asian sub-continent, the Caribbean, British born members of these groups and other people of mixed 'race', i.e. people with one black parent, *in other words people who are black*" (O'Neale, 2000, p 1 emphasis added).

This SSI report failed, therefore, to provide a proper overview of services for ethnic minority children and families on account of the shrinking of 'race' and ethnic minority to a black/white binary. How could, for example, the inspectors begin to form a view if services adequately take account of the cultural and identity needs of, for example, a second-generation 'white' Irish girl who is being 'looked after' by English foster carers? Similarly, in the context of the racism directed at Irish Travellers in both Ireland and Britain (Helleiner, 1998), how might the inspectors have perceived the services available for a 'white' boy from an Irish Traveller family who has been placed in a secure unit? More fundamentally, how does the SSI definition of 'ethnic minority' sit alongside the more embracing perception of the cultural component featured in Section 22.5 of the 1989 Children Act, which relates to 'looked after' children? A more recent report from the chief inspector of the SSI has called for all social services staff to "become culturally competent" (SSI, 2000, p 81), yet the suggestion here is that the continued promotion of a limited conceptual framework is likely to undermine this aspiration. Conceptually important, in this context, is social work's failure to engage with the how 'whiteness' is constructed and positioned in Britain's 'national story'.

'Whiteness', the British 'national story' and the myth of homogeneity

Enjoying the status of a reigning paradigm, social work's dominant approach situates Irish children *outside* of ethnic status and *inside* an homogenised 'white' category (see also, in this context, Kuhn, 1962). This suggests that there is still a need to unpack, or deconstruct, the conceptual assumptions found at the heart of the black/white binary. More generally, within the discourse of anti-discriminatory social work theory in Britain, skin colour remains embedded as the determining factor in terms of issues connected to diversity and difference (see, for example, Kirton, 2000; also 'Ethnic status not taken seriously', *The Irish Post*, (editorial), 27 January 2001).

Importantly, underpinning social work's approach to questions of 'race' and ethnicity is a perception of 'whiteness' as a universally dominant, homogeneous and static social category (Allen, 1994; see also Mac an Ghaill, 1999, 2002; Bonnett, 2000)[4]. Whiteness "certainly carries privileges, but they are not always guaranteed" and in order to "give back meaning to the apparent emptiness of the 'white' category it is necessary to explore the specificity of white experiences" (Walter, 2001, p 6; see also Brah, 1992; Maynard, 1994). Similarly, as the cultural critic Richard Dyer (1997, p 19) has suggested, in terms of historical and contemporary processes of racialisation, 'whiteness' has been "enormously, often terrifyingly effective in unifying disparate groups of people". Nonetheless, "some are more securely white than others" and this is reflected in the creation of people who are "sometimes whites" (Dyer, 1997, p 4). That is to say, some, such as Irish people and Jewish people, may be "let into whiteness under particular historical circumstances" (Dyer, 1997, p 19). In short, 'whiteness' as a category is socially constructed and contains a shifting border and internal hierarchies. Moreover, the social construction of Irish people has, of course, been inseparable from factors connected to British colonialism and the temper of Anglo-Irish relations at particular historical junctures (see Busteed, 1999, p 103).

In an historical sense, the denial of the specificity of the cultural and national background of Irish children in Britain can also be linked to social construction of the 'British childhood' (Hendrick, 1990). This exclusionary conceptualisation, reflected in the discursive practices of the welfare state, was dominant from the early 19th century until, perhaps, the late 1960s, and at its core was the hegemonic political construct of 'one nation' and the denial of heterogeneity and intra-national conflict, particularly class conflict.

In this context, Roman Catholicism played an important role in terms of how it intervened in the lives of Irish families in Britain. Fielding (1993, p 57) is certainly right to argue that it would be "simplistic to describe the Church as a 'bourgeois' institution intent on encouraging adherents to internalise capitalist doctrine". Nonetheless, astute commentators quickly recognised the role that the Church could fulfil among Irish immigrant communities and – on account of this – they tried to temper the anti-Catholic sentiments that featured as a strong current in Britain (see Neal, 1991-92). M.C. Bishop (1877, p 611), for example, writing in the *Contemporary Review*, asserted that the "million Irish, were, and still are, an unpleasant feature of English life". However, the fact that "this alien million is not an advanced cancer in the English body politic is due not to the policemen, but to priests [and to] the agents of Catholic charity" (Bishop, 1877, p 607). For him there was a need, therefore, to recognise and acknowledge "the use of Catholicism as a social cement" (Bishop, 1877, p 615). He concluded:

> The friction between labour and capital ... [is] mitigated by the culture of the emotions which is a special care of Catholic missionaries. A common brotherhood in the sacraments of the Church, in obligatory worship, in spiritual aim and discipline, and most of all in community of creed, restores equality between man and man in all higher interests, and redresses the inequalities as no mundane communism could do. It would be hard to over-estimate the service rendered by Catholicism ... in mitigating strikes and keeping the peace among the miners and navvies under its influence. (1877, p 616)[5]

Related to this promotion of industrial peace was the Church's "patriotic English character" (Fielding, 1993, p 40; see also Bunting, 1998). Indeed, Irish adherents of Roman Catholicism did not entirely approve of this emphasis and many were concerned about the "Church's attempt to anglicize Irish children" (Fielding, 1993, p 41). Indeed, for Hickman, (1993, p 298), the Roman Catholic Church in Britain can be perceived as seeking to "incorporate and denationalise" the Irish in Britain with Catholic schools, particularly, holding up "a mirror to their pupils in which was reflected their Catholicity rather than their Irishness". Recently, the ESRC-funded Irish 2 Project, looking at the experiences of second-generation Irish people, has also commented on the absence from the curriculum of reference to Irish history and culture in Catholic (and state schools) in England (see also Doyle, 2002; also, with a somewhat different emphasis, the Working Party on Catholic Education in a Multiracial, Multicultural Society, 1984).

The role and interventions of Catholic child welfare and 'rescue' organisations in Britain can also be viewed in a similar way in that the Catholicism of potential adopters was the prime factor in relation to adoptive placements for Irish children. Many Irish children, particularly in the 1950s and 1960s, were adopted, therefore, by English Catholics, but their Irish – national and cultural – heritage was apt to be lost to them (see Milotte, 1997). In this sense, these

Irish children, while retaining their Catholic heritage, were subjected to processes of 'incorporation' and 'denationalisation' and this has had consequences for some of these adoptees who now feel that their concept of self and sense of identity has been undermined (see Hosegood, 1993; Palme, 1998; see also Philpot, 2002). This, moreover, has had professional ramifications for post-adoption services in Britain and Ireland today[6].

Perhaps social work educators also need to recognise that the centrality of the black/white binary is related to the fallacious idea that, until the 1950s, Britain was a "homogeneous white county" (Alibhai-Brown, 2000, p 29). Integral to this myth of homogeneity and the "legitimizing identity" (Castells, 1997, p 6) associated with it, was the implicit assertion that all people "who were white assimilated into the 'British way of life' and that the problems all resided with those who migrated and possessed a different colour of skin" (Hickman, 1998, p 299). This idea helped to mask the "internal ethnic, regional and national differences which characterise the 'United Kingdom'" (Hickman, 1998, p 290; see also Hall, 2000, p 229; Commission on the Future of Multi-Ethnic Britain, 2000, p 61). Moreover, it served to bind together, within a gradually diminishing British Empire, internal forces with materially opposed class interests. Unsurprisingly, given this hegemonic 'national story', many of the analyses produced "about the impact and responses to the immigration of people from the Indian subcontinent and the Caribbean in the 1950s-1970s emphasised 'newness': new racism, new political discourses, new fears of an 'enemy within'" (Hickman, 1998, p 290). Nonetheless, running counter to such analyses, as we saw in earlier chapters, social work and associated sites of the welfare state were complicit in the racialisation and problematisation of Irish children and families in the 1950s and 1960s. Writing in the early 1970s and using the contemporary vocabulary, Kevin O'Connor, an Irish journalist working in London, observed:

> [T]he sharpening focus on increasing coloured [sic] immigrants distracted attention away from the Irish as an alien presence. With cyclic inevitability, coloured immigrants became the object of the same hostile platitudes of 'separateness' ie large families, eating habits, noisy parties that the Irish had been subjected to in previous generations. It was [also] noticeable during the early sixties the extent to which the accommodation notices in shop windows translated the slogan 'No Irish' to that of 'No Coloureds'. (O'Connor, 1972, p 98)

'Inclusive practice' and a framework for children in need and their families

Returning to the present day, New Labour's *Framework for the assessment of children in need and their families* has recently referred to "inclusive practice" (DoH et al, 2000, pp 26-27; see also Figure 4.1).

Figure 4.1: Framework for the assessment of children in need and their families

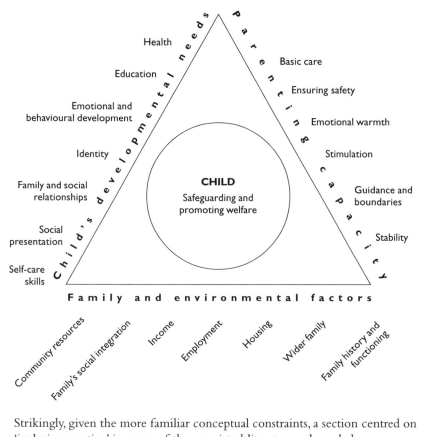

Strikingly, given the more familiar conceptual constraints, a section centred on 'inclusive practice' in some of the associated literature acknowledges:

> The population of England is comprised of many white minority ethnic groups as well as black minority ethnic groups and the differences in culture, religion, language and traditions for white minority groups have to be accounted for…. There are also a number of white minority ethnic groups who experience oppression on the basis of their ethnic, cultural or religious identity. In assessing families these experiences should be acknowledged and addressed. (Dutt and Phillips, 2000, p 37)

Clearly, this statement is to be welcomed since it explicitly begins to fracture the notion that 'white' people in Britain form an undifferentiated, homogeneous social category. This approach to 'white minority ethnic groups' also mirrors the more recent willingness to identify and respond to the heterogeneous nature of black experience(s) in Britain (see, for example, Modood et al, 1997). However, two problems still exist with the more 'inclusive' interpretative perspective of Dutt and Phillips. First, despite the critique featured in the Parekh report, there continues to be an unwillingness to *specifically* acknowledge Irish people in Britain (see Commission on the Future of Multi-Ethnic Britain, 2000). Second, it is asserted that while there "are some similarities and parallels in the experiences of black and white minorities in Britain there is also fundamental difference. Institutional racism has resulted in the impairment of the life opportunities of black people in this country" (Dutt and Phillips, 2000, p 37). This statement is accurate, yet there needs to be some qualification. Clearly, black people in Britain are subject to 'institutional racism' and Irish people can, of course, be the perpetrators of anti-black racism (McVeigh, 1996; Lentin, 2001). However, Dutt and Phillips risk obscuring the fact that Irish people in Britain are also subject to racism (Hickman and Walter, 1997; Commission on the Future of Multi-Ethnic Britain, 2000, p 61). Moreover, in the context of the research literature available, there is an inexcusable failure to acknowledge, as discussed in the introductory chapter of this book, that across a range of indices the 'life opportunities' of many Irish families in Britain are impaired and this is likely to impact on Irish children and families in contact with social services. Furthermore, none of the research findings in these areas would seem to support the 'ethnic fade' thesis that assumes that Irish people have been – and continue to be – rapidly assimilated and so are 'just the same' as 'white' British people[7].

Promoting changes to practice: placements and Irish children

Prior to investigating in more detail the current practice of social services departments (SSDs), the aim is to now briefly identify a range of factors that may provide part of the foundation for assessing Irish children who are in need of substitute care placements in Britain.

Sensibly and pragmatically, local authorities might begin to address the issue of 'identity' and Irish children by seeking to recruit more Irish substitute carers. Some local authorities, such as the London Borough of Southwark, use the Irish press to try to recruit adopters. A number of other local authorities, more generally, have begun to try to meet the needs of Irish service users. Perhaps not surprising, these initiatives have tended to be located in those areas with a history of Irish immigration. The London Borough of Brent, for example, works closely with the Brent Irish Advisory Service, which provides a children and families social work service, a consultancy service and a specific project for Irish travellers. Outside of the capital, in the late 1990s, Liverpool SSD had an Irish Workers' Group and there are, of course, a number of Irish 'community care' projects throughout the country.

Clearly, the placing of children with substitute carers is an immensely complex area of social work practice that must inescapably connect to the needs of *particular* children. Relevant issues will include:

- whether or not the placement is an adoptive placement or foster placement;
- whether it is a family or residential placement;
- whether or not the child has 'special needs';
- the age of the child or young person and their own wishes and feelings;
- the wishes of the birth parents;
- whether or not the child or young person is of mixed heritage and so on (in this context, see Prevatt Goldstein, 1999).

However, while remaining alert to the dangers of what Gilroy (1994) has dubbed 'ethno-dogma', it is still possible to try to map out how social workers might begin to pay attention to the specific cultural requirements of Irish children in need of out-of-home placements. In this context, Hosegood (1993, p 37) has asserted:

> To assume that British couples can rear Irish children with a full knowledge, understanding and respect for the complexities of their culture and can provide them with resources to cope with the prejudice attached to being Irish must be highly risky.

As observed earlier, DoH publications and guidance elide such considerations. Nonetheless, the statement in *Adoption now* that the requirement in the 1989 Children Act to "seek to place children with parents who are of a similar cultural and ethnic background and who can also meet their needs provides a sound basis for policy" could and should have practical resonance for Irish children in need of placements. In terms of assessment and care planning, an awareness of the specificity of Irish children and their families can be incorporated into the approach being promoted by the *Framework for the assessment of children in need and their families* (DoH et al, 2000). The materials associated with the framework certainly require social workers to monitor Irish ethnicity and to pay attention to the community networks available to children. As observed earlier, there are conceptual problems with some of the background papers and, more generally, issues related to 'race' and ethnicity are, perhaps, insufficiently emphasised. However, the framework also contains important guidance concerning the need to promote 'inclusive practice'. We are advised, for example:

> When assessing a child's needs and circumstances, care has to be taken to ensure that issues which fundamentally shape children's identity and well-being, their progress and outcomes are fully understood and incorporated into the framework for assessment. (DoH et al, 2000, p 26)

Guidance such as this can therefore be used creatively when working with Irish children and families. Importantly, there also needs to be operational change (as well as conceptual change) in other areas of service provision. Specifically in relation to, for example, the selection of potential carers, their training, led and facilitated by Irish professionals, carers, young people and their families, might include:

- an exploration of potential carers' responses to issues related to discrimination and the Irish community;
- the use of relevant case study material to generate discussion. (While being alert to the potential objectification of Irish people, these might be based on actual childcare 'cases', or be more general and culled from media 'stories');
- an exploration of how discrimination might impact on Irish children, specifically Irish children who are 'looked after'. (For example, what might also be the key factors in relation to first- and second-generation children and young people, and those from Irish Traveller families?);
- an exploration of how potential carers might seek to promote an Irish child's cultural and national heritage.

This awareness of the specificity of Irish experiences needs also to be applied to *particular* children in need of fostering or adoptive carers and this might be looked at in the context of other 'matching considerations' featured in the assessment documentation produced by BAAF. Does the individual profile of each applicant carer suggest that s/he is the most appropriate person to provide a placement for an Irish child or young person? Will there be available people and/or institutions in their support network where culturally sensitive assistance can be obtained? Hosegood (1993, p 38) has argued:

> Children of Irish birth parents ideally should be placed with families of Irish background, where they can be reared with an understanding and respect for their cultural heritage. They need to be equipped emotionally for the prejudice that will face them in British society against Irish people. In order to be fully integrated, they need (ideally) to love an Irish substitute parent.... Only within a child's cultural, ethnic and religious traditions can they reach a more whole understanding of themselves. As in all cases where transcultural placement becomes a necessity (e.g. where a suitable Irish family is not or will not be available), only couples who have examined their views about Irish people, realistically explored their prejudices and who make concerted efforts to learn about, maintain contact with and experience Irish culture, should be considered.

Fundamentally, however, social workers still need to assess such children as *individuals*. Therefore, this book is not simplistically suggesting that Irish children in need of substitute care *have to* be placed with Irish carers. Hosegood's important contribution also merits a caveat because, as Gilroy (1994) counsels, we should be wary of reifying 'race' and ethnicity so that they appear as *things* rather than *processes*. Furthermore, this understanding remains crucial when, as Brah (1992) suggests, social phenomena such as racism seek to fix and naturalise difference and create impervious boundaries between groups. Indeed, some of these complex issues will be returned to in the book's concluding chapter.

Conclusion

The Commission for Racial Equality has recommended that all institutions should now include an Irish category in monitoring exercises centred on 'race' and ethnicity. In addition, there was, as observed earlier, a self-identifying 'White Irish' category in the 2001 Census in Britain. On account of these developments, it might be argued that social services and other social care providers will, perhaps, slowly begin to become more attentive to the specificity of Irish people. Indeed, the next chapter will suggest that there has been some movement in SSDs monitoring procedures.

There are also some signs of change in terms of how the government is now attempting to gather data on services provided for ethnic minority children and their families. In February 2000, the DoH conducted the 'Children in Need' (CIN) Survey, the first comprehensive survey of all 'children in need' in England. Undertaken under the Quality Protects initiative, this was significant in that local authorities were asked to classify children according to the ethnic categories used in the subsequent 2001 Census (www.doh.gov.uk/cin/cin2000results.htm). The survey found that 16% (37,500) of 'children in need' were 'minority ethnic' children and 82% were 'white'. This approach again assumes that Irish children – *likely* to be white – are not a 'minority ethnic' group. However, because this survey deployed the categories used in the 2001 Census, the DoH was also able to provide information on 'White Irish' children. Here, estimates indicate that 1% (1,700) of 'children in need' in England fell into this category; 600 of these children were "looked after" and 1,100 were "supported in their families or independently". A similar DoH survey, conducted in September/October 2001, revealed that there were 1,600 'white' Irish children in need in England (www.doh.gov.uk/cin/cin2001results.htm). This figure was later revised to 1,500 Irish children[8]. Unpublished statistical information, derived from the September/October 2001 revised national figures and kindly provided by the CIN team at the DoH, has, however, usefully highlighted those SSDs with the highest numbers of Irish children receiving services in September/October 2001[9].

More generally, Pilkington (2003, p 1), surveying the social sciences as a whole, has maintained that it is "possible to detect the emergence in the last decade of a new framework guiding research on issues relating to 'race' and ethnicity in Britain". For much of the post-war period, it is suggested, the dominant framework was one of "racial dualism" (Modood, cited in Pilkington, 2003, p 1). This, what has been consistently referred to in this book as the 'black/white binary', took:

> [D]ifferent forms according to the preferred theoretical leanings of different
> social scientists [and] the primary emphasis was on the boundary between

people drawn on the basis of skin colour. 'White' people were envisaged as in a markedly more powerful structural position that that of 'Black' people. The role of researchers was therefore primarily to delineate and explain the disadvantages shared in common by black people. *This theoretical framework has lost its dominant position*, with the development of new theoretical approaches in the social sciences and the inclusion in social research of more sophisticated measures of ethnicity. (Pilkington, 2003, p 1; emphasis added; see also p 5)

In this context, there is perhaps an emerging willingness within mainstream social care discourses to examine the specificity of Irish experiences. For example, in terms of ethnic health inequalities, a national survey published in 2001 included Irish people and this highlighted issues related to tobacco and alcohol use and high cholesterol levels (DoH, 2001). Another report, looking at the impact of mental health services for black and minority ethnic communities, also included references to specific factors associated with the Irish community in England (National Institute for Mental Health in England, 2003)[10]. However, despite this new inclusiveness and the assertions of Pilkington, it can still be argued that social work and social care approaches in Britain, unacquainted with some of the historical and contemporary factors discussed earlier, remain dominated by 'racial dualism' (see, in this context, Airey et al, 1998; Alexander, 1999; Social Exclusion Unit, 2000). Pilkington's (2003) own assertions, in fact, are rather undermined on account of his own tendency often to remain locked within 'racial dualism' in his exploration of 'racial disadvantage' in Britain. Furthermore, his short, arid and misleading account of Irish immigration in the 19th century is sadly typical of how British textbooks have been apt to approach the subject. He observes, for example, that "in the nineteenth century, the combination of a rising population and *bad harvests* encourage a major movement of population from Ireland" (Pilkington, 2003, p 32; emphasis added). What is omitted here is the Irish *Famine* of 1845-52, which, partly caused by the rigid adherence of the British government to *laissez faire* economics, resulted in the death of one million people and forced a similar number to emigrate (see Kinealy, 1994).

In the next chapter, we will examine how SSDs are responding to Irish children and families in the early 21st century. More specifically, how is the question of Irish identity perceived by senior officers within SSDs? Have the changes to monitoring systems resulted in better recording of Irish ethnicity? How informed are departments about discrimination and the Irish community in Britain and what steps are being taken actively to engage with local Irish users of services? These are just some of the questions that will be explored in Chapter Five.

Notes

[1] At the level of institutional practices, British social work has, of course, failed adequately to respond to users of services who are black (Barn et al, 1997; Dutt and Phillips, 2000; Parekh, 2000). More generally, the killing of Stephen Lawrence and the subsequent publication of the Macpherson Inquiry highlighted the tenacity of anti-black racism and, of course, directed attention to the 'institutional racism' embedded in the police and other sectors of the state in Britain (Macpherson, 1999; see also Lea, 2000). The murder of Zahid Mubarek in Feltham Young Offenders Institute also points to the resilience of a type of racism, manifestly associated with fascist ideology that is rooted in a potentially lethal antipathy to black people in Britain (Sivanandan, 2000; see also 'Prison 'race' death blamed on shocking failures', *The Guardian*, 10 July 2003 and, in the same edition, 'Racism behind bars' [editorial]).

[2] Kirton (2000) has provided an overview of some of the main issues in relation to the same 'race' placement/transracial placement exchanges. In 2000, a special issue of the journal *Adoption & Fostering* (vol 24, no 1) endeavoured to analyse the issue and focus on complexities often omitted in a debate that has been not only polemical but also reductionist because of the centrality of arid 'black' and 'white' dichotomies.

[3] This was partly related to the cross-fertilisation of projects and strategies between Blair's New Labour and Clinton's Democrat administration.

[4] In the context of discourses in the US, Morrison's (1992) interventions on 'whiteness and the literary imagination' are also interesting.

[5] It also needs to be recognised that many Roman Catholic priests, in England, risked and gave their lives working among the impoverished and fever-stricken Irish poor who, on their arrival, were often placed in the Liverpool workhouses during the years of the Great Famine (Plumb, 1993; see also Kinealy, 1994; Gray, 1999). Furthermore, the role and success of the Church in determining the political affiliations of its members is a complex area. Fielding (1993, p 108) recounts the anecdote about one Irishman telling his priest "I'll see you at mass on Sunday Father, but I'll vote Communist on Thursday". O'Sullivan (2003) has argued that, in the early 21st century, the British government should seek to incorporate British Muslims in the way it incorporated Irish Roman Catholic immigrants in the 19th century.

[6] The sense of dislocation felt by some Irish adult adoptees could, however, help to inform professional practice in relation to children from Eastern Europe, adopted by Irish and British adopters (see also the editorial, 'Foreign adoptions', *The Irish Times*, 30 December 1998).

[7] However, as Campbell (1999, p 272) correctly suggests, in his analysis of the experiences of second-generation Irish people in Britain, we also need to remain mindful of 'positive' divergences, such as better educational achievement. In short, if only 'negative'

divergences are used to "demonstrate Irish difference, then this clearly restricts our understanding of the second-generation, who become textually constructed as a problem-centred presence". This, in turn, can then serve to reinforce, as we saw in earlier chapters of this book, historical constructs preoccupied with the 'otherness' of Irish people in Britain.

[8] 'Race' and ethnicity was not recorded for a very large proportion of children. Perhaps, more fundamentally, there is no indication *how* the identification 'Irish child' was arrived at. All of the figures have been rounded.

[9] See Tables A1-6 in Appendix A, which are derived from this information. HM Stationery Office (HMSO) granted me permission to reproduce Figure 4.1. This was originally published in DoH et al (2000).

[10] A useful summary of the research on the mental health of Irish people born in Britain is provided by the mental health charity MIND (www.mind.org.uk).

FIVE

Social services departments and Irish children and families in the early 21st century

So far, this book has investigated social work's historical responses to Irish 'unmarried mothers' and children in Britain and gone on to look at how today's dominant conceptualisation of 'race' and ethnicity has tended to omit an Irish dimension. In a contemporary context, however, it is clearly important to try to find out how social services departments (SSDs) are responding to Irish children and families. Indeed, to generate a more appropriate response it is important to try to ascertain what the current approach is in terms of social work practice in the various SSDs throughout England and Wales.

In what follows, the chief research instrument was a questionnaire, which was completed by SSD directors or delegated officers within their organisations. The support of the Association of Directors of Social Services (ADSS) was obtained in July 2001 in order for the questionnaire to be distributed among its members and it was agreed that no specific SSD would be identified in any research that was subsequently published. Initially, a pilot exercise was undertaken and a draft version of the questionnaire was mailed to five directors in geographically and demographically diverse areas of England and Wales. This included an authority in Wales, London, the Midlands, and in north-west and south-west England. Having obtained their views on the content of the questionnaire and the process of completing it, minor amendments were made. It was then mailed to the directors of SSDs in England and Wales in January 2002.

All SSDs who were are members of the ADSS network were mailed, excluding those in Northern Ireland, Guernsey, Jersey, the Isles of Scilly and the Isle of Man. That is to say, 171 SSD directors were sent a copy of the questionnaire. Seventy-five (44%) mailed it back. Using the regional structure adhered to by ADSS, it is also possible to identify those areas represented as providers of data in this chapter. For example, almost a quarter of questionnaires returned were from the Greater London region. The full regional breakdown of returned questionnaires was as follows:

North – 12%;
Yorkshire and Humberside – 5%;
North West – 14%;
East Midlands – 5%;

West Midlands – 8%;
East – 10%;
Greater London – 22%;
South East – 10%;
South West – 4%;
Wales – 10%.

The best response rates *within* regions were from the northern and West Midlands areas. Both regions returned 75% of questionnaires mailed to them. The poorest return rate was from Wales (36%) and the South East (38%). Five non-completing SSDs wrote and stated that this was due to lack of staff and other related pressures.

The questionnaire was limited in scope and comprised 25 questions, some with sub-sections. The majority of the questions looked for simple 'yes' or 'no' responses, but 'additional comments' were also invited. The questionnaire, as a whole, was divided into three parts and invited respondents to:

- answer questions on *policy and practice* in relation to Irish children and families;
- provide *quantitative information* on how many Irish children were being provided with a particular service;
- outline how the SSD was attempting to *engage with the Irish community*.

As a whole, despite the less than satisfactory response rate, it is perhaps possible to argue that what follows provides an accessible 'snapshot' that helps to illuminate how SSDs in England and Wales are currently responding to Irish children and families[1]. A number of themes are identifiable in relation to SSD responses to Irish children and families and, in what follows, the aim will be to refer to these themes and to provide a commentary.

Policy and practice

Evolving better monitoring systems

Social services department respondents had mixed opinions about the impact of the introduction of the 'White Irish' category, discussed earlier, in the 2001 Census. Some, appearing to pre-judge what the data would reveal, felt that it was "unlikely to have a significant impact". A number of other SSDs understood, however, that this change *was* likely to have an impact on perceptions, policy and practice:

> This should provide more accurate figures as we still rely on the 1991 Census
> – even though these only provide 'born in Ireland' figures. It will help us to
> build a better profile of our customers.

May have impact: we believe practice generally is to consider all white groups together. It will identify the size of this group within our community and lead us to reflect on whether specialist services might be required/requested.

The issue of Irish identity has made progress in being identified and accepted in Britain as separate issue (seriously down played over the years) and we will be forced to address the complex issues of Irish ethnicity in the development of services for children and families.

It should show a truer reflection of the numbers of people who classify themselves as Irish as opposed to being born in Ireland. There needs to be further work on whether – and what – difference this makes in terms of culturally appropriate training and service delivery.

It is indicative of recent changes, perhaps, including the 'Children in Need' (CIN) Surveys, referred to in Chapter Four of this book, that 62 SSDs (83%) reported that a specific 'Irish' category was now included in organisational documentation that was supposed to ascertain a child's 'race' and ethnicity (see Table B1, Appendix B). However, it was also clear that monitoring systems were severely impaired in terms of generating information about key aspects of service provision for Irish children and families.

Most SSDs were using the category 'White Irish' featured in the 2001 Census. At least one SSD reported, however, that the more limited 'born in Ireland' category was still being used, although the aim was eventually to include the more inclusive (but still problematic) 'White Irish' category. One London authority, like a number of other critics from within the Irish community, observed that there were still problems, however, with this latter categorisation in that 'white' and 'Irish' were coupled in this manner. This particular SSD reported that it had many users of services who would "identify as Irish, but not as white". Indeed, the 'White Irish' category founded on a narrow construction of 'Irishness' fails to embrace the complexity of diasporic identities in Britain. Importantly, and despite this inclusion of a 'White Irish' category, another SSD respondent felt, more generally, that "experience indicates significant under-reporting because children from these backgrounds are not always recognised as a separate group". Another SSD took the following position:

We do not really differentiate between White Irish and White British. Our priorities for developing ethnically sensitive services lie elsewhere. We probably have much bigger population of Irish extraction that is hidden in White British.

Planning

The Commission for Racial Equality's (CRE) *Racial equality means quality: Standards for local government* (1995) attempted to improve how local authorities performed in this area. Following the 2000 Race Relations (Amendment) Act, the CRE has published additional guidance for local authorities. This questionnaire attempted, however, to ascertain how the earlier CRE audit document was impacting on the planning and delivery of social services for Irish children and their families. Only 16 SSDs (23%) felt that *Race equality means quality* had an impact, with 53 (77%) of the view that it was having no impact (see Table B1, Appendix B). A number of SSDs maintained, however, that operational responses to questions of 'race' and ethnicity were audited using different benchmarks.

Local authority SSDs must produce overarching Children's Services Plans, which lay out how services are to be delivered. Related to this, Quality Protects (QP) was launched by the government in September 1998 and the aim of the programme, according to the Department of Health was to focus on the most vulnerable and disadvantaged children in society – those looked after, those in the child protection system and other children in need. A key part of QP is that SSDs must also furnish the DoH with Management Action Plans that identify how this objective is to be met. The questionnaire, therefore, asked SSDs if there were any specific references to Irish children in these two documents. Here, only four (5%) responded 'yes' with 71 (79%) stating 'no'. Some SSDs suggested, however, that policy was developing in this area (see Table B1, Appendix B).

Awareness of key issues

As recognised earlier, the major contemporary research, which has focused on discrimination and the Irish community in Britain, is Mary Hickman and Bronwen Walter's (1997) overview, *Discrimination and the Irish community in Britain*. Clearly, it is vital that policy makers at senior level within SSDs (and, indeed, other tiers of local government administration) are aware of this report and its implications in terms of service provision for Irish children and families. However, only 10 responding authorities (14%) reported that they had 'read' the report, with 64 (86%) stating it had not been 'read' (see Table B1, Appendix B). It seemed, however, that some SSDs had seen a summary of some of the key findings of the report – *The Irish in Britain* – published as an information pamphlet by the CRE (1997). Of the minority of SSDs that had read the main report or summary document, a number had an awareness of some of the key issues:

> The report highlighted the fact that the Irish in Britain were disadvantaged in terms of high unemployment, over reliance on private sector accommodation, limiting long term illnesses; and disadvantage was comparable

to the position of other ethnic minorities. The report also stated that one of the main inhibitions on the work of Irish and other community groups was the non-recognition of the Irish in Britain as an ethnic minority, which often leads to exclusion of the Irish as a specific group from strategic planning policy.

Another SSD respondent, although only having had access to the summary report, was making good use of its findings:

> I have read the CRE publication *The Irish in Britain*.... The evidence of discrimination against Irish people has been used in discussions. I have also circulated the publication to the relevant and interested people. Students on social care courses seeking advice have been informed about this publication.

Clearly, this response relates to SSDs' obligation to do more than simply improving monitoring, categorisation and 'awareness' of key research findings in relation to the Irish community. The question must surely be: how are more inclusive monitoring systems and – for some authorities – an acquaintance with key publications on the Irish community beginning to impact on day-to-day social work practice?

Training

The questionnaire asked if an Irish dimension was incorporated into anti-discriminatory training for staff who actually provide services for children and families in England and Wales. Here, only 14 SSDs (20%) reported that this was happening, with 56 (80%) indicating that there was no specific Irish dimension incorporated into training for childcare staff (see Table B1, Appendix B). A typical response was that there was "no specific Irish dimension to the training" since its "purpose is to raise awareness/sensitivity of staff to ethnicity issues generally". Others appeared to leave it to course participants to determine the direction of training:

> Issues relating to Irish families are not specifically addressed in the training, although there is always space for issues to arise during the two classes. If this is required I am happy to incorporate it at a more detailed level.

This more inclusive approach to training on 'race' and ethnicity issues for those working with children and families can, however, be contrasted with another SSD, which, evidencing some of the perceptions discussed earlier, reported:

> Race equality training [is] provided for all managers, but this focuses more on black minority groups.

However, a small number of SSDs – approximately a fifth of respondents – were now seeking to incorporate a specific Irish dimension into 'in-house' training programmes:

> We incorporate the Irish dimension when generally addressing issues of oppression. Currently some specific training is provided concerning the Irish Travelling community because of local needs and issues affecting children's education and support needs.

> Within our childcare courses there are two relevant courses which touch on the specifics of Irish families. One of the courses is 'Child protection: anti-racist practice' and the other is 'Working with Travelling families'. Although it is not included within the syllabus our 'anti-racist' training staff will often raise the question of Irish discrimination and there is often debate around the experiences of the Irish taking this course.

Another question also tried to establish if SSDs were incorporating an Irish perspective into anti-discriminatory training for substitute carers of children 'looked after' by local authorities. Here, only 15 SSDs (21%) responded that potential fostering and adoptive carers were receiving this type of training, with 56 (79%) stating this was not the case (see Table B1, Appendix B). One SSD baldly commented:

> [A]ny training is general i.e. does not refer to any specific ethnic, religious or national group.

Identity issues

The questionnaire asked SSDs how they were seeking to fulfil requirements under the 1989 Children Act relating to being attentive to a child's culture. A number of SSDs responded that a cultural dimension was, indeed, given 'due consideration' in terms of *all* children 'looked after'. One respondent, however, blandly – but, perhaps, honestly – stated "no expertise". Another SSD in Wales, somewhat tendentiously given the numbers of Irish people who have been stopped at Holyhead on their way to Ireland and questioned under the Prevention of Terrorism Acts, remarked:

> Irish people are not seen as that 'different' in Wales … in my experience. Maybe it's the Celtic connection.

Another SSD commented:

> Some of our children have mixed heritage where one parent is Irish and the other black. Often the Irish dimension is absent in their upbringing.

At least two SSDs used the Action and Assessment Records (AARs) that are part of the Looking After Children system (Parker et al, 1991) to enable its social workers to explore this aspect of a 'looked after' young person's 'identity'. This, however, may have been somewhat problematic because, as observed in Chapter Four, AARs have been criticised for failing to include *any* reference to Irish ethnicity (see Garrett, 1999). Specifically in terms of the placement of Irish children and young people, some authorities tried to "match them with a family with an Irish background" (in this context, see Hosegood, 1993; Garrett, 2000). A small minority of SSDs also placed advertisements in the Irish press for foster carers. Furthermore, it was apparent that some authorities were working hard to ensure that an Irish child's cultural background was respected. This, in practice, could include trying to "maintain links with [children's] own network/extended family". Important, in this context, for some Irish children, was the willingness of SSDs to fund journeys to and from Ireland. One SSD stated:

> We have recently funded 'holidays' for carers and taken Irish children to meet extended family; an Irish worker in a unit did some work on cultural issues with two children; one child has been placed with extended family in Ireland and we fund visits back to UK for contact with parents; two other children live in Ireland with father and we finance contact visits back in UK.

Thirty SSDs (42%) responded that staff in residential establishments and family centres were encouraged to "publicise and promote" Irish cultural festivals, such as St Patrick's Day (see Table B1, Appendix B). The majority, however, indicated – in answering 'no' – that this was not the case. Again, some respondents suggested, however, that there were likely to be developments in this area of policy and practice. Perhaps unsurprisingly, responses appeared to indicate that if the wider community/local authority as a whole was responsible for organising parades and related festivals, then this was likely to impact on how local facilities for children and their families, within SSDs, responded.

Irish Travellers

Recognising that the Irish community is complex and diverse, SSDs were also invited to respond to a query on their responses to Irish children and families who are part of Traveller communities. Here 27 SSDs (42%) stated that specific services were provided, with 41 SSDs (58%) indicating that no specific services were available (see Table B1, Appendix B). Some authorities' responses to Travellers were undifferentiated, in that Travellers' *specific* national or cultural backgrounds were assumed, it appeared, to be unitary (in this context, see Cemlyn, 2000). It was also apparent, explicitly in one instance, that responding to the welfare needs of children in these families was coupled with – and, perhaps, even rendered secondary to – more punitive corporate enforcement policies:

> Where Travellers occupy land or premises without lawful authority we will always assess the needs of any Traveller children before action is taken on eviction. There is an inter-departmental protocol to ensure that their welfare is protected.

It was clear from additional comments, included with responses from a number of authorities, that services for Travellers, if not located within the SSD were nonetheless becoming available from elsewhere within the corporate structure, for example, based within the educational or health services. In these instances, there was often "close collaboration with children and families social work services". The voluntary sector, of course, also played an important role. At least one SSD "commissioned a local Catholic organisation to provide services for a local Travellers' site". In other instances, more culturally sensitive services were beginning to evolve (see also Jordan, 2001).

Anti-Irish racism

For children who are in public care, bullying and related forms of harassment form a common and adverse part of their 'looked after' experience (Colton, 1989). Given the findings of Hickman and Walter (1997) on anti-Irish racism, and Ullah (1985), looking at anti-Irish racism among school children, SSDs were asked if they were aware of any harassment that could be related to this specific and historically rooted form of racism. Two SSDs (3%) stated that they were aware of bullying or harassment directly related to anti-Irish racism, with 55 (73%) responding 'no' (see Table B1, Appendix B). (A further 18 [24%] stated 'not known'.) However, an awareness of anti-Irish racism was, perhaps, implicit in the following response:

> By making their ethnicity widely known, they [Irish children and young people] may become subjected to discrimination and/or harassment within their local neighbourhood.

This remark also suggests that wariness on the part of some senior officers within SSDs could blunt efforts to promote an Irish dimension to policy and practice.

One SSD stated that "one young person from a Travelling family background reported such experience [racism] at school. She was supported here and it was acted upon by her carer" (see also Lloyd and Stead, 2001). Another SSD shifted the emphasis in its response and commented on how Irish childcare staff had, on occasions, been subjected to anti-Irish racism:

We are not aware of any bullying or harassment of young people being looked after which has been related to anti-Irish racism. However it should be noted that neither our residential nor fostering services could recall accommodating an Irish child (though there would be children on placement who were of Irish descent). Irish staff have experienced inappropriate comments from some young people (name calling and targeting). Staff have responded to this by providing young people with information about their culture and giving positive examples of what 'being Irish' means to them. The celebration of Irish cultural festivals is another way in which staff have promoted the positive aspects of being Irish.

Innovation

On a more general level, only three SSDs (4%) felt that they were able to identify "innovative projects" relating to Irish children and families (see Table B1, Appendix B). For one SSD, this involved working closely with the local Irish Centre. Another SSD, however, referred to a specific social work practice innovation that was found to be useful with Irish children and their families – family group conferences (see Marsh and Crow, 1998):

> [O]ur family group conferences project has a high rate of referrals for Irish families. Extended family members often live at a distance and have not previously been involved in planning for the care of the child. Resources are invested to allow either family members or professionals to travel to get together and make decisions about plans for the child's future, which may involve returning to Ireland.

Again, in terms of actual social work practice with Irish children and families, the recently introduced *Framework for the assessment of children in need and their families*, discussed in Chapter Four, has referred to 'inclusive practice' (DoH et al, 2000). Associated race and ethnic monitoring materials also include, as we have seen, a new 'White Irish' category and stress is placed on the community networks in which children are located. Social services departments were invited, therefore, to comment on ways in which the framework was likely to impact on their work with Irish children and families. Some respondents did not anticipate any change and some thought that the impact of the new assessment paradigm was still 'unclear'. One SSD asserted:

> We have not specifically identified this as an issue in relation to Irish children. There is *not really* an Irish community in this area. (Emphasis added)

A number of SSDs appeared, however, to recognise the potential significance of the framework:

> The assessment framework re-emphasises that importance of communities and culture and, therefore, underpins the department's requirement that staff work in an ethnically sensitive way.

> It will greatly effect practice as the focus of the initial assessment on ethnicity has moved away from being a purely tick box formality to a separate section that has to be addressed and completed in our assessments. The framework focuses on the network of child, family and community and the ethnicity of a child will be picked up to a much greater degree than in the individualistic focus of previous assessment formats.

However, another SSD perhaps failed to understand the significance of this approach to assessment. Here, the respondent felt that the new framework was promoting a form of social work practice that no longer needed to have regard to questions related to culture and ethnicity:

> We will promote 'inclusive practice' and do not draw a distinction with Irish families. My expectation is that they would receive the same levels of service as anyone else approaching us for a service.

Survivors of institutional abuse

Given the widespread concern about the physical and sexual abuse perpetrated in institutional settings in Ireland over many years (Raftery and O'Sullivan, 1999), SSDs were also asked to state if they were providing any services to 'survivors' of such abuse. Certainly in Britain, a fledgling survivors' movement, Survivors of Child Abuse, is active and has convened a number of public meetings (see also 'Specialist post to help abuse victims', *The Irish Post*, 5 May 2001). In addition, the Irish Survivors Outreach Service, referred to in the notes to the book's Introduction, provides support and assistance. It has also been suggested that there may be as many as 12,000 potential service users in London alone (see 'Three more centres for Irish victims', *Community Care*, 22-28 August 2002, p 7). Perhaps somewhat surprisingly, therefore, only one SSD reported providing services in relation to this issue. Arguably, this may have been a considerable under-representation since a number of directors, on receiving the questionnaire, delegated completion of the task to assistant directors in Children's Services who may not have been aware of social work support services being provided elsewhere in the department. As one SSD commented:

> Not to my knowledge. There may be people who worked with the adult mental health service, but I think no transparent recording aggregates this.

Quantitative information

Here, it was apparent that most SSDs *appeared* to deal with relatively few Irish children and families. However, it was also clear that a sizeable proportion of SSDs are simply unaware of the numbers of Irish children receiving a service. In addition, there is likely to be an under-recording of Irish ethnicity because of the entrenched tendency to include Irish children in a 'White British', or 'White Other' category.

Irish children receiving a service

Twenty-two SSDs were unaware of how many Irish children were receiving a service (see Table B2, Appendix B). Eight SSDs (17%) stated that there were no Irish children being provided with a service, but two (4%) were providing a service to 90+ Irish children.

In terms of those completing this part of the questionnaire, the data tended to be taken from the CIN Survey, which, as observed in Chapter Four, the DoH had required SSDs to undertake in February 2000 and September/October 2001. A number of additional comments provided by respondents indicated that where figures were furnished it was likely to be an underestimate of Irish children receiving a service.

> [We are] aware of significant historical connection between one town (port) in this Local Authority with Ireland. However, the number of users of services who would describe themselves as Irish is not currently known. *The Framework for the assessment of children in need and their families* will allow this to take place from April 2002.

> Referral data suggests 1% Irish, but we are still introducing our procedures for collecting ethnic information for service users.

> It is anticipated that most Irish children may be logged under 'White British'.

> The number of Irish children receiving a service is very small. Sampling of work undertaken by children's day centres and initial assessments indicate a percentage of 1-2%. There is likely to be significant under-reporting because information is not systematically recorded on children from Irish backgrounds.

> We are currently in the process of updating our ethnic monitoring processes and with the new *Framework for the assessment of children in need and their families* the ethnic question will require more than just a tick box to complete. At present our ethnic monitoring statistics are not good and our response rate is especially low so we are unable to determine how many Irish children receive a service.

Irish children 'looked after'

Here, 13 SSDs were unaware of how many Irish children were 'looked after' under the 1989 Children Act (see Table B3, Appendix B). Twenty-eight (47%) responded that there were no Irish children 'looked after', but one SSD had between 31 and 40 Irish children 'looked after'. Once again, however, a number of responses suggested that the data provided were resulting in an underestimate of the numbers of Irish children 'looked after'.

> We probably have children classed as white British who are of Irish descendency.

> It appears that this information is not being recorded systematically.

> Probably an under-estimate.

> [I]n due course our IT systems will give us this information.

Irish children on child protection registers

Here, 16 SSDs stated that it was 'not known' how many Irish children were featured on the local child protection register (CPR). Thirty-three (57%) had no Irish children on the CPR, but one authority had between 11 and 20 Irish children on the CPR (see Table B4, Appendix B).

> This information is not currently available electronically and we do not have the staffing capacity to collect this information manually as it would require someone going through each record of every child on the register.

> This is produced using the 1991 census definition of 'born in Ireland'.

Irish foster carers and adopters

Thirty-two SSDs did not know how many of its foster carers were Irish and 19 (48%) had no Irish foster carers. Three (8%) SSDs, however, had between seven and 10 Irish foster carers (see Table B5, Appendix B).

> Information is not currently collected.

> Our records I am told don't discriminate. This is something we need to rectify.

> Not recorded, but in due course our IT systems will give us this information.

Thirty SSDs did not know how many Irish adopters it had available; 24 (60%) had none and two (5%) stated that they had three (see Table B6, Appendix B).

Engaging with the Irish community

A key aspect of the survey was to try to ascertain how SSDs in England and Wales were currently engaging with the Irish community (see Table B7, Appendix B). Central here was the assumption that SSDs need to 'reach out' and make appropriate contacts with Irish people and Irish community organisations. Only seven of SSDs (10%), however, reported that they were using the Irish press (for example, the weekly *Irish Post*) to try to recruit temporary and permanent substitute carers for Irish children. Some authorities indicated, however, that this would be done if there were a need to 'match' a specific child with a family. In terms of child protection work with Irish children and families, only seven (10%) had an Irish representative on the local Area Child Protection Committee (ACPC). A number of SSDs did, however, have "people of Irish origin" on the ACPC, but "not specifically representing the Irish community".

Given the recent centrality of child adoption in the government's approach to 'looked after' children (Garrett, 2002), SSDs were also asked what steps were being taken to recruit more potential adopters who are Irish. Here, 'narrative' responses were invited, but this did not reveal any widespread activity, which was particularly targeted at the Irish community. One SSD respondent stated that this had not been "considered". However, "after completing this [questionnaire] I will pursue, particularly given our location [Wales]". The majority of respondents felt that there was insufficient need to mount this type of exercise. Here, typical responses included:

> We have detailed data on children needing adopting. Irish children are not significantly represented. If we did have Irish children needing adoption we would seek a match with an Irish family.

> We are not taking specific steps as we have a very small Irish community but would look at more relevant measures including the use of the Irish press, to meet any imminent needs.

> None, because we so very, very rarely have Irish children needing to be placed.

These statements may have been accurate. However, it might be countered that there was also too much complacency in some quarters about the accuracy of data systems logging children's 'race' and ethnicity. Indeed, as noted earlier in this chapter, embedded assumptions on these questions have frequently rendered Irish people in Britain 'invisible'.

Social services departments were asked if they were currently consulting local/national Irish community organisations to enable them to improve responses to the specific cultural requirements of Irish children and families. Twelve SSD respondents (16%) asserted that such consultation was taking place. A much higher percentage of respondents, however, were in contact with their counterparts in the Republic of Ireland and Northern Ireland. Thirty (41%) of SSDs reported that this type of contact took place and it was largely connected to child placement and child protection issues.

Directors and other senior officers completing the questionnaire were provided with an opportunity to identify what they perceived as *the* "major issue relating to service provision and Irish children and families". This produced a range of responses – some that related to issues already inquired about in the questionnaire, others that focused, albeit briefly, on areas not addressed. Here, most of the responses related to the failure to 'recognise' Irish children within this area of child welfare provision in Britain.

The failure to 'recognise' Irish children and families

We need to recognise the Irish in Britain as an ethnic minority in order to avoid the exclusion of the Irish as a specific group from strategic policy planning. We need to raise awareness and provide training to staff about the Irish in Britain and recognise that as with other ethnic minorities the Irish can suffer from discrimination in terms of the quality and accessibility of services they are provided with. We need to ensure we address the issues of anti-Irish harassment and discrimination. We also need to recognise and promote the ethnicity of Irish children and families and to establish activities and venues through which children of Irish parents can explore their cultural heritage and develop support and self-help groups.

Providing assessments, which meaningfully identify and address a child's cultural background and can be translated with service packages/intervention, which therefore improve outcomes for that child.

Being seen as having distinct cultural etc. needs outside the obvious areas of London, Birmingham and Liverpool.

Irish children and the children of Irish parents may feel that they are different and discriminated against, but professionals do not understand this in the same way as they understand difficulties experienced by other minority groups. They have not been identified as a disadvantaged group and staff are not trained in this area. Some development needs to take place on definitions if we are to record accurately and consistently.

The lack of appropriate services for Irish children and families is a general problem. The inability to apply culturally competent services as with other ethnic groups is an ongoing problem. Generally Irish children and families have been considered to belong to the general white group. This has resulted in a methodology of working ... that does not account for the potential needs of this group based on their ethnicity and cultural heritage e.g. in adoption services the Irish cultural heritage and identity is not often considered for potential families. Also within much elderly provision the needs of older people with Irish heritage is often not considered. Irish children and families with traveller ancestry face the additional problem of perceived lower social status and stigmatisation. For this group, in our local authority, substance misuse has been a particular problem for the younger generations.

In general, Irish children would not be seen as having any specific needs above a white British child. This may be something that needs reconsidering as needs may therefore be missed.

Irish children are not seen as a cultural minority and until this is recognised then specific services will be slow to develop.

Lack of understanding of the importance of promoting positive cultural identity.

There is not enough recognition of Irish children's heritage and culture, particularly of first generation Irish children who tend to be seen as white British. There is little acknowledgement of festivals, religious needs and differences in culture.

It is clear that our ethnic monitoring systems need to be improved so that we can identify how many Irish families we are working with. Following on from this with the implementation of the new Assessment Framework we will need to carefully consider the ethnicity of a child and the impact this has on their social networks more than we have ever done so before. In providing a service to Irish children and their families we should be mindful of language differences and cultural differences in relation to Irish travelling families who have extremely different customs and culture to other Irish families. We should also be aware of the discrimination experienced by Irish families and should strive to ensure that our practices in no way disadvantage them further.

However, and appropriately given the complexity associated with recognising an Irish dimension to theory and practice, a number of respondents were also willing to highlight specific factors.

Some of our children have mixed heritage where one parent is Irish and the other black. Often the Irish dimension is absent in their upbringing. Mixed heritage children in general appear to constitute a relatively high proportion of our looked after children.

An understanding of the historical and cultural background of the Irish people is important and it is equally important to be aware of and take full account of the diversities, which exist within such a broad-brush grouping.

General lack of awareness, although, as someone of Irish descent myself, I am aware of compartmentalising and inappropriately categorising individuals into groups.

Recognition of cultural differences with Irish children born in England. Our main aim is to treat all service users as individuals, and not to make assumptions and stereotypes.

Our ethnic minority community is so large and so diverse that we struggle to maintain a specific focus on each particular racial religious spiritual and cultural need...

Adoption and fostering: Religion has proved difficult – when a birth mother specifies Irish Catholic upbringing, we have to balance cultural needs – Irish – with religious needs. It is easier to find Irish families that are not Catholic (or perhaps one partner is Catholic) than families where both partners are Irish and practising Catholics. Needs should be better understood. There is also a need to analyse monitoring data and not just collect it.

Two respondents stated that facets of work with Irish Travellers were significant.

Contact arrangements for 'looked after' children and schools refusing to admit children from traveller communities.

Irish travellers children being defined out of the system: 'It's the way they live' means abuse is accepted which would not be in other cultures.

In addition, a range of disparate concerns was identified as 'major issues'.

Most aware of Irish women escaping domestic violence from Eire and N. Ireland and seeking refuge with this Local Authority.

We do have 37 so-called 'intentionally homeless families', which include some Irish people. These are inappropriately placed. There may also be a need for an Irish focus for our teenage pregnancy worker.

The major service provision issue facing Irish children and families is housing, benefits and support services. This can get into a difficult situation concerning who pays!

The issue, which arises most frequently, is related to support for families. Parents and children and young people may not have extended family support in the UK and their level of contact with the Irish community varies.

Only one respondent referred to the impact of 'terrorism' on the island of Ireland:

Stigma fuelled by misconceptions and prejudice about Irish values, traits etc. This is increased at times of terrorist incident or activity in Ireland.

Conclusion

The analysis in this chapter is rather limited in scope and does not provide any detailed exploration, for example, of how Irish children are responded to in relation to any other group of service users. Furthermore, *all* survey data should, of course, always be viewed with a certain scepticism and measured detachment.

Aside from reaching the fairly predictable viewpoint that more research of SSD practice is necessary, the SSD responses featured in this chapter do, however, suggest a number of conclusions. Although we have not rigorously analysed this dimension, questionnaire responses appear to indicate that where SSDs are located is a crucial factor. Important here is, perhaps, the size of the local Irish community and its will and ability to intervene in the formulation and implementation of social work and social care policies. One SSD, for example, when asked about responses to Irish children in the context of Section 22 of the 1989 Children Act, stated:

This is not a problem in a town where the Irish are the largest of the component of the white/European population in the town. Lots of Irish staff, carers etc.

However, if an Irish child is placed in an area with a small Irish community and few Irish staff and substitute carers, there may be less likelihood that this part of the Act will be adequately responded to, particularly if senior officers and policy makers have a poor awareness of the key issues for Irish children and families.

One of the more modest aims of the questionnaire, which forms the basis for the discussion in this chapter, was to prompt senior local government officers to begin to ponder their responses to Irish children and families. This type of reflection needs to take place among policy makers and practitioners inside of SSDs and related services. Furthermore, an Irish dimension should be built into operational planning, service planning and strategic planning (Pinnock and Garnett, 2002). Just as important is a willingness to bolster what can, on occasions, be perceived as fairly abstract commitments to provide culturally appropriate services with the funding of specific initiatives that will address the issue on a practical level, for example, in relation to contact issues and so on.

More broadly, given that organisationally social work with children and families is in flux, it may be a propitious moment to destabilise embedded approaches to social work practice and the issue of race and ethnicity (ADSS, 2002; Chief Secretary to the Treasury, 2003; Secretary of State for Health and the Secretary of State for the Home Department, 2003). The Social Services Inspectorate (SSI) has also called for services that are culturally sensitive and recognise and value diversity. Thus, maintains the SSI, black and ethnic minority community groups must "clearly be engaged in the planning of services" (SSI/DoH, 2001, p 14). Furthermore, the 2000 Race Relations (Amendment) Act, and the Race Equality Schemes it requires, provide a foundation for changes to SSD responses to Irish children and families (see also Home Office, 2002a, 2002b).

Responses to the questionnaire reveal that that alterations to systems relating to the monitoring of 'race' and ethnicity, prompted in part by changes introduced in the 2001 Census, do seem to be gradually producing a better recording of Irish ethnicity. However, it is apparent that a sizeable proportion of SSDs were simply unaware how many Irish children are receiving a service. This reflects a more general failure on the part of SSDs to satisfactorily monitor 'race' and ethnicity. Tunnard (2002, p 124), for example, has commented that "a sober finding in local authority audits is the generally poor level of recording of ethnicity". She goes on:

> It points to the continuing need for rigorous attention to sound ethnic monitoring if local authorities are to comply fully with the requirement of the Children Act 1989 to take account of race, religion, language and culture. The shocking gap, echoing findings from over a decade ago also highlights the undoubted need for training to boost professional understanding and confidence about why and how to ask families about ethnicity.

The DoH CIN Surveys carried out with SSDs in England in February 2000 and September/October 2001 further bolsters this assessment. Using the ethnic categories deployed in the 2001 Census, in the first of these surveys, 10% of 'children in need' were still not classified in terms of 'race' and ethnicity (www.doh.gov.uk/cin/cin2000results.htm). In the second survey, 11% of 'children in need' were located in a 'not stated' category (www.doh.gov.uk/cin/cin2001results.htm). There must, therefore, be a new attentiveness to this dimension. Furthermore, a more generalised failure to ascertain the 'race' and ethnicity of children may have particular adverse consequences for Irish children because, as argued earlier, of the customary failure to recognise their specificity in social work theory and practice.

Improved monitoring of 'race' and ethnicity is clearly vital, despite the wishes of those – often on the political right – with a deep antipathy to this form of monitoring (see, in this context, Williams, 2002). However, monitoring is not an end in itself since there is also a need to develop new practices and new approaches. Important here is willingness on the part of SSDs to improve the awareness of staff. Here, Irish staff are likely to be an invaluable resource, and Chapter Six of this book will turn to explore some of their views and perspectives on some of the book's key themes.

Note

[1] Using the Statistical Package for Social Sciences (SPSS) analysis software, the Survey Unit based at the University of Nottingham logged the data: all the percentages have been rounded. Some of the content of this chapter was published in a short report I completed for the All-Party Irish in Britain Parliamentary Group, *The invisible ethnic minority* (Action Group for Irish Youth et al, 2003).

SIX

'Maximising things for your community': the views of social workers

The second part of this book, which examines contemporary responses to Irish children and families, at first concentrated on dominant approaches to 'race' and ethnicity within social work in Britain. It then analysed some of the findings from a survey of directors of social services departments (SSDs) that looked at their organisation's involvement with Irish children and families in England and Wales. The data generated might be viewed, therefore, as providing a 'view from the top'. Now, however, the discussion will switch focus and examine the 'view from below' and look at what Irish social work practitioners regard as the key issues. The 'voices' featured derive from in-depth interviews conducted in early 2003. More specifically, eight Irish social workers involved in children and families social work were interviewed[1].

As observed in Chapter Five, almost a quarter of the returned questionnaires in the survey of directors of SSDs came from London. Indeed, more Irish-born people live in London than in any other city except Dublin and Belfast (Hickman, 2002, p 22), and in what follows *all* of the respondents live and work in the capital. Moreover, in this chapter, 'social worker' is used in a broad and inclusive manner. Three of the practitioners had attained a social work qualification – either a Certificate of Qualification in Social Work or the Diploma in Social Work. The other interviewees had different, though related, job titles. Previous research has revealed the relatively high proportion of Irish-born people who work in 'health and social care in Britain'. O'Connor and Goodwin (2002), for example, show that 17.9% of the Irish-born workforce are located in this sector as against 11.2% of those born in the UK. The vast majority of these are Irish women. Perhaps related to this, as Lloyd (1999, p 103) observes, it is "with the Philippines that Ireland is paired as the world's greatest exporters of female nursing and domestic service workers".

A short, semi-structured questionnaire formed the basis of the interviews and this had four components. First, it asked the interviewees to provide a self-description. Second, it looked for a description of the team, or project, in which the interviewee was located. Third, the questionnaire inquired about their perspectives, as Irish social workers, on working inside or alongside SSDs. Finally, the questionnaire focused on the future and improving services for Irish children and families. None of the interviewees was involved in the thematic construction of the questionnaire, or the formulation of particular questions. Prior to the interviews, however, the questionnaire was mailed to the interviewees to provide them with the opportunity to look at the questions and to locate the interviews within the context of the larger research endeavour that forms the basis of this book.

Importantly, the semi-structured questionnaire was not used in rigid or restrictive ways and it provided space for the interviewees to expand and talk about what *they* perceived as the significant issues. In short, these were not highly standardised interviews and there was no desire to "hide behind the question-answer format, the apparatus of the interview machine" (Denzin, 2000, p 30). Rather, the methodological position adopted was that each interview was "literally an *inter view*, an inter-change of views between two persons conversing about a theme of mutual interest" (Kvale, 1996, p 14, emphasis in original; see also pp 30-1). In this context, the metaphors of 'miner' and 'traveller' have been usefully deployed to illuminate contrasting approaches to interviews:

> The two metaphors – of the interviewer as a miner and a traveler – represents different concepts of knowledge formation.... In a broad sense, the miner metaphor pictures a common understanding in modern social sciences of knowledge as 'given'. The traveler metaphor refers to [an] understanding that involves a conversational approach to social research. The miner metaphor brings interviews into the vicinity of human engineering; the traveler metaphor into the vicinity of the humanities and art. (Kvale, 1996, p 5; see also Rosenau, 1992; Gudmundsdottir, 1996; Leonard, 2000)

The late Pierre Bourdieu (2002, pp 607-27) also provides an articulation of the research ethic, which was aspired to in these interviews. Thus, there was recognition that each interview was a social relationship. Important here, moreover, was a commitment to "active and methodical listening" as opposed to "half-understanding" based on a "distracted and routinized attention" (Bourdieu, 2002, pp 609, 614).

Bourdieu's important account of research interviews can, however, be criticised. He suggests, for example, "at the risk of shocking ... that the interview can be considered a sort of *spiritual exercise* that, through *forgetfulness of self*, aims at a true *conversion of the way we look at* other people in the ordinary circumstances of life" (Bourdieu, 2002, p 614, emphases in original). This is perhaps an overly reverential and somewhat quixotic perspective. Indeed, the notion that an "extraordinary discourse" can be fostered by offering the respondent "an absolutely exceptional situation freed from the constraints (particularly time) which weigh on most exchanges" (2002, p 614) is similarly rather problematic. Certainly, the interviews (extracts of which are featured in this chapter) were undertaken in busy workplaces where the social workers were temporally constrained and subject to a panoply of competing demands.

I was responsible for conducting all of the interviews, which were then audio taped. I then transcribed the tape[2]. It is acknowledged that "transcription cannot capture the rhythm and tempo of the spoken word.... It is clear that even the most literal form of redaction (the simplest punctuation, the placing of a comma, for example, can determine the whole sense of a phrase) represents a *translation* or even an interpretation" (Bourdieu, 2002, p 612; p 621, emphasis in original; see also Atkinson et al, 2001, p 12). That is to say, reporting interviews is a 'way of writing the world', not of providing "a mirror of the so-called external world, nor is it a window into the inner life" of those interviewed (Denzin, 2001, p 25).

All the interviews, as I have said, took place in the social workers' places of work. Although limited biographical information is provided on the respondents, the names used are not, however, their actual names. Likewise, no information is provided on the areas of London in which they work; neither are the correct names of the respondent projects or teams provided. This approach perhaps detracts from the significance of the specific context in which they are based and it might also serve to blur the importance of the matrix of relationships in which they are locally embedded. However, it is also important to safeguard the respondents' right *not* to be identified (see also D'Cruz, 2000).

Five of the respondents (Gemma, Geraldine, Mary, Caroline and Ciara) work in a refuge that was set up in the early 1990s in response to the increasing numbers of women identified as Irish, seeking support with regard to domestic violence. The other three respondents work for the same SSD. Tom and John work in a specialist team providing a service for Irish Travellers. Joe is based in a mainstream 'children and families' team. The themes that are highlighted and on which these workers talk expansively will be:

- the approach to 'race' and ethnicity in social work;
- Irish identities in Britain;
- racism and stereotyping;
- placements and the non-recognition of Irish children;
- social work with children and families who are Irish Travellers;
- an agenda for the future.

Learning how to *do* 'race' in social work

For the social workers interviewed, their experience of social work education was significant in terms of how an Irish dimension was simply excluded, or inadequately analysed, when discussions turned to the question of 'race' and ethnicity. Here, the black/white binary, referred to in previous chapters of this book, was dominant. Tom and John, now working in the same team, had been on the same social work course at the same time, and their experiences were also similar:

> We found the Irish dimension was neglected in the social work literature on anti-discriminatory training. We found there was a binary, which was a black/white binary and a particular view of racism, and there were tensions

on the social work course because of this approach. Us and other Irish social work students on the course would be expected to place ourselves in the 'white group', yet we would maintain that we came from a particular racialised group. There were some lecturers on the course who would find this idea difficult to take.... I did my MA thesis on anti-Irish racism so I had my eye on this whole area from the outset. There were interesting tensions that were not really addressed in the seminars. There would be discussions on anti-Irish racism and so on, but what I found was better were the discussions *outside* the seminars with social work lecturers at the university. There were some that were sympathetic and some that weren't. There was one person who was black, but also had an Irish background. She felt that because of her experience of racism from white Irish people that she shared the binary approach to racism. These discussions were fascinating, though, but were on the periphery of the course and not structured inside it.... An enriching dimension was left out.... People are now realising how fluid 'race' is and how it twists and turns in different historical periods. For example, look now at what is happening in Eastern Europe and what is happening in the Gulf [the US/Anglo led invasion of Iraq]. In the late 1990s, when we did our training, the black/white binary was, I think, more dominant. (John, second-generation Irish, with parents from the west of Ireland)

What is striking here, perhaps, is that the particular university John and Tom attended has an internationally respected 'Irish Studies' department, which was – and still is – seeking to develop theories on the racialisation of Irish people and anti-Irish racism. However, no attempts were made, it seemed, to integrate these perspectives into the social work programme. Tom maintained:

I think there are privileged identities within social work training around concepts of 'race', and the Irish are marginalised, and this became an area of tension in discussions around that and in trying to broaden it out. White-on-white racism simply couldn't be discussed – that was an issue we just didn't seem to get to ... because it was contentious, you dropped it. To confront it, you would end up in a row.... On my second placement, I was at the Irish Centre and the Macpherson Report had just been written. I had had my first placement with the Travellers' Team and I did my dissertation on anti-Traveller racism, which looked at ideas focused on settled and nomadic communities. Concepts started to open up and I was bringing all this to my discussions in college, but I found resistance and there was a certain amount of self-censorship in discussions.... The academic staff were quite clever at closing things down. The resistance lay with both them and with the ideology within the social work profession around 'race'. (Tom, originally from Belfast)

The previous chapter indicated how the vast majority of SSDs were failing to incorporate an Irish dimension into anti-discriminatory training for social workers located in 'children and families' teams. In this context, another social worker observed:

> Very rarely is there an Irish dimension. Most of training is strictly black and white.... The Irish in Britain Representation Group [IBRG], which I am involved in, has tried to have an input. In [one London borough], along with the Action Group for Irish Youth, we arranged specialised training providing a one-day off Irish Awareness Training for council staff across the board. The sad thing about that was that there was very little support across the council from a number of different departments. It was sort of boycotted. We got enough to fill the course, but then what you was getting was Irish staff coming along, or second-generation Irish staff, but the whole aim was to get *everybody* coming along. It was a pioneering effort, but it only continued for two or three years and is no longer going.... Generally, if you look at equal opportunities training, where it exists and where it is put on – and the whole move in the 1980s to provide anti-racist training mainly through the Greater London Council [GLC] – the Irish were either seen as a tag on at the very end, or else we had our own separate conference. If you go back to the GLC, although there was an Irish Liaison Unit and [a couple of boroughs] had Irish Policy Officers, the Irish were always separated from the mainstream.... It is not seen as any priority and is seen by mainstream managers as a 'non issue'. (Joe, arrived in Britain in the 1970s and, during the period of the GLC, was employed for a number of years as an Irish Policy Officer. Active in the IBRG Group and other groups campaigning on issues related to Irish people in Britain, civil liberties and criminal justice)

Joe was of the opinion that the "reality of 'race' politics in Britain" was such that the "colour dimension" was "always going to be dominant". Nonetheless, the courses he arranged had been generally well received:

> [The courses that focused on Irish people in Britain were] normally regarded very positively. Again, as I say, quite a number of [the participants] were second-generation Irish. There was a mixture of people from other different backgrounds and generally the feedback was very good. There was a feeling that they were totally unaware of the issue and some of them were deeply shocked to find out about say, Irish mental health figures or to look at economic disadvantage. The assumption was that the Irish, being a white group, would be very similar to the English and the Scots.... You find different awareness among different members of staff. It's the same with clients. When I visit Caribbean clients, they will often remark to you about 'No blacks, no Irish', so there is a consciousness about this common experience in the 1960s. (Joe)

One of the female social workers, working in a culturally specific Irish project, felt that, within social work and social care, the Irish dimension was excluded:

> There is, I think, little working knowledge of our separate identity – this is not to say that there are not Irish social workers. Alright, we may be largely white, blue-eyed and so on, but we have our own culture. *We are not English people, we are Irish people.* Now having to explain this, as an Irish woman, when you are running from an violent man, when you're sitting in front of someone who is doing an interview to decide if you are legally 'homeless' or not, it becomes very difficult, having to try and explain your cultural needs as well.... I went to a conference recently and they had workshops on ethnic minorities and they had a panel of speakers with no Irish people. I made the point, as an Irish woman, about Irish representation on the panel being conspicuously absent. Afterwards loads of women came up to me and said: "It was good you said that because we never even thought about things like that". This is because people think 'black' equals 'ethnic minority'. They don't see Irish people as having a separate, 'ethnic minority' identity. I think we are constantly up against that. (Geraldine, born in Dublin, but lived in England since childhood. Active in the women's movement. Currently director of a refuge for Irish women fleeing domestic violence and abuse).

Geraldine continued:

> I really believe whom shouts the loudest gets heard. I think we have to raise issues and to challenge *constantly* – our voice *has* to be heard. We are an active and able part of the community that we live in and that *has* to be recognised. Unless we go out there and do that, the world is not going to come knocking at our door.... I have actually been stopped at the door at conferences and told this is for "'black and ethnic minorities'".

For Joe, there were clearly potential adverse consequences for Irish workers questioning the dominant perspective on 'race' and seeking to introduce an Irish element:

> Its almost like if you are Irish and articulate and speak out on the Irish issue you will be parked there in terms of your career, you won't go any further. It may be changing now because of the Peace Process [in Northern Ireland], but that was certainly the issue in the 1980s. You were seen really as 'Irish with attitude'. So the idea was to keep your head down and get on with the job. The Irish issue is still, I think, 'ha ha', or 'funny peculiar' or 'don't bring it up', or 'don't annoy us', or 'go away with it'.

In Chapter Four, it was argued that there is now a more pervasive backlash against a professional sensitivity to 'race' and ethnicity in social work and in government protocols that focus, for example, on the issue of child placement (see, in this context, Chief Secretary to the Treasury, 2003; Garrett, 2003). It can also be argued that the notion of 'inclusive practice', which is central to *the Assessment framework for children in need and their families*, is somewhat ambiguous (DoH et al, 2000). Similarly, Joe felt that:

> Equalities issues are on the back foot across the board. They've moved on to this thing 'diversity' which they lifted from America. We are all very diverse. In fact, what they're trying to do is gloss over the whole area of equalities .... The problems with social services are, I think, more generic in that there is so much pressure that 'race' and lots of other issues 'go out the window' in terms of *any* community. You're just fire fighting all the time. So generally with 'race' and social work in the last 10 years ... there has been lip service paid to it, but, in reality, the workers are too busy to trying to meet government targets and so on.... In the current climate, you're just 'getting on with your jobs'.

Being Irish: Irish identities in Britain

Perhaps related to this 'lip service' is the failure to *truly* engage with complex issues that are connected to Irish identities in Britain. As observed earlier, this was one of the major problems with the 2001 Census that, with its 'tick-box' approach to identity, failed to take account of the fact that a sense of national or cultural identity is highly complex, always *in motion*. The Census did not capture such complexities, and failed to engage with ideas about cultural hybridity. This was apparent in some of the comments made by one of the second-generation Irish social workers interviewed.

> I struggled with the form. I found it very difficult to just tick a box because there wasn't like a 'mixed category'.... I wouldn't say I'm *completely* 'White Irish' because that ignores part of who I am. I'd also feel like a fraud to just tick 'White Irish' if I was, say, sat next to someone who was born in Dublin and raised there. I'm not as Irish as they are. I'd want to explain it a bit, but I'd never *ever* tick a 'White British' box either. I'm really Irish/English or English/Irish. I'm really torn. In terms of my ethnicity I'm Irish, but in terms of my nationality I am, I suppose, British because I was born here. My preference would be for a form which let me say something. I need to be able to explain myself and not just have boxes there. All of this worries me because I think it may well lead to an under-representation of Irish people when data from the Census is published. There are so many people who aren't first-generation Irish who would identify as Irish and this has implications for the funding of Irish projects. (Gemma)

A number of those interviewed also dwelt on the inaccurate assumption, reflected in the Census, that Irish people in Britain are exclusively a 'white' population.

One of the female workers, also aligning herself with some of the respondents to the questionnaire discussed in Chapter Six, took issue with this perspective, which denied her own sense of identity and heritage:

> [The Census approach is] not good enough anymore, there is a need for different categories. I obviously have a problem with the ['White Irish'] category. They need different boxes. Ireland itself is also changing. (Caroline, whose mother is Irish and father from South America)

As an Irish social worker who also had a 'black' identity, this had advantages, she felt, for the children she worked with at the refuge:

> The children sometimes say, "How come you are Irish?" I explain to them.... I think it is really important if you're working with Irish children and families that you do have some knowledge of Ireland. Its nice to able to say to the children that I'm not the same colour as them, but I know Ireland, my granny lives there, I've spent a lot of time there and so on.... Its good to be able to let them see that I'm obviously black and don't, perhaps, reflect more traditional ideas about what it means to be Irish. Travelling children, because I'm different, can often identify with that because they can feel on the outside. That said, I see myself as having an Irish background, but I am made up of lots of different backgrounds. (Caroline)

As can be seen from Gemma's comments earlier, related to the failure of the Census to grasp the range of Irish identities in Britain was a concern that Irish social care projects would lose out because funding decisions would still be made on the basis of inadequate data: despite the work that many of these workers had undertaken to ensure that their Irish service users completed the Census forms. In this context, Joe observed:

> It is unfortunate in that it [the Census] was done when Irish community is probably the lowest it has been since the Famine in terms of the number of Irish born here. So many people went back in the 1990s and the older ones are, in a sense, dying off quite quickly. I think also there is tremendous pressure on the Irish *not* to identify. The Irish community in Britain might identify with the Irish soccer team, or with Celtic [Football Club] and with the culture, which can be around a range of different things. I think the returns were very disappointing. I'm not sure, but it could be used as a way of saying the Irish community is quite small, quite tiny.

This, he felt, might compound problems for the Irish community, which was insufficiently recognised when similar national and more local counts had taken place in the past. He also suggested:

The dominant issue is that the Irish should become British in the second generation and I think this is almost an unspoken deal between the Irish and British governments. So 'OK, we'll recognise that the Irish who came over had some problems, particularly those who are now the older generation, with poverty and that'. Although to be fair to the [Irish] Embassy, over the last few years they have been more progressive.... Until the late 1980s, it was certainly hostile to the notion that the Irish suffered *any* form of discrimination or disadvantage here.

Racism and stereotyping

Throughout the book it has been argued that, in both and contemporary and historical contexts, many Irish children and families have been subjected to discrimination and multiple forms of disadvantage in Britain (see also Hickman and Walter, 1997). Indeed, it is clear that a failure to *recognise* Irish identity, reflected in some of the comments from interviewees, is a particular form of social injustice. For some, this failure to recognise was more emphatic in that it had involved, they felt, deliberate attempts to suppress or erase a sense of Irish identity:

> My experience ... of Irishness is one where people – your parents – kept their heads down. My mum was a nurse here during the war and she actually encountered those signs, 'No blacks, No Irish, No dogs' and so on. I know that had a effect on her.... What I've found with many Irish people in Britain is that it is a very profound, repressed experience.... Catholic education, for example, does not allow an Irish dimension. Where I was from, there was no cultural celebration of Irishness. You were known to be Irish, but you were almost totally alone with it. Most of my peer group rejected the Catholic dimension to their Irishness and so at the end of this process [supposed to produce] good Catholic citizens [they were] left without Catholicism and without Irishness. (John)

As to any overt anti-Irish racism levelled at them or at Irish people using social work and social care services, one respondent stated she felt that she was working in "a sheltered environment" in a "very PC [politically correct city]" (Ciara, from south-east Ireland). Similarly, Gemma, not audibly 'Irish' in accent, reported that she could not recall any racism directed at her. However, she did ponder if racism was having an impact on the quality of service some of the women at the refuge were likely to receive. Was this a 'variable' having an impact on how a service was being delivered for Irish children and families, or was it 'something else', such as social class? Frequently, she maintained, this was a zone of ambiguity that needed to be considered. Gemma gave the following example:

An Irish woman who was living here wanted something – I think it was a sunbed or something – and it required us to fund it. We said, "Yes, we'll provide the money, but you have to arrange it, go through the yellow pages and everything". Off the woman went, very happy and stuff and then she came back to me when she had found the company and said to me, "You call them". My response was, "Don't be daft", and I was just going to explain to her how to handle the telephone call and so on – I thought she just lacked the confidence to make the call. She just responded, though, "Yes, but I'm Irish, they'll treat me different". I was really taken aback, even though I've worked here for a number of years. Anyway, she did call and the outcome was negative. Then I called up and got it straight away. Another time – in fact it was the same woman – she needed an emergency appointment at the doctors for her son. She rang and was refused.... I called back, didn't mention her previous call and said I was phoning from a women's refuge, and I got her an appointment that day. I suppose I'll never know whether I got the appointment just because I'm a refuge worker and I'm from an agency or was it because I have English accent.... I don't know if service providers are being racist or have anti-Irish views, but I do know the women who we provide a service for perceive it as anti-Irish. They certainly believe that doctors, social services and so on tend to perceive them differently because of an Irish accent – treating them, in fact, like they are stupid.

Geraldine commented:

One of the interesting things about my own Irishness is that my children are 'mixed race' and I have a son who is in his mid-30s and we talk about racism. My experience of racism was that I had 'mixed-race' kids so when I wanted to rent a flat I couldn't because I was Irish, my man was black and there was this thing, 'No Irish, No blacks, No dogs', so I came up against all of this. My son says, "So what mum? I'm a black man. When I walk down the street, society's racism is aimed at me. If you want to wake up tomorrow and not be Irish you don't have to be". I respond, "Don't be minimising the racism I face in relation to that you face.... I'm proud of being Irish".... Because we were colonised, we were colonised *into* those people who did the colonising ... you talk the way they talk and you blend in. That's all part of being colonised and that's what those who colonised us expected us to do. This is constantly on my mind when I'm dealing with Irish women and children here.

A related issue that was prominent in the interviews was the notion of 'stereotyping'. As Pickering (2001, p 5) argues, stereotyping "imparts a sense of fixedness" and a number of the interviewees stated that they, or the service users they worked with, were stereotyped on account of being Irish. Gemma remembered, as a child, the idea that being Irish was associated with drunkenness. Geraldine also commented on the fact that Irish men are still constructed as people likely to "drink too much". Furthermore, she encouraged the women who worked and lived in the refuge to explore and talk about such stereotyping (see also McClintock, 1994, pp 52-3). Joe commented:

> Sometimes you also get references in court. A few weeks ago I did memorandum training and we were training with the police[3]. We were asked to do a, read a story to each other. So one person played the role of the child and the other the interviewer. So I agreed to read my bit and he [the police officer] replied, "That's fine so long as I can understand your thick Irish accent". This is from a serving police officer that is working in child protection. He also said something later in the day about when "the IRA were bombing the seaside" (which the IRA never, of course, did). But I didn't want to be put in the position of having to argue this. I have heard a lot of stuff like this over the years from police officers. I remember another police officer in the early 1980s saying to a young black kid, "You're not thick like some of these thick Paddies we get in here – you're an intelligent lad". Trying to play one community off against another. In another case in Brent, I remember a police officer in the radio car going on about how an Englishman came in to inquire about his Irish friend who had gone missing and he hadn't seen for days. The police officer started to go on about "pissed Paddy's friend" coming into complain. So now the Englishman had become contaminated and a problem because he had been drinking with an Irish guy.... In court as well, a legal officer came out with a very derogatory Irish remark, but you are put into the position of 'the Irish worker' having to challenge things, being on the defensive.

In terms of promoting derogatory stereotypes, Ciara felt that Irish television and films were often as culpable as British media. Moreover, it irritated her that she was always *assumed* to be Catholic. Joe also dwelt on this conflation of Irish identity with Catholicism and, reflecting some of the themes explored in earlier chapters of this book, suggested that this was then attached to ideas about sexuality and "dysfunctional", or "problem families":

> Even among staff there is also an assumption that because I am Irish, I'm a Catholic, yet I am a *complete* atheist. There is this feeling that because you are Irish you will have a certain set of beliefs, a lot of which will relate to sexuality and what you might do in terms of contraceptives and so on. Some of this impacts on families as well. You will often have the expression 'Irish Catholic Family' and there will be loads of assumptions there about their sexuality [and reproductive practices]. No reference is made to some sections of the Irish community, particularly the ones over here, *wanting* to retain certain traditions and *wanting* to have – perhaps unlike many families in Ireland these days – a large family.... That can be seen as, "Oh, they are Catholics and don't know how to look after their sexuality".

Joe also argued that, because of the power of historically rooted representations of Irishness, the mere mention of 'Irishman' in a criminal justice context, for example, could still carry a damaging connotation[4].

Placements and the non-recognition of Irish children

Did, therefore, the omission of an Irish dimension in anti-discriminatory theory and training, the complexity of Irish identities, racism and stereotyping have an impact on the placement of Irish children and families? This has, of course, been an area of central concern in this book, both in terms of historical and contemporary approaches. Joe argued:

> My experience is of not of non-recognition, but of total and deliberate denial. For example, I attended a case conference where the father of the children was Irish – no mention was made of that, whatsoever – and one of the grandparents happened to be Turkish. The chairperson of the conference went on at length about whether the children had access to their Turkish heritage, but at the same time completely ignored any Irish aspect. So there would be you as an Irish worker, put under pressure and having to fight your corner, even when you do raise it [the Irish dimension] it's sort of sidelined, or parked away somewhere so it's not discussed, or brought out. There is an intolerance about raising the Irish issue and you'll find there is often *no* recognition in the file, or elsewhere, that a family is Irish. There is almost – again – denial…. Irish children are not identified in the system. It may be professionals who are putting them down as 'English', but parents might put them down as 'English' also. This happened, I think, with the recent Census. There is a feeling that if they put themselves down as Irish they may well get discriminated against so they'll say they were born here…. If you explored it further with them, they probably say, "Of course, they're Irish".

Joe also asserted that the politics of 'race' sometimes led to a crude approach being taken to children's sense of identity and this could function in a way that worked to the disadvantage of individual children:

> [In one London borough] I was responsible for this young person who was 15 or 16 and they were trying to say to him, "You're black, you're black, you're black" – sort of downloading it, it was as heavy as that…. This kid, his mother was Irish and he was coming to me constantly, "Tell me about Ireland, lend me your books", but no provision was made whatsoever to balance the two [his black and Irish heritage]. It was almost a complete denial of this child's mother…. Okay, the child might be perceived as a black child … but I think you've got to go back to the needs of the child and that often is ignored where there is mixed relationships and the only aspect that is viewed as important is the skin colour aspect.

Children and families who are Irish Travellers

In the SSD directors' survey featured in Chapter Five, 42% of respondents stated that that specialist services were provided for Travellers. The situation of Irish Travellers was also a prominent issue, which featured in the Irish social worker responses. John stated the Irish Travellers are "a distinct community with a distinct way of life". The distinctive accents of the boys John and Tom worked with indicated, claimed the latter, how "bounded the community actually is". However, in terms of the data available to map the community and its needs, there were, maintained John, particular problems because "Irish Travellers can pass as Irish" and it is "often in their best interests when they apply for housing to do so". Such practices can, however, "make it hard to develop work in terms of evidenced-based practice because we don't get the data"[5].

At the refuge, a high proportion of the women using the service were Irish Travellers and all of those interviewed agreed with the assessment of Gemma that "Irish Travellers are definitely perceived as a separate group and are largely perceived in a negative way". Geraldine, the director of the refuge, asserted that Travellers are treated in "an appalling and racist way right throughout all the services". In terms of the perceptions of service providers, the same respondent stated:

> I think they are looked at as being very needy. So they are seen as having gangs of kids, they are regarded as being out of control, they're not going to send their kids to school, there will be an expectation that there will be issues to do with begging and so on. There will also be issues connected to their nomadic way of life — which is actually being taken away from them with all the laws that are coming out now. I think there is the feeling that children need to be 'settled'. Generally, Travellers are looked at as being very needy, but their culture is not recognised. If it is recognised, it is seen as something that needs to be broken.... There is no respect for nomadic culture.

Tom, located in the Travellers' Team insisted:

> Travelling families are commonly perceived as a problematic Irish family, an Irish family that is having difficulties. I've seldom come across explicit statements, but in conversation with other social workers it is clear that many haven't really understood *who* Travellers are and *what* they are and that's the difficulty — the fact that they can be seen as just a problematic Irish family.

Related to this, he felt, was the fear that Travellers generated:

> I have *never* come across a community that creates such fear in other people and that fear is manifested in a social worker going to visit — knock, knock

– no answer, so away they go. So a child may be there who needs a service, but does not get one because there is a fear, an anxiety. People tend to project so much onto this community. It's the most evident thing. All the phobias are projected onto this community and Traveller families experience incredible hostility. Irrational fear underpins a lot of the racism directed at Travellers. I'm most struck by that.... We've been trying, for example, to get a system going for years where admin[istrative] workers can do some very brief, initial assessment, but there seems to be almost a panic when a Traveller family comes in. It's "Go get John or Tom!".

Furthermore, asserted Tom, "all the negativity that is expressed towards this community can be turned onto you as a worker and you can get it in strange ways. For example, lack of cooperation". He also felt that some Irish Centres were keen "to pass Travellers on to specialist agencies" despite Travellers being a "part of the Irish community". More emphatically, Tom referred to the "intense prejudice still directed toward Travellers from within the Irish community" and the fact that "they have been left out in the cold in terms of Irish community organisations". However, he conceded that more recently the Irish voluntary sector has "used its resources in forwarding the Traveller Law Reform Bill"[6].

John believed that "Travellers have the right to access services just like any other community" and both he and Tom saw their role as facilitating this process. Thus, although located in a specialist team, they were still intent on challenging any "dumping" on the part of social work and social care providers. John stated that a Traveller's inability to read was often interpreted as being part of some elaborate "benefits scam". Literary was a key issue, however, for all the respondents who worked with Travellers:

> A lot of Irish travellers who come in are not able to read and write and that is something they often feel ashamed about going into social services, or homeless families or seeking an education service. They are going to feel embarrassed about that, or even ashamed. They feel a need to explain it and often they might fail to access services as a result. (Gemma)[7]

Ciara spoke about a headteacher wanting to *see* the children from a Travelling family before they could be considered for a place at one particular school. Another mother did not want social services involved because they "look down" on Travellers. Caroline stated:

> With Travelling families it can be very difficult because they have got a totally different lifestyle which a lot of the other agencies are not familiar with and the way the children are brought up is often seen very negatively – the choices that they have to make and so on.... Sometimes they [the agencies] don't recognise how hard it is for Travelling women to leave their

partners – for Travelling women it is *doubly* hard. When you mention social services to Travellers they get really scared, very *very* frightened.

The racism directed at Irish Travellers could also have an impact, however, on relationships *inside* the refuge.

> Racism from the Irish settled community is probably more intense than from the general community out there. So we can have issues here involving settled women and Traveller women living together. We had an incident here recently where a settled kid made real racist remarks about a Traveller kid…. At our house meeting, involving staff and residents, I brought this up. The Traveller woman cried throughout the meeting…. This is like a white woman being racist with a black woman. We do have issues to do with racism that we challenge immediately. (Geraldine)

John also spoke of the "levels of prejudice" they would encounter on having to liaise with services in the Republic of Ireland on issues related to particular Traveller families. Here, the *Gardaí Síochána* (the police) could present particular difficulties on account of discriminatory attitudes they often had and judgements they made about Travellers[8]. There were also, he maintained, "tensions *within* the Traveller community with regard to Irish Travellers". Hirst (1997, p 19) has commented on "Traveller culture, with its deeply religious, male-dominated rituals and mores" and a number of the respondents suggested that there were particular factors related to gender and Irish Travellers in Britain.

Irish social workers facing the future

When asked about how services for Irish children and families could be improved, a number of respondents focused on the Traveller issue. Gemma, for example, felt that there needed to be greater "awareness and services for Irish Travellers communities". Tom, when asked how social services might begin to evolve in a "more culturally responsive way" for Irish children and families, responded:

> What does a culturally sensitive service mean? I can't even grasp what that means for Irish people. I'm so wrapped up in the Travelling community and their needs are so extreme and their difficulties are so extreme, I can't even see the Irish community any more as having that level of need or as needing that level of awareness. If it means anything for me, cultural awareness is so paramount – knowledge of the community, its history, where the individuals are coming from, the complexity of the community…. My experience of the voluntary sector – working with the homeless – suggests that having Irish workers, at the very least, is important. They are likely to bring with them an awareness of Irish culture and of relevant issues likely to be having an effect on someone here – in England – in difficulties…. With Travellers,

there is immense unmet need out there. If you are ever to tackle the black/white binary you have to show that discrimination has an impact and it can be mapped out. It is structured in the society. I think, with the Travelling community, it has never been mapped. With the Irish community, we have started to map it and it is only when you map the need that you realise the impact of discrimination.... For me, it is important that social work training addresses that, it is built in and it is acknowledged.

His colleague, John, echoed these remarks and added:

With Hickman and Walter (1997) there is some reference to Irish Travellers, but this is an area where there is a need for more evidence-based research which could improve social services. Raising the profile of Irish Travellers in social work literature would, I think, enrich that literature as well and lead to reflection on other forms of practice. There is also a need to look at the Irish Traveller diaspora. It is unique and special, but still needs to be properly researched.... We are dealing with a nomadic culture and an unusual form of prejudice. To raise this whole area in social work training is very relevant because it would also give people a handle on aspects of eastern European migration and white-on-white racism. It's also important to support the community social work initiatives, which are currently being provided with Travellers. Furthermore, there is a need to see that Irish Traveller culture is a *culture under threat* and to have social workers become aware of that dimension. Importantly, though, social work is not a means of pathologising, or victimising this community. It's not a case of: 'There are Travellers here so there must be a need for social workers'. Instead, Travellers, like any other group, have a *right* to appropriate services and there should be social workers that understand their role as helping Travellers access these services.

It was crucial here that social workers and social work educators evolved a complex and dynamic approach to understanding the fluidity of cultural identity:

All cultures are very dynamic and are evolving and this is the case with the Travelling community.... There is a need to engage with theories of need in a way, which doesn't patronise this community and doesn't freeze them in time. There is a need to work in an enabling way that allows them to face the challenges that are ahead of them and to decide in what ways they will seek to preserve and develop their culture. This will involve looking at how they might want to better use education systems. In the future, Traveller women may play a more decisive role in shaping the community. The challenge for outsiders will be to develop ways of working in partnership with Travelling communities rather than coming in from outside with paternalist, assimilationist or colonialist attitudes. (John)

Joe felt that certain policy "innovations" being introduced by the New Labour administration might adversely impact on the Irish community (see, for example, Home Office, 2003[9]. The current focus on "street activity was targeted at the working class", but Irish people in Britain because of certain "patterns of socialisation" and attempts to create "back home" are likely to face difficulties in this regard. The fact that many Irish people live in poor or substandard housing can also be related to this, he suggested, because, for many, there is a greater reliance on socialising *outside* the home.

A number of the respondents stressed that there was a need for a 'joined-up' approach to improving social work and social care services for Irish people in Britain. Here, schools, for example, had a role to play in terms of promoting Irish culture and highlighting "what Irish people are proud about. This should be in the curriculum and celebrated" (Geraldine). Joe felt that the resources of the Roman Catholic Church could be "released" or opened up to greater community participation and activities, given that churches are left largely empty and unused during the day. In relation to social welfare and social care provision provided by and for the Irish community, he was also of the view that a number of these agencies needed to be modernised given that many are, he asserted, still modelled on the 1950s approach with "someone coming off the boat" and many of the staff are low-paid. There was, for him, a need for a "far more sophisticated service, including legal advice, employment advice.... Nothing is recorded adequately with the Irish community – it is all hidden away".

When looking to the future, one dimension that was considered related to the wider and changing historical and political context. More specifically, could the Peace Process in Northern Ireland have positive consequences for the Irish community in terms of social work and social care provision in England? Joe took a pessimistic position on this question.

> The Irish started to go home in large numbers just as the Peace Process was kicking in: a lot of the political leadership went back. The Irish in the IBRG, for example, lost 50% of its members and it is probably the most able ones who have gone back. The same happened in the 1970s when the political climate here was getting very difficult.... The IBRG came into being in 1981, after the hunger strikes.... There was no political leadership in the Irish community in Britain, they had all run to the hills or they had gone back into music and culture and stuff. In theory it should be much easier now ... but I find the whole situation now more complex and the goalposts have been moved. The government is still condensing groups down into black and white and you still find most of the research coming through focuses on black and white.... What you've never really got in Britain is any resources to address any of the issues.

Tom, however, articulated a more optimistic position:

> The Good Friday Agreement and the whole peace settlement have had a profound impact on the Irish community across Britain. It has definitely 'opened up' the Irish community. They celebrate their identity more ... the Good Friday Agreement has had a knock-on effect over here.... The changing demographics of Irish society is going to be a difficult issue for the Irish voluntary sector, in terms of how they are going to manage migration *now*. They are still dealing with the legacy of the huge migration of the 1950s and 1960s. They need to focus also on other vulnerable elements within the Irish community. The Good Friday Agreement has taken a huge weight off them in the sense that the political situation is clearly no longer as intense as it was in the late 1980s – it was in hyper-drive then, the state was still at war. The resolution of the political crisis has freed up the Irish community to explore other things with energy. All those activists, all those people out there, what do they turn to? They need to turn to map the discrimination faced by the community. It's not as glamorous as a war for national liberation, but it is a significant issue.

Important, on a practical level, was also a certain 'organisational nous' that flowed from direct involvement in wider political struggles:

> For me as an Irish social worker from Belfast and over here, it is almost like you *brought with you* the background that you experienced. You may not have been heavily an activist, but there is a culture of resistance and a culture of self-help and a culture of struggle and of fighting for things.... I'm not saying nobody else has this, but there is something about the idea that you are looking to *maximise things for your community*. That is, I think, what the Irish community here may have also. It makes it more than the individuated social worker's role. You are always thinking in those terms. You are thinking in a multi-layered way. For example, with the Traveller Law Reform issue, you're thinking of the social exclusion of the boys you work with and of ways of dealing with that because of what our communities have experienced – it's a sense of solidarity. That's how you are engaging with it. (Tom; emphasis added)

Conclusion

Conceptually, this group of Irish social workers – although internally differentiated – can be viewed collectively as a 'muted group' whose opinions and interpretations are apt to be omitted within the dominant discourse on social work, 'race' and ethnicity (in this context, see Atkinson et al, 2001, pp 13-14). Indeed, as we have seen, many felt that their perspective, as Irish people in Britain, was often disparaged when issues of 'race' and ethnicity were discussed or were key social work practice issues.

Some of Bourdieu's thoughts on the methodology surrounding research interviews were referred to at the beginning of the chapter and drawing on, but refining, the same writer's concept of habitus, David Parker (2000) has helpfully articulated some of the key issues related to micro-interactions where ethnicity is significant. More specifically, he has explored how individuals from ethnic minority groups, providing a service, engage with others located within dominant ethnic categories that are in receipt of a service.

Habitus, for Bourdieu, refers to internalised or embodied social structures. Houston (2002, p 157) maintains that Bourdieu:

> defines habitus as our 'cultural unconscious' or mental habits' or 'internalised master depositions' which lead to particular perceptions and actions that are durable in character. Implicit within the concept ... is an acknowledgement that the social structure is deeply ingrained within us all, that our ways of interpreting the world are influenced by our social milieus. However, pervasive this influence may be, though, Bourdieu reminds us that we are not automatons or mindless vehicles of our governing habitus. Rather, habitus acts as a very loose set of guidelines permitting us to strategize, adapt, improvise or innovate in response to situations as they arise.

The habitus formulation tries to capture, therefore, how social action is "simultaneously regulated and improvised, while neither wholly determined or spontaneous" (Parker, D., 2000, p 83). The chief problem, however, is that habitus, as described by Bourdieu, fails satisfactorily to embrace the "lived experiences of racialized hierarchy" because his "topology of social space prioritises the mapping of class positions". On account of Bourdieu's failure to "specify the non-class modes of exposure to the world defined by habitus", Parker coins the phrase "diaspora habitus" (Parker, D., 2000, p 83). This refers to the "scheme of perception, appreciation and action which governs everyday practice in diaspora" (Parker, D., 2000, p 82). Here, the "diasporic social location adds an extra element which he [Bourdieu] cannot accommodate in his model" (Parker, D., 2000, p 82). It is also "forces a closer investigation" of how "imperial legacies structure exchanges" (Parker, D., 2000, p 74).

Parker then goes on to assert that in their exchanges with Chinese people, "white people" in Britain are able to deploy "imperial capital". This refers to "the legacies of imperial dominance in the form of conceptions of servitude and stereotypical deformations of cultural difference" (Parker, D., 2000, p 86). Elsewhere, it is maintained that "imperial capital" is the "accumulated historical advantage of colonial power" (Parker, D., 2000, p 88). Importantly, however, "the diasporic habitus does not simply predispose those without imperial capital to a stoic and passive acceptance of the hand dealt to them" (Parker, D., 2000, p 85). Neither does the 'diasporic habitus' simply "give rise to a conformism which equips people for subordination, it also offers resources between the legacies of the past, the imperatives of the present, and the possibilities of the future" (Parker, D., 2000, p 74).

In his empirical work, Parker examined interactions taking place within 'Chinese takeaways' and – quite clearly – the situation of Irish social workers and Chinese people working in this type of environment is radically different. With his reference to 'white people', he can also be seen to be working with the black/white binary criticised throughout this book. However, Parker's contribution remains important because a number of his insights are, perhaps, conceptually suggestive if they are viewed in the context of the Irish social workers' comments. Both the Chinese interviewees he interviewed and the Irish social workers who are the focal interest of this chapter can be viewed, for example, as being involved in forms of 'work' and both are subject to (different forms of) racialisation during the course of that activity (see also Pratt, 1993, ch 1). In the Introduction to this book, the conceptual utility of the 'diaspora' construct was referred to and Parker's 'diaspora habitus' sheds more light on some of the interactions mentioned by the social workers and way in which accumulated 'imperial' or 'colonial' capital can be deployed against them and some of the people for whom they provide services. Furthermore, perhaps the interviews with the Irish social workers also reveal how strategies of resistance can operate within 'diaspora habitus' and within a particular sphere of social welfare.

Importantly, the relatively small group of respondents cannot, however, be seen as representative of *all* Irish social workers in Britain. The interviews at the core of this chapter are best interpreted, therefore, as an exploratory venture that could provide a foundation for a more widespread research initiative focusing on a larger group of children and families social workers based in locations other than London. Nonetheless, the views of the workers interviewed do provide further insights into a number of themes that have been circulating preoccupations of this book. Moreover, partly on account of their work locations, the respondents identified additional factors relating to working with Irish Travellers. The next chapter, the Conclusion, forms an overview of some of the key themes to have emerged in the book.

Notes

[1] In 2002, I was asked to present some of the emerging findings from the survey of SSDs, featured in Chapter Five, at two meetings. These were the Irish Youth Forum convened by the Action Group for Irish Youth and the Irish Equalities Working Group, which meets at the CRE (see also, 'New group to act as bridge to the CRE', *The Irish Post*, 8 November 1997). Both meetings, attended by Irish social workers and people working in associated fields, provided opportunistic recruiting locations for the interviews. Two of the interviewees I had met, very briefly, on a previous occasion before the interviews took place. The other six, I had never met before.

[2] Denzin (2001, p 24) observes that the "reflexive interview in a not an information gathering tool per se. It is not a commodity that you hire someone to collect for you, or that you pay someone to give you. It belongs to a moral community". No computer software package was used to aid the analysis of the interviews. Copies of the transcripts were sent to all the respondents to enable them to check that they

agreed that their comments had been accurately rendered (in this context, see also Atkinson et al, 2001, pp 15-16). Atkinson and Silverman (1997, p 305) provide helpful cautionary remarks on the "neo-Romantic celebrations of the speaking subject" that is frequently implicit in some of the literature on research interviews.

[3] *The memorandum of good practice*, published by the Home Office in 1992, provides guidance on how children, who are the subject of child abuse investigations are to be interviewed by police officers and social workers. See also Aldridge and Wood (2000) and Garrett (2003, ch 4).

[4] In this context, the case of Christy McGrath is pertinent. He was sentenced to life imprisonment for murder and the events surrounding the murder and conviction have sparked a campaign for his freedom. The widely supported Justice for Christy McGrath Campaign has drawn attention to how the phrase and designation 'Irish lad' was used throughout the course of the police investigation. Similarly, the way the phrase 'Irishman' was deployed in report of the child abuse inquiry examining the circumstances surrounding the death of Maria Colwell in the 1970s is also interesting (see Committee of Inquiry into the Care and Supervision Provided in Relation to Maria Colwell, 1974).

[5] In relation to the absence of data, John observed: "I also deal with a lot of mental health issues that have been under-researched in the Irish Travelling community".

[6] Furthermore, in February 2003, the Irish Traveller Movement in Britain presented a Traveller Culture and Heritage Day at the London Irish Centre in Camden Square.

[7] Social work with children and families increasingly demands that people using services are able to read and write. On form filling and social work, see Garrett (2003).

[8] Jim MacLaughlin (1996) has written about anti-Traveller racism in Ireland (see also, Helleiner, 1997, 1998). See also 'Parents to remove children at schools over travellers', *The Irish Times*, 1 May 2001; 'Threat to ban Travellers from pubs lifted', *The Irish Times*, 14 August 2002. A number of features and articles in both the Irish and British press have also commented on the racism directed at migrants, refugees and asylum seekers in present-day Ireland (Nic Suibhne, 1998; Coulter, 2003; see also 'Asylum seekers face growing distrust and animosity', *The Sunday Tribune*, 25 May 1997; 'No refuge in the land of the welcomes', *The Sunday Independent*, 19 July 1998; 'I hear it every day: Nigger, go home', *The Sunday Tribune*, 9 August 1998; 'Services swamped by a human tide', *The Sunday Independent*, 28 November 1999; 'Arson and abuse: Ireland's greeting for immigrants', *The Observer*, 19 August 2001; 'The victims of race hate's rising tide', *The Sunday Independent*, 18 June 2000; 'Violent deaths of non-nationals rise with growth of minority communities', *The Sunday Tribune*, 2 March 2003; 'Africans flee Ulster homes after attacks', *The Guardian*, 5 July 2003). However, a range of individuals, groups and organisations in Ireland are combating this racism (see Fanning, 2002). Lloyd (1999, p 106) has astutely observed, "As the Irish elites rush towards further

integration into the new, racialized 'Fortress Europe', and the incidence of racist violence against our own immigrant and minority communities climb, we emigrants need to reinvoke our colonized past" (see also Mac an Ghaill, 2002; Crowley and MacLaughlin 1997; Connolly and Keenan, 2002).

[9] This includes so-called Anti-Social Behaviour Orders (see Home Office, 2003). A Traveller education practitioner in Manchester has observed, "I am aware that significant numbers of Irish Traveller lads are being considered for Anti Social Behaviour Orders" (in Vanderbeck, 2003, p 377).

Conclusion

In Britain, social work has no memory. That is to say, the social work, as a constellation of discourses rhetorically founded on safeguarding and promoting the welfare of the vulnerable, often appears oddly amnesiac. Partly because of this condition, the profession has tended to lack interest in unearthing historical patterns of engagement with the Irish community in Britain. For this reason, this book began with an examination of social work's historical responses to Irish children and families in Britain. Initially, the focus was on how Irish women and their children were responded to in the 1950s and 1960s. It then went on to examine more contemporary responses; here, it was maintained that Irish children and families are largely rendered 'invisible' by mainstream discourses on 'race' and ethnicity. In the early 21st century, some changes are detectable. However, empirical research exploring the policies of social services departments (SSDs) throughout England and Wales and the perspective of a number of Irish social workers indicates that Irish children and families receiving services (and Irish providers of social work and social care services) are still not properly recognised.

This book can be seen, therefore, as a modest attempt to reshape British social work's dominant approach to issues of 'race' and ethnicity. In this sense, the aim has been to question the black/white binary that lies at the heart of the profession's approach. Although not a central concern in the foregoing discussion, social work's dominant theoretical understanding also fails adequately to conceptualise the situation of many recent migrants seeking refuge and asylum in Britain (see Castles and Davidson, 2000; Parker, J., 2000; Simms, 2004). Even worse, it provides political opportunists with the conceptual space to assert that punitive policies directed at refugees and asylum seekers are not racist because some of the people in these categories cannot be identified as 'black' (Yuval-Davis, 2001).

The tentative and concluding remarks presented in this chapter look at how some of the issues raised in the book might be addressed in the future both by social workers and those working in related fields of activity. Here, as Joe pointed out in Chapter Six, it is accepted that morale is apt to be low in SSDs and that issues related to 'race' and ethnicity are not, in the early 21st century, central concerns within the dominant managerialist approach (see Jones, 2001; Chief Secretary to the Treasury, 2003; Garrett, 2003). It is also acknowledged that a number of local authorities have to provide services for populations that are becoming increasingly diverse. With about 165,000 people, Hammersmith and Fulham, for example, is "one of London's smallest boroughs. However, more than 130 languages are spoken and 22% of residents describe themselves as from an ethnic minority, including a significant proportion of asylum seekers" (Salter, 2003, p 33).

Initially, the focus will be on how contemporary social theory might aid our understanding of issues related to cultural identity. It then moves on to try to identify how social work and more embracing discourses have recognised, or not recognised, Irish children and families in Britain during the period discussed in the book. This chapter argues that the Irish identities in Britain are complex, but that an emerging legal framework might contribute to the evolution of more appropriate policies and practices and to the ending of Irish 'invisibility'.

Irish children and families in Britain and the need to 'risk essentialism'

In acknowledging that social theory can help us to grapple with what have been some of this book's circulating concerns, there is no intention to retreat into a realm of intellectual abstraction divorced from practical realities. More fundamentally, the book remains committed to promoting changes to policy and practice. Here, it is simply suggested that some of the issues relating to social work and Irish children and families in Britain are highly complex. Thus, conceptualisations emerging from contemporary social theory can assist our understanding (see, for example, Calhoun, 1995; Hall and du Gay, 1996).

Clearly, one of the key arguments in this book is that social work and related social care professions need to begin to take account of the specificity of Irish children and families in Britain (see also Hickman and Walter, 1997). Throughout the discussion, it has been accepted, however, that Irish identities in Britain are socially constructed. As Manual Castells (1997, p 7) maintains:

> It is easy to agree on the fact that, from a sociological perspective, all identities are constructed. The real issue is how, from what, by whom, and for what. The construction of identities uses building materials from history, from geography, from biology, from productive and reproductive institutions, from collective memory and from personal fantasies, from power apparatuses and religious revelations. But individuals, social groups, and societies process all these materials, and re-arrange their meaning, according to social determinants and cultural projects that are rooted in their social structure, and in their space/time framework.

Put more succinctly, this book has not attempted to promote a simple understanding of Irish identity. Furthermore, throughout the discussion there has been an aversion to championing a crude interpretation of Irish cultural identity, which might then provide a resource for anyone seeking to install a reductive and arid approach to social work with Irish children and families in Britain. In addition, it remains important to recognise the temporal, economic and political contexts in which debates are unfolding and to look *beyond* social work. As Gilroy (2000, p 107), ever sceptical about recourse to essentialist notions of 'identity' and 'community', has asserted:

Identity has come to supply something of an anchor amid the turbulent waters of de-industrialization and the large-scale patterns of planetary re-construction that are hesitantly named 'globalisation'. It would appear that recovering or possessing an appropriately grounded identity can provide a means to hold these historic but anxiety-inducing processes at bay. Taking pride or finding sanctuary in an exclusive identity affords a means to acquire certainty about who one is and where one fits, about the claims of community and the limits of social obligation.

Wariness about the lure of 'certainty' when seeking to engage with questions of cultural identity remains vital. Moreover, the argument here is that the perspective of social theorists, such as Castells and Gilroy, should underpin how issues related to Irish children and families in Britain are framed by those seeking to destabilise the dominant approach to 'race' and ethnicity within social work and social welfare discourses in Britain.

Nonetheless, while being mindful of the complexities attached to this book's main themes, there are also risks, perhaps, associated with too great an emphasis on how identity is 'shifting', 'contingent' – socially constructed. That is to say, the deployment particularly of some post-structuralist influenced contributions on identity can perhaps be used to mask realities related to the experiences (and material disadvantages) of being Irish in Britain (Hickman and Walter, 1997). The comments of Kincheloe and Steinberg (1997), although written in an American context, are not untypical. They maintain that in "the postmodern condition individuals must wear several identities, as they travel in and out of multiple locales. Gone is the memory of 'genuine cultures' who pass along their mores and folkways unchanged to the next generation" (1997, p 216). Such interventions are, in part, helpful, but also rather banal and unconvincing. In this and similar contributions there is also a tendency to privilege travel and movement.

Similarly, no matter how much talk there might be about individuals possessing 'multiple' or 'competing' identities, Irish children and families still remain largely *absent* identities within social work's dominant perspective on 'race' and ethnicity. On account of this 'absence' (that is, this rendering of Irish children and families as 'invisible'), it is justifiable, therefore, to "risk essentialism" (Calhoun, 1995, p 17) when seeking to promote awareness and recognition[1]. In this sense, Calhoun's remarks on the strategy of several feminist thinkers are insightful and significant:

> They do not have in mind a simple return to uncontested categories or uncritical assumptions of the biological determination of true identity. Rather the point is to see that *under certain circumstances – mainly identified as political but I think arguably intellectual – self critical claims to strong basic and shared identity may be useful. At it simplest, the argument suggests that where a particular category of identity has been repressed, delegitimated or devalued in dominant discourses, a*

> vital response may be to claim value for those labelled by that category, thus implicitly invoking it an essentialist way. (1995, p 17; emphasis added)

Perhaps these remarks can also be understood as aligned with Spivak's acceptance of the utility of 'strategic essentialism'. Calhoun (1995, p 18) also counsels against allowing the "critique of essentialism" to become "a prohibition against the use of all general categories of identity".

As we have seen throughout the course of this book, Irish identities in Britain have certainly been repressed, delegitimated and devalued in social work and social welfare discourses in Britain. Moreover, there has also been wilful ignorance about how, historically, social work and social welfare professionals have often engaged with Irish families.

Recognition and Irish children and families in Britain

For a number of writers, questions of identity are enmeshed in what has been referred to as the 'politics of recognition' (Taylor, C., 1997). Moreover, some of the interventions in this debate can inform our understanding of social work with Irish children and families in Britain in the early 21st century. Charles Taylor (1997, p 75) has argued that identity

> designates something like a person's understanding of who they are, of their fundamental characteristics as a human being. The thesis is that our identity is partly shaped by recognition or its absence, often the misrecognition of others, and so a person or group of people can suffer real damage, real distortion if the people or society around them mirror back to them a confining or demeaning or contemptible picture of themselves. Non recognition can inflict harm, can be a form of oppression, imprisoning someone in a false, distorted or reduced mode of being.

For Taylor, therefore, the failure to recognise a "person's understanding of who they are they are, of their fundamental characteristics as a human being" is harmful, oppressive and prevents self-realisation. Honneth (2001) also relates recognition claims to a psychology of human needs. However, Fraser (2001) has made important contributions by her insistence that recognition must also be regarded as enmeshed in social justice issues and not, simply, ethics. For her, "misrecognition is wrong because it constitutes a form of institutionalized subordination – and thus, a serious violation of justice" (Fraser, 2001, p 26). Eschewing the type of 'psychologisation' that could be said to characterise the approach of Taylor and Honneth, she maintains:

> What makes misrecognition morally wrong ... is that it denies some individuals and groups the possibility of participating on a par with others in social interaction. The norm of *participation parity* invoked here ... locates the wrong in social relations, not in individual or interpersonal psychology.

To be misrecognized, in this view, is not simply to be thought ill of, looked down on, or devalued in others' conscious attitudes or mental beliefs. It is rather to be denied the status of a full partner in social interaction and prevented from participating as a peer in social life as a consequence of institutionalized patterns of cultural value that constitute one as comparatively unworthy of respect or esteem. (Fraser, 2001, p 26; emphasis in original; see also Fraser and Honneth, 2003)[2]

Accepting the importance of recognising a person's sense of identity and how this relates to the struggle for social justice, it is possible to go on to try to conceptualise how forms of recognition/misrecognition have had an impact on social work with Irish children and families in Britain during the period covered in this book. It is not possible, of course, easily to separate out the various types of recognition afforded to Irish children and families, yet for heuristic purposes it is possible perhaps to identify and track four approaches in the area of social work and, more broadly, social welfare[3].

First, we can observe a form of *adverse* or *negative recognition*. This type of recognition was founded on historically rooted stereotypes and typologies and it can be associated with the racialisation of Irish people in Britain and anti-Irish racism. Here, it was accepted that Irish people are a distinct national or cultural group in Britain. However, as a result of this type of recognition, policies and practices (methods of social welfare intervention) were put into place that led to Irish users of welfare services being stigmatised or penalised. Here we might refer, for example, to the policy of repatriating 'unmarried mothers' and to the discharge from care of Irish children to Ireland in the 1950s and 1960s. Related to this approach was the failure to engage with Irish children and families and a tendency to respond in a 'top-down' way that had little regard for service users' own wishes and feelings.

Second, it is possible to refer to *non-recognition* or *denial*. Within this perspective, Irish people in Britain are simply perceived as part of the dominant 'white' group, and this relates to what has been described as the black/white binary. This approach can be seen, perhaps, to have influenced child adoption policies pursued by Catholic adoption societies in the 1950s and 1960s when many English couples adopted Irish children. Catholic schools were also central in the evolving policies and practices that contributed to the 'denationalisation' of Irish children (Hickman, 1995). Non-recognition or denial of Irish specificity has also, of course, characterised the Department of Health approach to social work with Irish children and families. It is also a feature, as the Irish social workers described, of social work education's approach to the teaching of 'race', ethnicity and anti-discriminatory social work practice.

Third, it is possible to detect the evolution of *bureaucratic* or *'tick-box' recognition*. This emerging form of recognition is reflected, for example, in the new and problematic 'White Irish' category featured in the 2001 Census. Here, the aim is to integrate an Irish 'category' in monitoring procedures, but a failure to have the data generated impact on policy formulation, practice and the manner of engagement with the Irish community. This approach relies heavily on forms that require welfare professions to 'record' the ethnicity of service users by ticking boxes that can easily be put into and stored on computer databases (see, in this context, Garrett, 2003). Consequently, this approach does not engage with the complexity associated with personal accounts of Irish identity. A related problem with this form of recognition is that it perceives Irish people in Britain in a static and simplistic way and reflects a "tendency towards homogenising categorization" (Lewis, 2000, p 262). It is also possible to argue that this bureaucratic recognition can be associated with a more relaxed attitude on the part of the British State to Irish people as a result of the Peace Process in Northern Ireland. This type of recognition can be viewed as something of an improvement on the two other forms of recognition outlined, but it still results in an eviscerated form of recognition.

Finally, it might be suggested that *positive* or *complex recognition* represents an aspirational form of recognition. This approach retrieves elements of the approach associated with bureaucratic recognition: the desire to monitor and to assess the extent of vulnerability and need within the Irish community; but it seeks to make use of any data that is generated. More fundamentally, this approach seeks to *complicate* the monitoring task by stressing that a person's self-definition and own narrative of Irish identity is central. This approach is now also embedded in some of the more recent research literature focusing on Irish people in Britain, such as that undertaken under the auspices of the Irish 2 Project (see Walter et al, 2002b). Here, there is a meaningful engagement with individuals and with Irish community organisations. In terms of social work with Irish children and families, this approach seeks to restore the centrality of 'talk' in social work engagements with children and families (see, for example, Parton and O'Byrne, 2000). In more expansive terms, positive or complex recognition, however, is also located alongside a commitment to 'critical univeralism' (McLennan, 2001)[4].

Importantly, therefore, this form of recognition is underpinned by the acknowledgement that the Irish community is complex and diverse.

The complexity of Irish identities in Britain

> I had those long spells when by sort of instinct I knew who I really was, could stand aside and watch myself coming up the road after my day's work with relaxed and measured steps. (O'Connor, 1967, p 52)

It was argued earlier in this chapter that there was a need to 'risk essentialism' when seeking to promote recognition of the cultural specificity of Irish children and families in Britain. However, it is accepted that Irish identities in Britain are complex. Consequently, it is important that this understanding should form a basis for social workers' relationships with Irish children who might, for example, be 'looked after' under the 1989 Children Act and where issues related to 'identity' are being explored.

In Goldberg's *Multiculturalism: A critical reader*, Caws (1997, p 397) questions

> the emphasis on identity as something *needed*, hence, by implication as
> something *lacking*. The allegation of needs in cases like this – usually, it is to
> be noted, the needs of others (it is hard to imagine the people who make
> this kind of argument admitting to deficiencies in their own identities) –
> seem to me to run a great risk of being patronizing.

In contrast to Caws, here it is accepted that within social work, what is often
referred to as 'identity work' (involving, for example, the construction of 'life-
story' books) is often an important feature of work with children and young
people who are in public care, who may have no contact with birth parents
and who may be at risk of loosing a sense of their cultural heritage. How SSDs
and individual social workers seek to the address 'identity' questions related to
children 'looked after' is clearly vital (this question was explored in Chapter
Four). However, this area should not be approached in a crude or simplistic
manner, nor should professional engagement pivot on stereotypical, constraining
or anachronistic constructs of 'Irishness'. Here, it might be argued, as a number
of SSD directors and Irish social workers pointed out earlier, that the '*White*
Irish' category is unable to house the complexity of Irish identities in Britain
in the early 21st century. Equally important, the notion of bonds/bondage,
developed by Goldberg (1997, p 12), is pertinent. He asserts that identity is
generally conceived

> as a bond ... as the affinity and affiliation that associates those so identified,
> that extends to them a common sense or space of unified sameness. It is a
> tie that holds members of the collective together. These at least are the
> elements that may go into what might be deemed an affirmative conception
> of identity. [However, the bond] can also be bondage; the tie that holds
> someone in. It can keep people in who don't want to be in.

Waldron (2000, p 101) has observed that a person should have the freedom to
'renounce' their cultural heritage. Perhaps these comments can also be associated
with the remark of James Joyce's hero, Stephen Dedalus, in *A portrait of the artist
as a young man*. Dedalus famously declared:

> When a soul of a man is born in this country there are nets flung at it to
> hold it back from flight. You talk to me of nationality, language and religion.
> I shall try to fly these nets.

Fraser (2001, p 31) has also referred to what she terms "excessive ascribed or
constructed distinctiveness", and this is likely to impact on how a person
perceives themselves and their relationship to 'their' culture. Moreover, in this
context, it should, of course, be acknowledged that for some people from the
island of Ireland, living in Britain, cultural identity (because of issues related to

the Troubles in Northern Ireland) may be founded on a sense of 'Britishness' and a *renunciation* of Irish identity.

Clearly, there is a range of complexities and ambiguities associated with being Irish in the 'diaspora space' (Brah, 1996) that is Britain in the early 21st century. This was reflected in some of the comments of Irish social workers explored earlier[5]. Indeed, as Hickman (2002, p 22) has observed, "ethic repertoires are constructed within a context, which constrains what is available". She goes on:

> There has never been a way to be Irish British or British Irish in England, Wales or Scotland in the manner which people can claim to be Irish-American in a totally acceptable way. People of Irish descent in Britain who identify wholly or in part as Irish have had particular difficulties in that they have been excluded from public categories of multi-belongings in an increasingly multi-ethnic Britain.

However, many people with an Irish identity in Britain *do* perceive themselves as being located 'between camps' (Gilroy, 2000): both Irish and British, neither *entirely* Irish nor British. As the researchers involved in the Irish 2 Project have reported:

> We found that second-generation Irish identities lie at the *intersection* of two hegemonic national domains, each of which represents their Irish identifications as inauthentic. England/Britain cannot countenance any dilution of whiteness or weakening of the hegemonic national subject and thus insists on their Englishness, and Ireland rejects these 'hybrids' as not Irish and in fact English. Our data shows that there are a range of claims made by second-generation Irish people, from being English to being Irish, but many articulated allegiances to both domains. (Irish 2 Project, *Newsletter 3*, September 2002, p 2; see also Walter et al, 2002b)

Some of the comments in Chapter Six also highlight the cultural specificity of children and families who are Irish Travellers. Here, the comments of John, a social worker, about the risks of "freezing" the Travelling community and culture "in time" are important. There are, however, specific forms of oppression and disadvantage being encountered that social work and social care professions need to address. In this context, anti-Traveller racism, for example, is a distinct and virulent current within what Fekete (2001) has termed 'xeno-racism' in contemporary Britain. Anti-Irish Traveller racism appears to combine a culturally embedded anti-Irish racism with a more pervasive antipathy toward the unsettled, strangers and migrant populations (Bauman, 2002, pp 110-18; Hawes and Perez, 1995; see also 'Arrests for burning of "Gypsy caravan"', *The Guardian*, 12 November, 2003). Indeed, what is striking here is that exclusionary practices formerly directed at Irish people in general, but no longer countenanced, can still be directed at Irish Travellers[6].

What is to be done?

Having looked at some of the more abstract considerations relating to Irish children and families and their relationship with SSDs in Britain, and having called for a sensitive and reflexive approach to some of the issues raised, it is now appropriate to refer to how the law might frame policy and practice.

The UN Convention on the Rights of the Child suggests that social workers and other social care professionals should take the specificity of the cultural needs of children more seriously. In this sense, the preservation and promotion of an Irish child's sense of national and cultural identity can be situated within a more embracing human rights framework. Article 8 calls on states to "respect the right of the child to preserve his or her identity" including "nationality". Similarly, the substitute care of children calls for "due regard" to be paid to the "desirability of continuity in a child's ethnic, religious, cultural and linguistic background". The 1989 Children Act also directs SSDs to be alert to the significance of the cultural aspects of a young person's life, national background and cultural heritage.

Furthermore, the 2000 Race Relations (Amendment) Act (RRAA), which came into force in April 2001, should influence policy and practice with Irish children and families in Britain (see Home Office, 2002a)[7]. The RRAA, partly prompted by the Stephen Lawrence Inquiry, extends the "battle against racism in a new direction" (Home Office, 2002a, p 6). 'Institutional racism' is defined as:

> The collective failure of an organisation to provide an appropriate and professional service to people because of their colour, culture or ethnic origin. *It can be seen or detected in processes, attitudes, and behaviour which amount to discrimination through unwitting prejudice, ignorance and thoughtlessness and racist stereotyping which disadvantage* minority ethnic people. (Home Office, 2002b, p 1; emphasis added)

As we saw in Chapter Five, many SSDs are undertaking creative and sensitive work with Irish children and families, and it is clear that the Irish community has many allies who are strategically placed with social work and social care bureaucracies. However, this book also suggests that some SSDs risk being labelled as 'institutionally racist' on account of their responses to Irish children and families in Britain. This assertion, moreover, is not made in a causal or unduly emotive way, but it is a conclusion that it reached after simply scrutinising what is occurring in terms of policy and practice.

The RRAA placed new requirements on public bodies to have "due regard to the need to eliminate unlawful discrimination and to promote equality of opportunity and good relations between persons of different racial groups" (Home Office, 2002a, p 6). Under the legislation, public authorities also had a duty to produce Race Equality Schemes by the end of May 2002. This is a public statement about how authorities plan to meet their duties. These schemes, moreover, will be "living documents and will be reviewed on a regular basis" (Home Office, 2002a, p 5; see also 'Few councils have equality schemes', *Community Care*, 6-12 June, 2002, p 6). In these Racial Equality Schemes, public bodies such as SSDs have to set out clear arrangements for:

- assessing and consulting on the impact of 'race' equality of the proposed policies;
- monitoring any adverse impact of their policies on the promotion of 'race' equality;
- publishing the results of assessments, consultation and monitoring;
- ensuring public access to information and services; training staff on issues relevant to the duty.

The Commission for Racial Equality (CRE) can also take enforcement action against a public body failing to comply with its specific duties.

The RRAA, therefore, can provide one of the factors prompting change in relation to social work with Irish children and families in Britain. It is claimed, for example, that:

> Diversity and equality are central to the Government's policy on social services, and are the key to the provision of high quality services. Services should be available to all those who need them, and should take account of the 'race', culture and religion of users. (Home Office, 2002a, p 53)

Statements such as this, together with ideas about 'inclusive practice' (DoH et al, 2000) discussed in Chapters Four and Five could furnish, therefore, part of the foundation for change. Similarly, the Parekh report, as observed in the Introduction, might help to promote alternative ways of working in 'multi-ethnic' Britain, a community of communities (Commission on the Future of Multi-Ethnic Britain, 2000).

Clearly, social work does not exist in a social, political and intellectual vacuum. So, for example, a number of issues raised in this book call for changes across the social sciences and in public policy. However, in terms of the immediate future, how might SSDs begin to evolve better ways of working with Irish children and families in Britain? And this in the context of the social work and social care sector, more generally, being subject to change and 'modernisation' (Chief Secretary to the Treasury, 2003; Garrett, 2003; Secretary of State for Health and the Secretary of State for the Home Department, 2003)[8].

It is neither appropriate nor realistic, of course, to try to assemble a 'blueprint' for change, but some areas do seem to warrant particular attention. First, there needs to be more research undertaken with Irish children and families who are engaging with social work and children's services in Britain. As the government of the Republic of Ireland has recently observed, there is a clear need for more research, at both the macro and micro levels, into the needs of the Irish Abroad. This is vital in order to evaluate the nature and scale of the responses required. (Task Force on Policy regarding Emigrants, 2002)

This book, which is rather modest in scope and aspiration, has not featured, for example, a 'user dimension'; this would seem to be particularly important both in terms of the Irish community and the Irish Traveller community.

Second, mindful of some of the criticisms made earlier about 'bureaucratic or "tick-box" recognition', SSDs need to improve their monitoring of Irish ethnicity. In the context of fluid boundaries inside local authorities, this should also be reflected within other departments, such as Housing and Education and the envisaged Children's Trusts (Chief Secretary to the Treasury, 2003). Furthermore, monitoring should no longer be restricted to the use of a 'born-in-Ireland' category. Reference to Irish ethnicity should also be included in all equal opportunities/anti-discriminatory practice statements. This monitoring needs, moreover, to enhance service provision for Irish children and families and should not become an end in itself. The monitoring of Irish ethnicity should also extend to job applications and employment practices. This occurs in some places at present, but such initiatives can appear rather haphazard.

Third, there should be improvements in the area of education and training for social work and social care. For example, an Irish dimension should be covered in all equal opportunities/induction training for staff. In addition, a bibliography including Irish aspects of anti-discriminatory social work practice could form a part of the induction pack for new staff. An Irish dimension should be incorporated into anti-discriminatory training for other service providers, such as foster carers. Within social work education, the General Social Care Council should ensure that providers of social work courses embrace, at the level of theory and practice, recognition of Irish people in Britain. This should be mandatory for all institutional providers of social work education. Given the comments of some of the respondents in Chapter Six, it would also seem to be important for the various Irish Studies Centres in Britain to have some input into social work education and training. Irish social work staff are likely to be an invaluable resource and SSDs need to recognise this and draw on their experience and skills.

Fourth, there is a need for the government and senior professional organisations to begin to fulfil – resorting to the lexicon of managerialism – a 'leadership' role. Consequently, there should be more prominence given to Irish ethnicity in policy documents that tend, at present, to render Irish children and families 'invisible' in literature concerned with 'race' and ethnicity. Within influential bodies such as the Association of Directors of Social Services there should also be a willingness to foster and promote best practice and to highlight those SSDs working hard to provide culturally sensitive services for the Irish community. That association could also begin to engage more actively with national organisations that are seeking to promote the needs of Irish people in

Britain, such as the Federation of Irish Societies, the Action Group for Irish Youth and the Irish Equalities Working Group at the CRE. It should also be publicly committed to opposing anti-Irish racism. Relevant trade unions and similar associations within SSDs could also begin to formulate positions on issues relating to Irish people in Britain.

Finally, it is, of course, recognised that ethnicity is only one of the domains informing the social and psychological formation and wellbeing of children and young people (see Prevatt Goldstein, 2000). Nonetheless, this book's argument echoes that of Stuart Hall, when he maintains:

> We all speak from a particular place, out of a particular history, out of a particular experience, a particular culture.... We are all, in that sense, ethnically located and our ethnic identities are crucial to our subjective sense of who we are. (Hall, 1996, p 447)

This perspective is conceptually persuasive and should begin to inform public policy and social workers' engagement with Irish children and families in Britain.

Notes

[1] More broadly, Pearson (1994) appropriately highlights how there have been constant attempts to suppress Irish culture across history by Britain (see also, for example, Berresford Ellis, 1985, ch 3). Even within the privileged setting of self-proclaimed 'leading universities' in Britain, it is also not uncommon to hear anti-Irish remarks and comments that seek to belittle Irish staff.

[2] In relation to Fraser's approach, Bauman (2001, p 145) correctly observes:

> Placing the issue of recognition in the frame of social justice, instead of 'self-realization' (where, for instance, Charles Taylor and Axel Honneth prefer to put it) has a detoxicating effect: it removes the poison of sectarianism (with its unprepossessing consequences like social separation, communication breakdown and self-perpetuating hostilities) from the sting of recognition claims.

Walby (2001), however, has provided an incisive critique of Fraser's conceptualisation of recognition (see also Lister, 2001). Hall is right to claim, perhaps, that the "double demand for equality and difference appears to outrun our existing political vocabularies" (Hall, 2000, p 232; see also Williams, 1992).

[3] Here it is conceded that there is fluidity and overlap and these loosely constructed categories can operate concurrently.

[4] McLennan (2001, p 405) observes that it "is important to recover some element of critical universalism as both defensible and indispensable, all the more so in the context of the shared predicaments and perils that currently constitute our planetary prospect.

Differences need not be obliterated, nor cultural specificity disrespected, nor power relations left unexposed; but 1980s and 1990s thought underwrote difference at the expense of the commonalties which exist across human societies and individuals, and it is time to reverse that emphasis". This point is surely accurate, yet Irish 'difference' was, of course, *not* positively recognised in social work and social care discourses during the 1980s and 1990s. Eagleton's (1998, p 25) pithy comments on the celebration of 'difference', perhaps particularly within some areas of 'cultural studies', are also worth noting. He observes that "not all differences are positive, not all exclusions are pathological (excluding racists or neo-Nazis?), some forms of hybridity are painful and disabling, and by no means all strangers are to be welcomed. Occupying imperialist forces, for example".

[5] Brah (1996, pp 208-9) asserts:

> Diaspora space is the point at which boundaries of inclusion and exclusion, of belonging and otherness, of 'us' and 'them', are contested. My argument is that diaspora space as a conceptual category is 'inhabited', not only by those who have migrated and their descendants, but equally by those who are constructed and represented as indigenous. In other words, the concept of *diaspora space* (as opposed to that of diaspora) includes the entanglement, the intertwining of the genealogies of dispersion with those of 'staying put'. The diaspora space is the site where *the native is as much a diasporian as the diasporian is the native.* (emphases in original)

[6] This is, of course, starkly evidenced by the 'No Travellers' signs in pubs and shops, by dominant cultural representations and by the violence directed at the Irish Traveller community ('"Starve out travellers", says Tory councillor', *The Irish Post*, 6 March 1999; 'Sheffield pub in "no travellers" row', *The Irish Post*, 5 February 2000; see also 'Brutal death of travelling child', *The Guardian*, 10 June, 2003). Refer also to the portrayal, in the late 1990s, of a family of Irish Travellers involved in a so-called 'air rage' incident. Here what was significant was how even the more liberal broadsheets constructed the family (see the piece by John Sweeney 'Into the lair of the air rage travellers', *The Observer*, 7 February 1999; also 'Fighting family set to fly home', *The Guardian*, 3 February 1999). Vanderbeck (2003) discusses the representation of Travellers in the 'Tony Martin Affair'. In April 2000, Martin was convicted of the murder of 16-year-old Fred Barras, a Traveller, who had broken into his farmhouse.

[7] See also, however, reports of statements by the Home Secretary that act as a counterweight to this notion ('Blunkett: racism tag is aiding racists', *The Guardian*, 15 January 2003; 'Momentum in fight against racism "wanes"', *The Guardian*, 19 April 2003).

[8] In summer 2003, for example, responsibility for social work with children and families moved from the Department of Health to the Department for Education and Skills.

References

Abbotts, J., Williams, R., Ford, G., Hunt, K. and West, P. (1999) 'Morbidity and Irish Catholic descent in Britain: relating health disadvantage to behaviour', *Ethnicity and Health*, vol 4, no 4, pp 221-30.

Ackers, L. (1996) 'Internal migration and the negotiation of citizenship: the struggle for reproductive self-determination in Ireland', *Journal of Social Welfare and Family Law*, vol 18, no 4, pp 413-28.

Action Group for Irish Youth, The Bourne Trust, Federation of Irish Societies (1997) *The Irish community: Discrimination and the criminal justice system*, London: Irish Commission for Prisoners Overseas, National Association of Probation Officers.

ADSS (Association of Directors of Social Services) (2002) *Tomorrow's children: A discussion paper on UK child care services in the coming decade*, London: ADSS.

Airey, C., Bruster, S., Erens, B., Lilley, S.J., Pickering, K. and Pitson, L. (1998) *National surveys of NHS patients: General practice 1998*, London: National Centre for Social Research.

Akenson, D. (1996) *The Irish diaspora: A primer*, Belfast: Institute of Irish Studies.

Aldridge, M. and Wood, J. (2000) 'Interviewing child witnesses with memorandum guidelines', *Children & Society*, vol 14, pp 168-81.

Allen, K. (1999) 'The Celtic Tiger, inequality and social partnership', *Administration*, vol 47, no 2, pp 31-55.

Allen, T.W. (1994) *The invention of the White Race. Volume one: Racial oppression and social control*, London: Verso.

Alleyne, B. (2002) 'An idea of community and its discontents: towards a more reflexive sense of belonging in multicultural Britain', *Ethnic and Racial Studies*, vol 25, no 4, pp 607-27.

Alexander, C. and Alleyne, B. (2002) 'Framing difference: racial and ethnic studies in twenty-first-century Britain', *Ethnic and Racial Studies*, vol 25, no 4, pp 541-51.

Alexander, Z. (1999) *Study of Black, Asian and ethnic minority issues*, London: DoH.

Alibhai-Brown, Y. (2000) 'Muddled leaders and the future of British national identity', *The Political Quarterly*, vol 71, no 1, pp 26-31.

Anderson, B. (1991) *Imagined communities*, London: Verso.

Anthias, F. (2002) 'Where do I belong? Narrating collective identity and translocational positionality', *Ethnicities*, vol 2, no 4, pp 491-514.

Anthias, F. and Yuval-Davis, N. (1993) *Racialised boundaries*, London: Routledge.

Armstrong, S. (1996) 'Driving people to drink', *The Guardian*, 23 September, p 21.

Arnold, M. and Laskey, H. (1985) *Children of the poor Clares: The story of an Irish orphanage*, Belfast: Appletree Press.

Arrowsmith, A. (1999) 'Debating diasporic identity: nostalgia (post) nationalism, "critical traditionalism"', *Irish Studies Review*, vol 7, no 2, pp 173-83.

Aspinall, P.J. (2002) 'Collective terminology to describe minority ethnic populations: the persistence of confusion and ambiguity in usage', *Sociology*, vol 36, no 4, pp 803-17.

Atkinson, P., Coffey, A. and Delamont, S. (2001) 'A debate on our canon', *Qualitative Research*, vol 1, no 1, pp 5-21.

Atkinson, P. and Silverman, D. (1997) 'Kundera's immortality: the interview society and the invention of the self', *Qualitative Inquiry*, vol 3, no 3, pp 304-25.

Banks, S. (1995) *Ethics and values in social work*, Houndsmill: Macmillan.

Barn R., Sinclair, R. and Ferdinand, D. (1997) *Acting on principle: An examination of race and ethnicity in social services provision for children and families*, London: British Agencies for Adoption and Fostering.

Barrett, C.J. (1952) *Adoption*, Dublin: Clonmore and Reynolds.

Barrett, C.J. (1955) 'The dependent child', *Studies*, vol 44, pp 419-28.

Barton, A. (2000) 'Wayward girls and wicked women: two centuries of "semi-penal" control', *Liverpool Law Review*, vol 22, pp 157-71.

Bauman, Z. (2001) 'The great war of recognition', *Theory, Culture & Society*, vol 18, no 2-3, pp 137-50.

Bauman, Z. (2002) *Society under siege*, Oxford: Polity.

Berresford Ellis, P. (1985) *A history of the Irish working class*, London: Pluto.

Bew, P. and Patterson, H. (1982) *Sean Lemass and the making of modern Ireland 1945-66*, Dublin: Gill & Macmillan.

Biestek, F.P. (1975) 'Client self-determination', in F.E. McDermott (ed) *Self determination in social work*, London: Routledge & Kegan Paul, pp 17-33.

Bishop, M.C. (1877) 'The social methods of Roman Catholicism in England', *The Contemporary Review*, March, pp 603-35.

Bloch, A. and Schuster, L. (2002) 'Asylum and welfare: contemporary debates', *Critical Social Policy*, vol 22, no 3, pp 393-415.

Bonnett, A. (2000) *White identities: Historical and international perspectives*, Harlow: Prentice Hall.

Bourdieu, P. (2002) *The weight of the world: Social suffering in contemporary society* (1st reprint), Cambridge: Polity Press.

Bowlby, J. (1990) *Child care and the growth of love* (3rd edn), Harmondsworth: Penguin.

Brah, A. (1992) 'Difference, diversity and differentiation', in J. Donald and A. Rattansi (eds) *'Race', culture and difference*, London: Sage Publications, pp 126-46.

Brah, A. (1996) *Cartographies of diaspora: Contesting identities*, London: Routledge.

Brah, A., Hickman, M.J. and Mac an Ghaill, M. (1999) *Global futures: Migration, environment and globalisation*, Houndsmill: Macmillan.

Braziel, J.A. and Mannur, A. (2003) *Theorizing diaspora*, Oxford: Blackwell.

Breen, R., Hannan, D., Rottman, D. and Wheelan, C. (1990) *Understanding contemporary Ireland*, Dublin: Gill & Macmillan.

Brooks, D., Barth, B.P., Bussiere, A. and Patterson, G. (1999) 'Adoption and race: implementing the Multiethnic Placement Act and interethnic adoption provisions', *Social Work*, vol 44, no 2, pp 167-79.

Bunting, M. (1998) 'The old man and the See', *The Guardian*, 24 February, pp 2-4.

Busteed, M. (1999) 'Little islands of Erin: Irish settlement and identity in mid-nineteenth-century Manchester', *Immigrants & Minorities*, vol 18, no 2-3, pp 94-128.

Byrne, D. (1999) *Social exclusion*, Buckingham: Open University Press.

Calhoun, C. (ed) (1995) *Social theory and the politics of identity* (1st reprint), Oxford: Blackwell.

Campbell, S. (1999) 'Beyond the "plastic Paddy": a re-examination of the second generation Irish in England', *Immigrants & Minorities*, vol 18, no 2-3, pp 268-89.

Carey, M. (2002) 'Six deaths and no answers', *Magill*, September, pp 15-19.

Carr, M. (1999) *Assessment report on the health and social needs of Travellers in Ealing*, London: London Borough of Ealing Social Services/Ealing and Hounslow Health Authority.

Castells, M. (1997) *The information Age: Economy, society and culture. Volume 2: The power of identity*, Oxford: Blackwell.

Castles, S. and Davidson, A. (2000) *Citizenship and migration*, London: Macmillan.

Caws, P. (1997) 'Identity: cultural, transcultural, and multicultural', in D.T. Goldberg (ed) *Multiculturalism: A critical reader* (3rd reprint), Oxford: Blackwell, pp 371-88.

CCETSW (Central Council for Education and Training in Social Work) (1995) *Assuring quality in the Diploma in Social Work 1. Rules and requirements for the DipSW*, London: CCETSW.

Cemlyn, S. (2000) 'Assimilation, control, mediation or advocacy? Social work dilemmas in providing anti-oppressive services for traveller children and families', *Child and Family Social Work*, vol 5, pp 327-41.

Cheetham, J. (1972) *Social work with immigrants*, London: Routledge & Kegan Paul.

Chief Secretary to the Treasury (2003) *Every child matters*, London: The Stationery Office (www.dfes.gov.uk/everychildmatters).

Clark, S. (1993) 'Adoption decision gets DoH approval', *Community Care*, vol 16, September, p 3.

Cleaver, H. and Freeman, P. (1995) *Parental perspectives in cases of suspected child abuse*, London: HMSO.

Collins, B. and Hanafin, P. (2001) 'Mothers, maidens and the myth of origins in the Irish Constitution', *Law and Critique*, vol 12, pp 53-73.

Colton, M. (1989) 'Foster and residential children's perceptions of their social environments', *British Journal of Social Work*, vol 19, pp 217-35.

Commission on Emigration and Other Population Problems (1955) *Commission on Emigration and Other Population Problems 1948-54 Reports*, Dublin: The Stationery Office.

Committee on the Criminal Law Amendment Acts (1931) *Report of the Committee on the Criminal Law Amendment Acts 1880-85 and Juvenile Prostitution* (1931) Dublin: The Stationery Office (document held at the National Archives in Dublin, ref S5998).

Commission on the Future of Multi-Ethnic Britain (2000) *The future of multi-ethnic Britain*, London: Runnymede Trust.

Commission on the Relief of the Sick and Destitute Poor, including the Insane Poor (1927) *Report of the Commission on the Relief of the Sick and Destitute Poor, including the Insane Poor*, Dublin: The Stationery Office.

Connolly, P. and Keenan, M. (2002) 'Racist harassment in the white hinterlands: minority ethnic children and parents' experience of schooling in Northern Ireland', *British Journal of Sociology of Education*, vol 23, no 3, pp 341-56.

Committee of Inquiry into the Care and Supervision Provided in Relation to Maria Colwell (1974) *Report of the Committee of Inquiry into the Care and Supervision Provided in Relation to Maria Colwell*, London: HMSO.

Conroy Jackson, P. (1992) 'Outside the jurisdiction: Irish women seeking abortion', in A. Smyth (ed) *The abortion papers*, Dublin: Attic Press, pp 119-38.

Cope, H. (2001) *Still beyond the Pale? The response of social landlords to the housing and related needs of London's Irish community*, London: Irish Housing Forum.

Coulter, C. and Coleman, S. (eds) (2003) *The end of Irish history? Critical reflections on the Celtic Tiger*, Manchester: Manchester University.

Coulter, J. (2003) 'Ireland – the orange swastika: the rise of a new millennium Loyalist Nazism', *Searchlight*, November, pp 28-30.

CPRSI (Catholic Protection and Rescue Society of Ireland) (nd) *Annual reports* (1914-73), Dublin: CPRSI.

CRE (Commission for Racial Equality) (1995) *Racial equality means quality: A standard for local government in England and Wales*, London: CRE.

CRE (1997) *The Irish in Britain*, London: CRE.

Creegan, M.F. (1967) 'Unmarried mothers: an analysis and discussion of interviews conducted in an Irish Mother and Baby Home', Unpublished MSocSc Dissertation, Dublin: University College Dublin.

Crowley, E. and MacLaughlin, J. (eds) (1997) *Under the belly of the tiger: Class, race, identity and culture in a global Ireland*, Dublin: Irish Reporter Publications.

Culchane, R. (1950) 'Irish Catholics in Britain', *The Furrow*, vol 1, no 8, pp 387-415.

Cullen, M. (1991) 'Women's history in Ireland', in K. Offen et al (eds) *Writing women's history*, Bloomington and Indianapolis: Indiana University Press, pp 429-42.

Curtis, L.P. (1997) *Apes and angels in Victorian caricature* (revised edn), Washington, DC: Smithsonian Institute.

D'Cruz, H. (2000) 'Social work research as knowledge/power in practice', *Sociological Research Online*, vol 5, no 1 (www.socresonline.org.uk/5/1/dcruz.html).

Delaney, E. (1999) '"Almost a class of helots in an alien land": the British state and Irish immigration, 1921-45', *Immigrants and Minorities*, vol 18, no 2-3, pp 240-65.

Delaney, E. (2000) *Demography, state and society: Irish migration to Britain, 1921-1971*, Liverpool: Liverpool University Press.

Denzin, N.K. (2001) 'The reflexive interview and a performative social science', *Qualitative Research*, vol 1, no 1, pp 23-46.

Department of Local Government and Public Health *Annual Reports (1928-45)*, Dublin: The Stationery Office.

Devine, T. (ed) (2000) *Scotland's shame? Bigotry and sectarianism in modern Scotland*, Edinburgh: Mainstream Publishing.

Diaz, R. (2000) *Irish people and housing – Factsheet*, London: Shelter.

DoH (Department of Health) (1990) *The care of children: Principles and practice in regulations and guidance*, London: HMSO.

DoH (1991) *Patterns & outcomes in child placement*, London: HMSO.

DoH (1998) *Adoption – Achieving the right balance*, LAC (98) 20, London: The Stationery Office.

DoH (1999) *Adoption now: Messages for the research*, Chichester: Wiley.

DoH (2000) 'Social services for children from ethnic minorities must be improved', Press Notice, 11 July.

DoH (2001) 'Minister welcomes report on ethnic health inequalities', Press Notice, 24 January.

DoH, DfEE, HO (Department of Health, Department for Education and Employment, Home Office) (2000) *Framework for the assessment of children in need and their families*, London: The Stationery Office.

Dominelli, L. (1996) 'Deprofessionalising social work: anti-oppressive practice, competencies and postmodernism', *British Journal of Social Work*, vol 26, pp 153-75.

Dominelli, L., Lorenz, W. and Soydan, H. (eds) (2001) *Beyond racial divides: Ethnicities in social work practice*, Aldershot: Ashgate.

Douglas, R.M. (2002) 'Anglo-Saxons and Attacotti: the racialization of Irishness in Britain between the World Wars', *Ethnic and Racial Studies*, vol 1, pp 40-63.

Downey, R. (1997) 'Access refused', *Community Care*, 10-16 July, p 12.

Doyle, A. (2002) 'Ethnocentrism and history textbooks: representation of the Irish Famine 1845-49 in history textbooks in English secondary schools', *Intercultural Education*, vol 13, no 3, pp 315-31.

Drakeford, M. and Morris, S. (1998) 'Social work with linguistic minorities', in C. Williams, H. Soydan and M.R.D. Johnson (eds) *Social work and minorities*, London: Routledge, pp 93-110.

Dudley Edwards, R. (1998) 'Britain blameless says historian', *The Irish Post*, 12 December, p 32.

Duncan, D. (2002) 'A flexible foundation: constructing a postcolonial dialogue', in D.T. Goldberg and A. Quayson (ed) *Relocating postcolonialism*, Oxford: Blackwell, pp 320-34.

Dunne, T. (2002-03) 'Penitents', *The Dublin Review*, vol 9, pp 74-83.

Dutt, R. and Phillips, M. (2000) 'Assessing black children and their families', in DoH *Assessing children in need and their families: Practice guidance*, London: The Stationery Office.

Duvell, F. and Jordan, B. (2002) 'Immigration, asylum and welfare: the European context', *Critical Social Policy*, vol 22, no 3, pp 498-518.

Dyer, R. (1997) *White*, London: Routledge.

Eagleton, T. (1998) 'Postcolonialism and "postcolonialism"', *Interventions*, vol 1, no 1, pp 24-6.

Earner-Byrne, L. (2003) 'The boat to England: an analysis of the official reactions to the emigration of single expectant Irishwomen to Britain, 1922-1972', *Irish Economic and Social History*, vol 30, pp 52-70.

Edge, S. (1995) 'Women are trouble, did you know that Fergus?', *Feminist Review*, vol 50, pp 173-86.

Eisenstadt, N. (1998) 'Changing times', *Community Care*, 3-9 September, p 16.

Engels, F. (1926) *The condition of the working class in England in 1844*, London: Allen & Unwin (trans F.K. Wischnewetzky).

Fanning, B. (2002) *Racism and social change in Ireland*, Manchester: Manchester University.

Farrell, E. (1996) *The hidden minority: Mental health and the Irish experience in Britain*, London: Brent Irish Advisory Service and Equal Access.

Fekete, L. (2001) 'The emergence of xeno-racism', *Race & Class*, vol 43, no 2, pp 23-40.

Ferguson, S. and Fitzgerald, H. (1954) *History of the Second World War: Studies in the social services*, London: HMSO and Longmont.

Fielding, S. (1993) *Class and ethnicity: Irish Catholics in England 1880-1939*, Buckingham: Oxford University Press.

Fink, J. (2000) 'Natural mothers, putative fathers and innocent children: the definition and regulation of parental relationships outside of marriage, in England, 1945-1959', *Journal of Family History*, vol 25, no 2, pp 178-95.

Fink, J. and Holden, K. (1999) 'Pictures from the margins of marriage: representations of spinsters and single mothers in the mid-Victorian novel, inter-war Hollywood melodrama and British film of the 1950s and 1960s', *Gender and History*, vol 11, no 2, pp 233-55.

Fish, S. (1997) 'Boutique multiculturalism or why liberals are incapable of thinking about hate speech', *Critical Inquiry*, Winter, pp 378-96.

Fletcher, R. (1995) 'Silences: Irish women and abortion', *Feminist Review*, vol 50, pp 44-66.

Forrest, D. (2000) 'Theorising empowerment thought: illuminating the relationship between ideology and politics in the contemporary era', *Sociological Research Online*, vol 4, no 4 (www.socresonline.org.uk/4/4/forrest.html).

Foster, J.H. (2003) 'The Irish alcohol misuser in England: ill served by research and policy? Some suggestions for future research opportunities', *Drugs: Education, Prevention and Policy*, vol 10, no 1, pp 57-64.

Fraser, N. (2000) 'Rethinking recognition', *New Left Review*, May/June, pp 107-21.

Fraser, N. (2001) 'Recognition without ethics', *Theory, Culture & Society*, vol 18, no 21-42.

Fraser, N. and Honneth, A. (2003) *Redistribution or recognition: A political–philosophical exchange*, London: Verso.

Gaffney, M. (2001) *Needs analysis of the Travelling community in Southwark*, London: Social Inclusion Unit, London Borough of Southwark.

Garrett, P.M. (1998) 'Notes from the diaspora: anti-discriminatory social work practice, Irish people and the practice curriculum', *Social Work Education*, vol 17, no 4, pp 435-49.

Garrett, P.M. (1999) 'Mapping child-care social work in the final years of the twentieth century: a critical response to the "looking after children" system', *British Journal of Social Work*, vol 29, pp 27-47.

Garrett, P.M. (2000) 'Responding to Irish "invisibility": anti-discriminatory social work practice and the placement of Irish children in Britain', *Adoption & Fostering*, vol 24, no 1, pp 23-34.

Garrett, P.M. (2002) 'Getting "a grip": New Labour and the reform of the law on child adoption', *Critical Social Policy*, vol 22, no 22, pp 174-202.

Garrett, P.M. (2003) *Remaking social work with children and families*, London: Taylor & Francis.

Garvin, T. (1996) *1922: The birth of Irish democracy*, Dublin: Gill & Macmillan.

Gibbon, P. (1973) 'Arensberg and Kimball revisited', *Economy and Society*, vol 2, pp 279-432.

Gibbon, P. and Curtin, C. (1978) 'The Stem family in Ireland', *Comparative Studies in Society and History*, vol 20, pp 429-53.

Giles, J. and Middleton, T. (eds) (1995) *Writing Englishness, 1900-1950: An introductory sourcebook on national identity*, London: Routledge.

Gilley, S. (1999) 'Roman Catholicism and the Irish in England', *Immigrants & Minorities*, vol 18, nos 2-3, pp 147-68.

Gilroy, P. (1994) 'Forward', in I. Gaber and J. Aldridge (eds) *In the best interests of the child: Culture, identity and transracial adoption*, London: Free Association, pp ix–xiii.

Gilroy, P. (2000) *Between camps: Nations, cultures and the allure of race*, Harmondsworth: Penguin.

Gilzean, N. and McAuley, J. (2002) 'Strangers in a strange land?: (Re)constructing "Irishness" in a northern English town', *Irish Journal of Sociology*, vol 11, no 2, pp 54-77.

Giroux, H.A. (1997) 'Insurgent multiculturalism and the promise of pedagogy', in D.T. Goldberg (ed) *Multiculturalism: A critical reader* (3rd reprint), Oxford: Blackwell, pp 325-44.

Gledhill, A. (1989) *Who cares?*, London: Centre for Policy Studies.

Glynn, Sir J. (1921) 'The unmarried mother', *Irish Ecclesiastical Record*, vol xviii, pp 461-7.

Godfrey, W. (1956) 'The Irish emigrant: apostle of the faith in England', *Christus Rex*, vol 10, no 4, pp 358-66.

Goldberg, D.T. (ed) (1997) *Multiculturalism: A critical reader* (3rd reprint), Oxford: Blackwell, pp 325-44.

Goulding, J. (1999) *The light in the window* (2nd reprint), Dublin: Poolbeg.

Graham, C. and Maley, W. (1999) 'Introduction: Irish studies and postcolonial theory', *Irish Studies Review*, vol 7, no 2, pp 149-53.

Gray, B. (1996) 'The home of our mothers and our birthright for ages? Nation, diaspora and Irish women', in M. Maynard and P. Purvis (eds) *New frontiers in women's studies: Knowledge, identity and nationalism*, London: Taylor and Francis, pp 164-87.

Gray, B. (1997) 'Unmasking Irishness: Irish women, the Irish nation and the Irish diaspora', in J. MacLaughlin (ed) *Location and dislocation in contemporary Irish society*, Cork: Cork University Press, pp 209-32.

Gray, B. (2000) 'Gendering the Irish diaspora: questions of enrichment, hybridization and return', *Women's International Review*, vol 23, no 2, pp 167-85.

Gray, B. (2002) 'The Irish diaspora: globalised belonging(s)', *Irish Journal of Sociology*, vol 11, no 2, pp 123-45.

Gray, B. (2003) *Women in the Irish diaspora*, London: Routledge.

Gray, P. (1999) 'Shovelling out your paupers: the British state and Irish famine migration 1846-50', *Patterns of Prejudice*, vol 33, no 4, pp 47-65.

Greenslade, L. (1992) 'White skin, white masks: psychological distress among the Irish in Britain' in P. O'Sullivan (ed) *The Irish in the new communities*, London: Leicester University.

Gudmundsdottir, S. (1996) 'The teller, the tale and the one being told: the narrative nature of the research interview', *Curriculum Inquiry*, vol 26, no 3, pp 293-307.

Hall, M.P. (1960) *The social services of modern England*, London: Routledge & Kegan Paul.

Hall, S. (1990) 'Cultural identity and diaspora', in J. Rutherford (ed) *Identity: Community, culture, difference*, London: Lawrence and Wishart, pp 222-38.

Hall, S. (1996) 'New ethnicities', in D. Morley and Kuan-Hsing Chen (eds) *Stuart Hall: Critical dialogues in cultural studies*, London: Routledge, pp 441-50.

Hall, S. (2000) 'Conclusion: the multi-cultural question', in B. Hesse (ed) *Un/settled multiculturalisms: Diasporas, entanglements, transruptions*, London: Zed Books, pp 209-42.

Hall, S. and du Gay, P. (eds) (1996) *Questions of cultural identity*, London: Sage Publications.

Hall, S., Critcher, C., Jefferson, T., Clarke, J. and Roberts, R. (1978) *Policing the crisis: Mugging, the state and law and order*, London: Macmillan.

Harlow, E. and Hearn, J. (1996) 'Educating for anti-oppressive and anti-discriminatory social work practice', *Social Work Education*, vol 15, no 1, pp 5-18.

Harrison, L. and Carr-Hill, R. (1992) *Alcohol and disadvantage among the Irish in Britain*, London: Federation of Irish Societies.

Hawes, D. and Perez, B. (1995) *The gypsy and the state: The ethnic cleansing of British society*, Bristol: SAUS Publications.

Helleiner, J. (1997) 'Women of the itinerant class: gender and anti-Traveller racism in Ireland', *Women's Studies International Forum*, vol 20, no 2, pp 275-87.

Helleiner, J. (1998) 'Contested childhood: the discourse and politics of Traveller childhood in Ireland', *Childhood*, vol 5, no 3, pp 303-25.

Hendrick, H. (1990) 'Constructions and reconstructions of British childhood: an interpretative survey, 1800 to the present', in A. James and A. Prout (eds) *Constructing and reconstructing childhood: Contemporary issues in the sociological study of childhood*, London: Farmer, pp 34-63.

Hickman, M.J. (1993) 'Integration or segregation? The education of the Irish in Britain in Roman Catholic voluntary-aided schools', *British Journal of Sociology of Education*, vol 14, no 3, pp 285-301.

Hickman, M.J. (1995) *Religion, race and identity*, Aldershot: Avebury.

Hickman, M.J. (1998) 'Reconstructing deconstructing "race": British political discourses about the Irish in Britain', *Ethnic and Racial Studies*, vol 21, no 2, pp 288-307.

Hickman, M.J. (2002) 'Locating the Irish diaspora', *Irish Journal of Sociology*, vol 11, no 2, pp 8-27.

Hickman, M.J. and Walter, B. (1995) 'Deconstructing whiteness', *Feminist Review*, vol 50, pp 5-20.

Hickman, M.J. and Walter, B. (1997) *Discrimination and the Irish community in Britain*, London: CRE.

Hickman, M.J., Morgan, S. and Walter, B. (2001) *Second generation Irish people in Britain: A demographic, socio-economic and health profile*, London: Irish Studies Centre, University of North London.

Hillyard, P. (1993) *Suspect community*, London: Pluto.

Hirst, J. (1997) 'New ways', *Community Care*, 13-19 February, pp 18-20.

Hobsbawm, E. (1994) *Age of extremes: The short twentieth century 1914-1991*, London: Michael Joseph.

Hobsbawm, E. (1996) 'Identity politics and the left', *New Left Review*, vol 217, pp 38-48.

Home Office (2002a) *Race equality in public services*, London: Home Office.

Home Office (2002b) *Training in racism awareness and cultural diversity*, London: Home Office.

Home Office (2003) *Respect and responsibility – Taking a stand against anti-social behaviour*, London: Home Office.

Honneth, A. (2001) 'Recognition of redistribution? Changing perspectives on the moral order of society', *Theory, Culture & Society*, vol 18, no 2-3, pp 43-55.

Hopton, J. (1997) 'Anti-discriminatory practice and anti-oppressive practice', *Critical Social Policy*, vol 17, no 3, pp 47-61.

Hosegood, C. (1993) 'Issues in the adoption of Irish children', *Adoption and Fostering*, vol 17, no 1, pp 37-40.

Houston, S. (2002) 'Reflecting on habitus, field and capital: towards a culturally sensitive social work', *Journal of Social Work*, vol 2, no 2, pp 149-67.

Howe, D., Sawbridge, P. and Hinings, D. (1992) *Half a million women*, Harmondsworth: Penguin.

Humphries, S. (1988) *A secret world of sex*, London: Sedgewick and Jackson.

Hunter, M. (2002) 'Search for redress', *Community Care*, 19-25 September, pp 34-6.

Ingman, H. (2002) 'Edna O'Brien: stretching the nation's boundaries', *Irish Studies Review*, vol 10, no 3, pp 253-66.

Joint Committee of the Royal College of Obstetricians and Gynaecologists and the Population Investigation Committee (1948) *Maternity in Great Britain: A survey of social and economic aspects of pregnancy and childbirth*, London: Oxford University.

Jones, C. (2001) 'Voices from the front line: state social workers and New Labour', *British Journal of Social Work*, vol 31, pp 547-62.

Jordan, E. (2001) 'From interdependence to dependence and independence: home and school learning for Traveller children', *Childhood*, vol 8, no 1, pp 57-74.

Kanya-Forstner, M. (1999) 'Defining womanhood: Irish women and the Catholic Church in Victorian Liverpool', *Immigrants & Minorities*, vol 18, no 2-3, pp 168-89.

Kearney, R. (1997) *Postnationalist Ireland: Politics, culture, philosophy*, London: Routledge.

Keating, A. (2003) 'The legalisation of adoption in Ireland', *Studies*, vol 92 (www.jesuit.ie/studies/articles/2003/030601a.htm).

Kelleher, P., Kelleher, C. and Corbett, M. (2000) *Left out on their own: Young people leaving care in Ireland*, Dublin: Oak Tree Press.

Kelly, K. and Nic Giolla Choille, T. (1997) 'Listening and learning; experiences in an emigrant advice agency', in P. O'Sullivan (ed) *Irish women and Irish migration*, London: Leicester University, pp 68-192.

Kenny, K. (2003) 'Diaspora and comparison: the global Irish as a case study', *Journal of American History*, June, pp 134-63.

Kiberd, D. (1996) *Inventing Ireland: The literature of the modern nation*, London: Vintage.

Kincheloe, J.L. and Steinberg, S.R. (1997) *Changing multiculturalism*, Buckingham: Open University.

Kinealy, C. (1994) *The great calamity: The Irish Famine 1845-52*, Dublin: Gill & Macmillan.

Kirkby, P., Gibbons, L. and Cronin, M. (2002a) 'Introduction: the reinvention of Ireland: a critical perspective', in P. Kirkby, L. Gibbons, M. Cronin (eds) (2002) *Reinventing Ireland: Culture, society and the global economy*, London: Pluto, pp 1-21.

Kirkby, P., Gibbons, L. and Cronin, M. (2002b) *Reinventing Ireland: Culture, society and the global economy*, London: Pluto.

Kirton, D. (1996) 'Race and adoption', *Critical Social Policy*, vol 16, no 1, pp 123-37.

Kirton, D. (2000) *'Race', ethnicity and adoption*, Buckingham: The Open University.

Knight, T. and Caveney, S. (1998) 'Assessment and action records: will they promote good parenting?', *British Journal of Social Work*, vol 28, pp 29-43.

Kowarzik, U. (1994) *Developing a community response: The service needs of the Irish community*, London: Action Group for Irish Youth/Federation of Irish Societies.

Kowarzik, U. (1997) *Irish community services: Meeting diverse needs*, London: Action Group for Irish Youth/Federation of Irish Societies.

Kuhn, T. (1962) *The structure of scientific revolutions*, Chicago, IL: University of Chicago.

Kvale, S. (1996) *Interviews: An introduction to qualitative research interviewing*, London: Sage Publications.

Lash, S. and Featherstone, M. (2002) 'Recognition and difference: politics, identity, multiculture', *Theory, Culture & Society*, vol 18, no 2-3, pp 1-19.

Lea, J. (2000) 'The Macpherson Report and the question of institutional racism', *The Howard Journal*, vol 39, no 3, pp 219-33.

Lee, J. (1991) 'The Irish Constitution of 1937', in S. Hutton and P. Stewart (eds) *Ireland's histories: Aspects of state, society and ideology*, London: Routledge, pp 80-94.

Lennon, M., McAdam, M. and O'Brien, J. (1988) *Across the water: Irish women's lives in Britain*, London: Virago.

Lentin, R. (2001) 'Responding to the racialisation of Irishness: disavowed multiculturalism and its discontents', *Sociological Research Online*, vol 5, no 4 (www.socresonline.org.uk/5/4lentin.html).

Leonard, P. (2000) *Postmodern welfare: Reconstructing an emancipatory project* (1st reprint), London: Sage Publications.

Lewis, G. (2000) 'Discursive histories, the pursuit of multiculturalism and social policy', in G. Lewis, S. Gewirtz and J. Clarke (eds) *Rethinking social policy*, London: Sage Publications/Open University.

Lewis, J. (1986) 'Anxieties about the family and the relationships between parents, children and the state in twentieth century England', in M. Richards and P. Light (eds) *Children of social worlds: Development in a social context*, Cambridge: Polity Press, pp 31-55.

Lister, R. (2001) 'Towards a citizens' welfare: the 3+2 Rs of welfare reform', *Theory, Culture & Society*, vol 18, no 2-3, pp 91-111.

Lloyd, D. (1999) *Ireland after history*, Cork: Cork University Press.

Lloyd, G. and Stead, J. (2001) 'The boys and girls not calling me names and the teachers to believe me: name calling and the experiences of Travellers in school', *Children & Society*, vol 15, pp 361-74.

Logan, J. (1996) 'Birth mothers and their mental health: uncharted territory', *British Journal of Social Work*, vol 26, pp 609-35.

Luddy, M. (1995) *Women and philanthropy in nineteenth-century Ireland*, Cambridge: Cambridge University Press.

Luddy, M. and Murphy, C. (eds) (1990) *Women surviving*, Dublin: Poolbeg Press.

Lunn, K. (1992) 'Irish labour recruitment schemes 1937-1948', *Labour History Review*, vol 57, no 3, pp 20-3.

MacAmhlaigh, D. (1966) *An Irish navvy: The diary of an exile*, London: Routledge & Kegan Paul.

MacAmhlaigh, D. (2001) *Selected short stories of Donal MacAmhlaigh*, Northampton: Northampton Connolly Association.

Mac an Ghaill, M. (1999) *Contemporary racisms and ethnicities*, Buckingham: Open University.

Mac an Ghaill, M. (2002) 'Beyond a black-white dualism: racialisation and racism in the Republic of Ireland and the Irish diaspora experience', *Irish Journal of Sociology*, vol 11, no 2, pp 99-123.

Macauley, M. (1955) 'Our children', *Christus Rex*, vol 9, no 2, pp 126-33.

MacInerny, M.H. (1922) 'A postscript to the souper problem', *Irish Ecclesiastical Record*, vol xix, pp 246-62.

MacLaughlin, J. (1996) 'The evolution of anti-Traveller racism in Ireland', *Race & Class*, vol 37, no 3, pp 47-64.

MacLaughlin, J. (ed) (1997) *Location and dislocation in contemporary Irish society*, Cork: Cork University Press.

Macpherson, Sir William of Cluny (1999) *The Stephen Lawrence Inquiry*, London: Stationery Office.

McClintock, A. (1994) *Imperial leather: Race, gender and sexuality in the colonial conquest*, London: Routledge.

McCollum, S. (1994) *Alcohol and the Irish in the London Borough of Brent*, London: Brent Irish Advisory Service.

McCormack, W.J. (ed) (1992) *Austin Clarke: Selected poems*, Harmondsworth: Penguin.

McGahern, J. (2002) *That they may face the rising sun*, London: Faber.

McGovern, M. (2002) 'The "craic" market: Irish theme bars and the commodification of Irishness in contemporary Britain', *Irish Journal of Sociology*, vol 11, no 2, pp 77-99.

McLennan, G. (2001) 'Can there be a "critical" multiculturalism?', *Ethnicities*, vol 1, no 3, pp 389-422.

McVeigh, R. (1996) *The racialization of Irishness: Racism and anti-racism in Ireland*, Belfast: Centre for Research and Documentation.

Maddox, B. (1996) 'A fine old Irish stew', *New Statesman*, 29 November, pp 21-3.

Maguire, M.J. (2002) 'Foreign adoptions and the evolution of Irish adoption policy, 1945-52', *Journal of Social History*, vol 36, no 2, pp 387-405.

Mahon, E., Conlon, C. and Dillon, L. (1998) *Women and crisis pregnancy*, Dublin: Government Publications Office.

Mahood, M. (1990) *The Magdalenes: Prostitution in the nineteenth century*, London: Routledge.

Mallinson, I. (1995) 'Moving from anti-racist practice to non-oppressive practice?', *Issues in Social Work Education*, vol 15, no 1, pp 60-7.

Margolin, L. (1997) *Under the cover of kindness: The invention of social work*, Charlottesville, VA: University of Virginia.

Marks, L. (1992) 'The luckless waifs and strays of humanity: Irish and Jewish immigrant unwed mothers in London, 1870-1939', *Twentieth Century British History*, vol 3, no 2, pp 113-38.

Marriot, J. (1999) 'In darkest England: the poor, the crowd and race in the nineteenth-century metropolis', in P. Cohen (ed) *New ethnicities, old racisms*, London: Zed Books, pp 82-101.

Marsh, P and Crow, G. (1998) *Family group conferences in child welfare*, Oxford: Blackwell.

Marston, S.A. (2002) 'Making difference: conflict over Irish identity in the New City St Patrick's Day parade', *Political Geography*, vol 21, pp 373-92.

Mason, D. (1995) *Race and ethnicity in modern Britain*, Oxford: Oxford University.

Mayer, E. (2003) '"An outsider's view of modern Ireland": Michel Houllebecq's atomised', *Studies*, vol 92, no 365, pp 27-34.

Maynard, M. (1994) 'Race, gender and the concept of difference in feminist thought', in H. Afshar and M. Maynard (eds) *The dynamics of 'race' and gender*, London: Taylor & Francis, pp 9-26.

Miles, R. (1982) *Racism and migrant labour*, London: Routledge & Kegan Paul.

Miles, R. (1993) *Racism after 'race relations'*, London: Routledge.

Milotte, M. (1997) *Banished babies*, Dublin: New Island Books.

Moane, G. (2002) 'Colonialism and the Celtic Tiger: legacies of history and the quest for vision', in P. Kirkby, L. Gibbons and M. Cronin (eds) (2002) *Reinventing Ireland: Culture, society and the global economy*, London: Pluto, pp 109-24.

Modood, T., Berthoud, R., Lakey, J., Nazroo, J., Smith, P., Virdee, S. and Beishon, S. (1997) *Ethnic minorities in Britain: Diversity and disadvantage*, London: Policy Studies Institute.

Mooney J. and Young J. (1999) *Social exclusion and criminal justice*, Middlesex: Centre for Criminology, Middlesex University.

Morrison, T. (1992) *Playing in the dark: Whiteness and the literary imagination*, London: Picador.

MPRH (1941) 'Illegitimate', *The Bell*, vol 2, no 3, pp 78-88.

Mullen, K., Williams, R. and Hunt, K. (1996) 'Irish descent, religion and alcohol and tobacco use', *Addictions*, vol 91, no 2, pp 243-54.

Murphy, J.J. (1996) 'The health needs of the Irish in Manchester: a report by the Director of Social Services to the health policy sub-committee of Manchester City Council', Unpublished.

Murphy, P. (1994) 'The invisible minority: Irish offenders and the English criminal justice system', *Probation Journal*, March, pp 2-8.

Myles, J. (2003) 'Census figures may not tell the real story', *Irish Post*, 18 January.

Nash, C. (1993) 'Remapping and renaming new cartographies of identity, gender and landscape in Ireland', *Feminist Review*, issue 44, pp 39-58.

Nash, C. (2002) 'Genealogical identities', *Environment and Planning D*, vol 20, pp 27-52.

National Institute for Mental Health in England (2003) *Improving mental health services for black and minority ethnic communities in England*, Leeds: DoH.

National Statistics (2003) 'Census 2001 – new detailed view includes picture of children's backgrounds' (www.statistics.gov.uk/census).

Neal, F. (1988) *Sectarian violence: The Liverpool experience 1819-1914*, Manchester: Manchester University Press.

Neal, F. (1991-92) 'English-Irish conflict in the North West of England: economics, racism, anti-Catholicism or simple xenophobia?', *North West Labour History*, vol 16, pp 14-26.

Newman W.A. (1951) 'Legal adoption', *The Bell*, vol 16, no 4, pp 59-66.

Nicolson, J. (1968) *Mother and baby homes*, London: George Allen & Unwin.

Nic Suibhne, M. (1998) 'Fortress Ireland', *The Guardian Weekend*, 3 October, pp 32-40.

Norman, A. (1985) *Triple jeopardy: Growing old in a second homeland*, London: Centre for Policy on Ageing.

Oaks, L. (2002) 'Abortion is part of the Irish experience, it is part of what we are: the transformation of the public discourses on Irish abortion policy', *Women's Studies International Forum*, vol 25, no 3, pp 315-33.

O'Brien, O. and Power, R. (1998) *HIV and a migrant community: The Irish in Britain*, London: Action Group for Irish Youth/University College London Medical School.

O'Connor, F. (1967) *My Oedipus complex and other stories*, Harmondsworth: Penguin (2nd reprint).

O'Connor, H. and Goodwin, J. (2002) 'Work and diaspora: locating Irish workers in the British labour market', *Irish Journal of Sociology*, vol 11, no 2, pp 27-54.

O'Connor, K. (1972) *The Irish in Britain*, London: Sidgwick and Jackson.

O'Flynn, E. (1992) *Under Piccadilly's neon: Irish and homeless in London – A six month survey*, London: Piccadilly Advice Centre.

O'Hagan, K. (2001) *Cultural competence in the caring professions*, London: Jessica Kingsley.

O'Hare, A. et al (1983) *Mothers alone? A study of women who gave birth outside of marriage*, Dublin: Federation of Services for Unmarried Parents and their Children.

O'Neale, V. (2000) *Excellence not excuses: Inspection of services for ethnic minority children and families*, London: DoH.

Osborough, N. (1975) *Borstal in Ireland*, Dublin: Institute of Public Affairs.

O'Seaghdha, B. (2002) 'The Celtic Tiger's media pundits', in P. Kirkby, L. Gibbons and M. Cronin (eds) (2002) *Reinventing Ireland: Culture, society and the global economy*, London: Pluto, pp 143-60.

O'Sullivan, J. (1996) 'If you're hip, you must be Irish', *The Independent*, 1 July.

O'Sullivan, J. (2003) 'British Muslims are the new Irish', *New Statesman*, 3 November, pp 25-7.

O'Sullivan, P. (2003) 'Developing Irish diaspora studies: a personal view', *New Hibernia Review*, Spring, pp 130-48.

O'Toole, F. (1994) *Black hole, green card: The disappearance of Ireland*, Dublin: New Island Books.

O'Toole, F. (1997) *The ex-isle of Erin: Images of global Ireland*, Dublin: New Island Books.

Palme, C. (1998) 'Adopting an Irish identity', *The Irish Post*, 10 October, p 35.

Parker, D. (2000) 'The Chinese takeaway and the diasporic habitus: space, time and power geometrics', in B. Hesse (ed) *Unsettled multiculturalism*, London: Zed Books, pp 73-96.

Parker, J. (2000) 'Social work with refugees and asylum seekers: a rationale for developing practice', *Practice*, vol 12, no 3, pp 61-77.

Parker, R., Ward, H., Jackson, S., Aldgate, J. and Wedge, P. (1991) *Looking after children: Assessing outcomes in child care*, London: HMSO.

Parton, N. and O'Byrne, P. (2000) *Constructive social work*, London: Macmillan.

Patel, N. (1999) 'Endemic racism? Lessons from the campaign against CCETSW', Unpublished paper presented at the 'Anti-Racism and Anti-Oppressive Practice' Conference, University of Leeds, 9 June.

Pearson, M. (1994) *Irish identity and children's rights*, Birmingham: Stylewrite Press.

Pearson, M., Madden, M. and Greenslade, L. (1991) *Generations of invisibility: The health and well-being of the Irish in Britain*, Liverpool: Institute of Irish Studies, University of Liverpool.

Philp, A.F. and Timms, N. (1957) *The problem of 'the problem family'*, London: Family Service Units.

Philpot, T. (2002) 'The secret is out', *Community Care*, 22-28 August, pp 35-7.

Pickering, M. (2001) *Stereotyping: The politics of representation*, London: Palgrave.

Pilkington, A. (2003) *Racial disadvantage and ethnic diversity in Britain*, Houndsmill: Palgrave Macmillan.

Pilkington, L. (2002) '"Religion and the Celtic Tiger": the cultural legacies of anti-Catholicism in Ireland', in P. Kirkby, L. Gibbons, and M. Cronin (eds) (2002) *Reinventing Ireland: Culture, society and the global economy*, London: Pluto.

Pinnock, M. and Garnett, L. (2002) 'Needs-led or needs must?', in H. Ward and W. Rose (eds) *Approaches to needs assessment in children's services*, London: Jessica Kingsley.

PIU (Performance and Innovation Unit) (2000) *The Prime Minister's review of adoption: A Performance and Innovation Unit report*, London: The Stationery Office.

Plumb, B. (1993) 'Catholicism in the Workhouse', *North West Catholic History*, vol 20, pp 1-12.

Pochin, J. (1969) *Without a wedding ring: Casework with unmarried parents*, London: Constable.

Pooley, C.G. (1999) 'From Londonderry to London: identity and sense of place for Protestant Northern Irish women in the 1930s', *Immigrants & Minorities*, vol 18, no 2-3, pp 189-214.

Powell, F.P. (1992) *The politics of Irish social policy 1600-1990*, Dyfed: Edwin Mellen Press.

Pratt, M.L. (1993) *Imperial eyes: Travel writing and transculturation* (1st reprint), London: Routledge.

Preston-Shoot, M. (1995) 'Assessing anti-oppressive practice', *Social Work Education*, vol 4, no 2, pp 11-30.

Prevatt Goldstein, B. (1999) 'Black, with a white parent, a positive and achievable identity', *British Journal of Social Work*, vol 29, pp 285-301.

Prevatt Goldstein, B. (ed) (2000) *Adoption & fostering – Special issue: Ethnicity in placement*, vol 24, no 1, pp 9-15.

Raftery, M. (2003) 'Restoring dignity to Magdalens', *Irish Times*, 21 August, p 14.

Raftery, M. and O'Sullivan, E. (1999) *Suffer the little children: The inside story of Ireland's industrial schools*, Dublin: New Island Books.

Ramirez, F.O. and McEneaney, E.H. (1997) 'From women's suffrage to reproduction rights? Cross-national considerations', *International Journal of Comparative Sociology*, vol 38, no 1-2, pp 6-25.

Rose, M.E. (1976) 'Settlement, removal and the new poor law', in D. Fraser (ed) *The new poor law in the nineteenth century,* London: Macmillan, pp 25-44.

Rose, N. (1989) *Governing the soul: The shaping of the private self*, London: Routledge.

Rosenau, P.M. (1992) *Postmodernism and the social sciences*, Chichester: Princeton University.

Roskill, C. (2000) 'Lest we forget', *Community Care*, 26 October-1 November, pp 26-28.

Rossiter, A. and Sexton, M. (2001) *The other Irish journey: A survey of Northern Irish women attending British abortion clinics, 2000/1*, London: Marie Stopes.

Russell, M. (1964) 'The Irish delinquent in England', *Studies*, Summer issue, pp 136-149.

Ryan, L. (2001a) 'Irish female emigration in the 1930s: transgressing space and culture', *Gender, Place and Culture*, vol 8, no 3, pp 271-82.

Ryan, L. (2001b) 'Aliens, migrants and maids: public discourses on Irish immigration to Britain in 1937', *Immigrants & Minorities*, vol 20, nos 3, pp 25-42.

Ryan, L. (2002a) 'I'm going to England: women's narratives of leaving Ireland in the 1930s', *Oral History*, Spring issue, pp 42-54.

Ryan, L. (2002b) 'Sexualising emigration: discourses of Irish female emigration in the 1930s', *Women's Studies International Forum*, vol 25, no 1, pp 51-65.

Ryan, L. (2003) 'Moving spaces and changing places: Irish women's memories of emigration to Britain in the 1930s', *Journal of Ethnic and Migration Studies*, vol 29, no 1, pp 67-82.

Ryan, M. (1994) *War and peace in Ireland*, London: Pluto Press.

St Louis, B. (2002) 'Post-race/post politics? Activist-intellectualism and the reification of race', *Ethnic and Racial Studies*, vol 25, no 4, pp 652-75.

'Sagart' (1922) 'How to deal with the unmarried mother', *Irish Ecclesiastical Record*, vol xx, pp 145-54.

Salter, T. (2003) 'Birth of a children's trust', *Community Care*, 26 June-2 July, pp 32-5.

Scannell, Y. (1988) 'The constitution and the role of women', in B. Farrell (ed) *De Valera's constitution and ours*, Dublin: Gill & Macmillan, pp 123-37.

Scraton, P. (ed) (1987) *Law, order and the authoritarian state*, Milton Keynes: Open University.

Secretary of State for Health and the Secretary of State for the Home Department (2003) *The Victoria Climbie inquiry – Report of an inquiry by Lord Laming*, London: The Stationery Office.

SEU (Social Exclusion Unit) (2000) *National strategy for neighbourhood renewal: Minority ethnic issues in social exclusion and neighbourhood renewal*, London: SEU.

Simms, A. (2004) 'The new serfs', *New Statesman*, 16 February, pp 20-2.

Sivanandan, A. (2000) 'Reclaiming the struggle', *Race & Class*, vol 42, no 2, pp 67-74.

Small, J. (1982) 'New black families', *Adoption & Fostering*, vol 6, no 3, pp 35-40.

Small, J. with Prevatt Goldstein, B. (2000) 'Ethnicity and placement: beginning the debate', *Adoption & Fostering*, vol 24, no 1, pp 9-15.

Smart, C. (2000) 'Reconsidering the recent history of child sexual abuse 1910-1960', *Journal of Social Policy*, vol 29, no 1, pp. 55-71.

Smith, G. (2000) 'Meeting the placement needs of Jewish children', *Adoption & Fostering*, vol 24, no 1, pp. 40-47.

Smyth, A. (1992) *The abortion papers*, Dublin: Attic Press.

Spensky, M. (1992) 'Producers of legitimacy: homes for unmarried mothers in the 1950s', in C. Smart (ed) *Regulating womanhood: Essays on marriage, motherhood and sexuality*, London: Routledge, pp 100-19.

Spinley, B.M. (1953) *The deprived and the privileged*, London: Routledge & Kegan Paul.

Spivak, G.C. (2002) 'Resident alien', in D.T. Goldberg and A. Quayson (eds) *Relocating postcolonialism*, Oxford: Blackwell, pp 47-66.

SSI (Social Services Inspectorate) (2000) *Modern social services: A commitment to people. The 9th annual report of the chief inspector of social services 1999/2000*, London: DoH.

SSI/DoH (2001) *Co-ordinated service planning for vulnerable children and young people in England*, London: DoH.

Stallybrass, P. and White, A. (1986) *The politics and poetics of transgression*, London: Methuen.

Starkey, P. (2000) 'The feckless mother: women, poverty and social workers in wartime and post-war England', *Women's History Review*, vol 9, no 3, pp 539-59.

Steele, L. (1998) 'Keeping a precarious balance', *Community Care*, 10-16 September, pp 2-9.

Stevens, L., Brown, S. and Maclaren, P. (2000) 'Gender, nationality and cultural representations of Ireland', *The European Journal of Women's Studies*, vol 7, pp 405-21.

Stevenson, O. (1998) 'It was more difficult than we thought: a reflection on 50 years of child welfare practice', *Child and Family Social Work*, vol 3, pp 153-61.

Task Force on Policy regarding Emigrants (2002) *Ireland and the Irish abroad*, Department of Foreign Affairs, Government of Ireland (www.gov.ie/iveagh).

Taylor, A. (1997) 'Ethnic identities', *Community Care*, 11-17 September, p 16.

Taylor, C. (1997) 'The politics of recognition', in D.T. Goldberg (ed) *Multiculturalism: A critical reader* (3rd reprint), Oxford: Blackwell, pp 75-107.

Thoburn, J., Norford, L. and Rashid, S.P. (2000) *Permanent family placement for children of minority ethnic origin*, London: Jessica Kingsley.

Thompson, N. (1993) *Anti-discriminatory practice*, London: Macmillan.

Thompson, S. (2001) 'Introduction: towards an Irish cultural studies', *Cultural Studies*, vol 15, no 1, pp 1-11.

Tilki, M. (1996) *The health of the Irish in Britain*, London: Federation of Irish Societies.

Tilki, M. (1998a) *Elderly Irish people in Britain*, London: Federation of Irish Societies.

Tilki, M. (1998b) 'The health of the Irish in Britain', in I. Papadopoulos, M. Tilki and G.Taylor (eds) *Transcultural care: A guide for health professionals*, Wiltshire: Quay Books, pp 125-52.

Torode, R. and O'Sullivan, E. (1999) 'The impact of *Dear Daughter*', *Irish Journal of Feminist Studies*, vol 3, no 2, pp 85-99.

Travers, P. (1997) 'There was nothing for me there: Irish female immigration, 1922-71', in P. O'Sullivan (ed) *Irish women and Irish migration*, London: Leicester University, pp 146-68.

Tunnard, J. (2002) 'Matching needs and services', in H. Ward and W. Rose (eds) *Approaches to needs assessment in children's services*, London: Jessica Kingsley, pp 99-127.

Ullah, P. (1985) 'Second generation Irish youth: identity and ethnicity', *New Community*, vol 12, pp 35-50.

Valios, N. (1997) 'Report blasts politically correct adoption myths', *Community Care*, 16-22 October, p 5.

Valios, N. (1998) 'Staff hit back at allegations of obsession with political dogma', *Community Care*, 23-29 April, pp 6-7.

Valios, N. (2002) 'The lot of the Irish', *Community Care*, 3-9 October, pp 34-5.

Vanderbeck, R.M. (2003) 'Youth, racism, and place in the Tony Martin affair', *Antipode*, vol 35, pp 363-84.

Vertovec, S. (2000) *The Hindu diaspora: Comparative patterns*, London: Routledge.

Viney, M. (1966) *No birthright: A study of the Irish unmarried mother and her child*, Dublin: Irish Times.

Walby, S. (2001) 'From community to coalition: the politics of recognition as the handmaiden of the politics of equality in an era of globalization', *Theory, Culture & Society*, vol 18, no 2-3, pp 113-35.

Waldron, J. (2000) 'Minority cultures and the cosmopolitan alternative', in W. Kymlicka (ed) *The rights of minority cultures* (reprint), Oxford: Oxford University.

Wallace, J. (1995) 'Unmarried mothers in Ireland in the middle decades of the twentieth century', Unpublished MPhil dissertation, Trinity College Dublin.

Walls, P. (1996) *Researching Irish mental health: Issues and evidence – A study of the mental health of the Irish community in Haringey*, London: Muintearas Irish Health Group/Haringey Cultural and Community Centre.

Walls, P. and Williams, R. (2003) 'Sectarianism at work: accounts of employment discrimination against Irish Catholics in Scotland', *Ethnic and Racial Studies*, vol 26, no 4, pp 632-62.

Walter, B. (1995) 'Irishness, gender and place', *Society & Space*, vol 13, pp 35-50.

Walter, B. (2000) 'Shamrocks growing out of their mouths: language and racialisation of the Irish in Britain', in A.J. Kershen (ed) *Language, labour and migration*, Aldershot: Ashgate, pp 57-74.

Walter, B. (2001) *Outsiders inside: Whiteness, place and Irish women*, London: Routledge.

Walter, B. with Gray, B., Almeida Dowling, L. and Morgan, S. (2002a) *A Study of the existing sources of information and analysis about Irish emigrants and Irish communities abroad*, Department of Foreign Affairs, Government of Ireland (www.gov.ie/iveagh).

Walter, B., Morgan, S., Hickman, M.J. and Bradley, J.M. (2002b) 'Family stories, public silence: Irish identity construction amongst the second-generation Irish in England', *Scottish Geographical Journal*, vol 118, no 3, pp 201-17.

Ward, H. (ed) (1995) *Looking after children: Research into practice*, London: HMSO.

Warnes,T. and Crane, M. (2001) *Profile of London's single homeless people*, London: St Mungo's, Thamesreach and Bondway Housing Association.

Welshman,J. (1999) 'The social history of social history: the issue of the "problem family", 1940-70', *British Journal of Social Work*, vol 29, pp 457-76.

West, P. (2002) 'The new Ireland kicks ass', *New Statesman*, 17 June, pp 20-2.

Wheeler,W. (1998) *Imagining home: Gender, 'race' and national identity, 1945-64*, London: UCL Press.

Wheen, F. (2000) *Karl Marx* (1st pbk edn), London: Fourth Estate.

Whyte,J.H. (1971) *Church and state in modern Ireland*, Dublin: Gill & Macmillan.

Wickham,J. (1998) 'The golden geese fly the Internet: some research issues in the migration of Irish professionals', *The Economic and Social Review*, vol 29, no 1, pp 33-54.

Williams, F. (1992) 'Somewhere over the rainbow: universality and diversity in social policy', in N. Manning and R. Page (eds) *Social Policy Review 4*, London: Social Policy Association.

Williams, P.J. (2002) 'Racial privacy', *The Nation*, 17 June, p 9.

Wimperis,V. (1960) *The unmarried mother and her child*, London: George Allen & Unwin.

Woods, A. (1956) 'Safeguards in England for the Irish emigrant', *Christus Rex*, vol 10, no 4, pp 366-83.

Working Party on Catholic Education in a Multiracial, Multicultural Society (1984) *Learning from diversity: A challenge for Catholic education*, London: Catholic Media Office.

Yuval-Davis, N. (1997) *Gender and nation*, London: Sage Publications.

Yuval-Davis, N. (2001) 'Contemporary agenda for the study of ethnicity', *Ethnicities*, vol 1, no 1, pp 11-13.

Information derived from the Department of Health 'Children in Need' (CIN) survey, September-October 2001

Table A1: Those local authorities in London with the highest number of Irish children 'looked after'

London authority	Number of Irish children
Islington	35
Southwark	35
Barnet	20
Camden	20
Hammersmith & Fulham	20
Haringey	20

Table A2: Those local authorities elsewhere in England with the highest number of Irish children 'looked after'

Authority elsewhere in England	Number of Irish children
Birmingham	25
Manchester	20
Wirral	20

Table A3: Those local authorities in London with the most Irish children being 'supported in families or independently'

London authority	Number of Irish children
Islington	65
Camden	55
Hammersmith & Fulham	20
Lewisham	20
Westminster	20
Barnet	20
Haringey	55
Hillingdon	20
Hounslow	20

Table A4: Those local authorities elsewhere in England with the most Irish children being 'supported in families or independently'

Authority elsewhere in England	Number of Irish children
Birmingham	25
Hertfordshire	25
Oxfordshire	20
Wigan	20

Table A5: Those local authorities in London providing the highest number of Irish children with services ('looked after' plus 'support in families or independently')

London authority	Number of Irish children
Islington	100
Camden	75
Haringey	75
Barnet	50
Southwark	45
Hammersmith & Fulham	35
Hounslow	35
Hillingdon	30
Enfield	25
Westminster	30
Croydon	20
Ealing	20
Hackney	20
Kensington & Chelsea	20
Lambeth	20
Lewisham	20
Tower Hamlets	20
Waltham Forest	20

Table A6: Those local authorities elsewhere in England providing the highest number of Irish children with services ('looked after' plus 'support in families or independently')

Authority elsewhere in England	Number of Irish children
Birmingham	50
Hertfordshire	40
Manchester	35
Oxfordshire	25
Wirral	25
Brighton & Hove	20
Derby	20
Sheffield	20
Wakefield	20
Wigan	20

Statistical responses to the questionnaire mailed to social services departments in England and Wales

Table B1: Policy and practice

	Yes Number	%	No Number	%	Response
Does your department include a specific Irish category in 'race' and ethnic monitoring systems?	62	83	13	17	75
Has *Race equality, means quality: The CRE's standard for local government* had an impact on how you deliver services to those who are Irish?	16	23	53	77	69
Have you read *Discrimination and the Irish community in Britain* (Hickman and Walter, 1997)?	10	14	64	86	74
Is there an Irish dimension incorporated into anti-discriminatory training provided for childcare staff in your department?	14	20	56	80	70
Is there an Irish dimension incorporated into anti-discriminatory training provided for potential fostering and adoptive carers?	15	21	56	79	71
Is there specific reference to Irish children and families in either your most recent plan for children's services or the most recent Management Action Plan submitted to the Department of Health as part of the Quality Protects initiative?	4	5	71	79	75
Are you aware of any bullying or harassment that has been related to anti-Irish racism?[a]	2	3	55	73	57
Are staff encouraged to publicise and promote Irish cultural festivals, such as St Patrick's Day, in, eg, residential establishments and Family Centres?	30	42	41	58	71
Does your department provide services for Irish children and families who are part of Traveller communities?	27	42	41	58	68
Does your department provide any innovative project that relates specifically to Irish children and families?	3	4	71	96	74

Note: [a] Eighteen (24%) stated that they 'did not know'.

Table B2: The number of Irish children receiving a service from SSDs

Number of Irish children receiving a service	Number of SSDs	% of SSDs
0	8	17
1 or 2	8	17
3-6	10	21
7-10	4	8
11-20	8	17
21-30	4	8
31-50	2	4
51-70	1	2
71-90	1	2
91+	2	4
Total	48	100
Not known	22	

Table B3: The number of Irish children 'looked after'

Number of Irish children 'looked after'	Number of SSDs	% of SSDs
0	28	47
1 or 2	13	22
3-6	11	18
7-10	3	5
11-20	1	2
21-30	3	5
31-40	1	2
Total	60	100
Not known	13	

Table B4: Irish children on local authority Child Protection Registers (CPRs)

Number of Irish children on CPR	Number of SSDs	% of SSDs
0	33	57
1 or 2	10	17
3-6	10	17
7-10	4	7
11-20	1	2
Total	58	100
Not known	16	

Table B5: Irish foster carers

Number of Irish foster carers	Number of SSDs	% of SSDs
0	19	48
1 or 2	12	30
3-6	6	15
7-10	3	8
Total	40	100
Not known	32	

Table B6: Irish adopters currently approved by the Adoption Panel in the local authority area

Number of Irish adopters	Number of SSDs	% of SSDs
0	24	60
1 or 2	14	35
3	2	5
Total	40	100
Not known	30	

Table B7: Engaging with the Irish community

	Yes		No		
	Number	%	Number	%	Response
Does your department use the Irish press (eg *Irish Post*) to recruit Irish adoptive and foster carers?	7	10	66	90	73
Does your department consult with any local/national Irish community organisation to enable you to improve your response to the specific cultural requirements of Irish children?	12	16	63	84	75
Is there an Irish representative in the Area Child Protection Committee?	7	10	63	90	70

Index

Page numbers in *italics* refer to tables; those followed by f refer to 'notes'